TWO MINUTE WARNING

Handbook of Effective Christianity for the 4th Quarter of Life

Bernie Lutchman

TWO MINUTE WARNING
by Bernie Lutchman

Printed in the United States of America

ISBN 978-1-60266-561-3

Official Dictionary used: www.websters-online-dictionary.org

www.xulonpress.com

To Nancy S.

God bless you

Thanks for your service to the Lord

Bennie Hinn
psalm 27:4

ENDORSEMENT

"*Two Minute Warning* offers a powerful reminder of the hope we have in the Living God by giving the insight and motivation to live sold out for your Savior to the very end. Bernie Lutchman gives an outside perspective on the life of Fourth-Quarter Christian and uses basic truths to convey a deep, moving and inspirational message! Living in the world and not of the world is a daily challenge and God is using Bernie Lutchman to help Christians like you and me embrace that challenge and end this life on earth victorious!"
Joe White
President, Kanakuk Kamps

About Joe White……

Joe attended college at Southern Methodist University in Dallas, Texas, where he won the Heart Award as a two-year starting defensive tackle for the ***SMU Mustangs****. He earned a B.A. in Biology in 1970. He then became a football coach at* ***Texas A & M University****.*

In 1972 Joe married the love of his life, Debbie-Jo. Together they started working in the family business - ***Kanakuk Kamps****. His charisma and compelling style of speaking over the years brought him many opportunities and invitations to speak at a variety of events, most of which were aimed at young people. Joe has spoken before many NFL football and professional baseball teams, as well* *as countless churches, youth conferences, high school graduations, FCA banquets, Young Life events, etc.*

Joe has written a total of 15 books designed to reach teens and families. He has been a guest speaker for Dr. Dobson's family talk show many times. He hosted the live call-in talk show for teens sponsored by ***Focus on the Family*** *called "Life On the Edge Live" for 4 years and spoke at the "Life on the Edge" conferences around the country. In 1991 he was awarded an honorary Doctor of Education from Southwest Baptist University, then was ordained by University Baptist Church, Fayetteville, AR, on May 3, 1992.*

Joe conducts a series of college crusades called ***AfterDark****, taking evangelistic sermons to college campuses across the country. He has also embarked on a PureExcitement tour in which he takes the purity until marriage challenge to junior high and high school students all over America. He recently walked across Egypt with a Cross!*

"Joe White knows more about teenagers than anyone in North America." Dr. James Dobson, founder, Focus on the Family

(All information courtesy:
http://www.kanakuk.com/about/JoeWhiteBio.aspx)

Table of Contents

ACKNOWLEDGEMENTS:

This book is dedicated to my dear wife Vicki Lee Lutchman, whom the Lord chose for me before the Foundation of the earth! Our three dear talented children Bernie III, Sam and Sarah.

They were dedicated to the Lord many years before they were even born. May the Lord bless you all. There are many people who inspired me, helped in my discipleship and understanding of God's word and are simply dear friends and fellow believers in Christ.

I thank Dr. Joe White, President of Kanakuk Camps, Branson, Missouri for your trust in me and your blessing through your Endorsement of this book. Thanks to your assistant Kara Britt as well. Thank you, sir and May God bless you with long life and all Joy!

I am grateful to Dr. Steve Farrar for his kindness in putting up with my emails and questions. I admire his honesty, integrity and wisdom. Thank you for allowing me to quote your books

To John and Norma Woolridge, thank you for your hard work and love in editing this work. Your advice was heeded!

To Gene Grman, my mentor, thank you for the many late hours spent talking past midnight about matters of the Lord. To his wife, Kathe, for putting up with that!!

Thank you to Dave Rosche, Tom Cheshire, Doug Ryherd, and Dan Boyer. To my prayer warrior brother James Nesbit, Doc Powell, Scott Beauchamp of the Springfield International House of Prayer.

Thank you to Lori Wagner (author of "Gates and Fences"); Sue Stoltz, Lisa Crump and Claudia Dunne. These are my compatriots in the Service of the Lord through the National Day of Prayer Task

Force. Lisa is based at the Focus on the Family Campus in Colorado Springs, Colorado.

Thank you to Ron Wightman of Salt Lake City, Utah. He is a fine gentleman of his word and the closest you can get to the Founders of American Christianity – Roger Williams and Obadiah Holmes! His family are also relatives of our greatest president, Abraham Lincoln!

To Harold Dameron, who is a brother from way back when we organized men's' retreats in the mid 1990's without much support!

Thank you to the folks of Springfield Bible Church led by John Standard, the Eastvolds and others. Both the Standards and Eastvolds are fine examples of walking the talk.

To brother Bryan McKenzie (former linebacker for the Atlanta Falcons) and his dear family from Grace Bible Church in Lake Jackson, Texas.

I acknowledge Pastor/author Gary Gilley of Southern View Chapel who unknowingly was one of my inspirations in writing a regular web column on www.businessmeninChrist.com and for opening my eyes to the heresies and false prophets in modern Christianity.

I thank Bob Warren, former San Antonio Spur (National Basketball Association) whose teachings taught me how to study the Full Counsel of the Word of God! Thanks Bob! We all need to have bright eyes, bright smile so everyone will want what we got! His influence is all through this book!

Thank you to my dear family, mother Cynthia and all the Lutchmans all over the world.

To my dear mother- and father -in-laws Joyce and Verlin. To my brother in law Pastor Dennis Morgan, Sheryl and the Morgan's and the Reaves family.

To Toni and Peter Martin, to the Knox's of Springfield, Howard Fouks and John McBride of WLUJ 89.7FM for a decade of friendship as well as Lonnie Lein. Hey, to new brothers Jeremiah Beck and Rob Regal of WIBI FM. May the Good Lord bless us all.

Finally thank you to all my Pastoral brothers in Christ who have had significant fellowship and influence in my life today – Frederick D. Nettles; Scott Payne; Scott Brindley; Warren Brosi; Dan Boyer;

Milton Bost and brother Randy Heinsch! By the time you read this, Randy would have pushed a wheelbarrow of tracts 75 miles from Peoria to Springfield, Illinois over 7 days! He comes from a family tradition of D.L. Moody Bible Institute grads and is in the footsteps of the great Evangelists like Arthur Blessitt and Sammy Tippitt! This man is warrior with a heart of gold.

There are so many people I can name from the present and the past I apologize if your name was inadvertently left out... Men like Joe Craggs, Scott Keck and others who have crossed my path, whether through Bible studies I led (like Cora Bethard and Carolyn Brown etc).

To my brother, hermano Douglas K. Turner from the Petah Tikvah Messianic Congregation. Shalom alechem. One of my most precious memories is the many times Rabbi Avram asked me to read the Haftarah (Readings, Prophets) during the many Shabbat services I attended as we glorified Yeshua!

I acknowledge all the Bible teachers who have been my mentors over the Radio and TV and whom the Holy Spirit used to instruct me for the past 17 years: Doctors Charles Stanley, John MacArthur, James Merritt, Tony Evans, Michael Youssef and Adrian Rogers. Thanks, most of all to the great Ray Comfort. His books and teachings have opened my eyes to the greatness of the preaching of Charles Spurgeon, D.L. Moody, and Jonathan Edwards.

His book "Revival's Golden Key" was the defining book on the Theology of Evangelism and Revival for me. Together with the teachings of Claude King on Revival, I gained a broader picture of sin, repentance and Revival. Claude King is such a kind and humble man and I sense the Holy Spirit working through him to teach the ways of Revival to a wayward church!

Thank you, Lord, for the true Evangelical church in America: the Southern Baptist Convention, the Bible Church movement and other solid, independent and denominational Evangelicals .To every fire and brimstone preacher who ever preached at tent revival, you are my heroes. From the dirt road church in the red clay of Sweet Home Alabama to the city church surrounded by high tech equipment - to you, I tip my hat. You have helped to make the difference to millions between heaven and hell. Shalom.

INTRODUCTION

The name of this book is "Two Minute Warning". It is basically a handbook on most of the major issues facing both men and women in the maturing stages of life – the 4th Quarter, if you will. While it is written to the Christian, any seeker can grasp the Truths contained here.

The major credible translations of the English Bible are deployed. All doctrine employed is solid and can stand the test of time. All doctrine is taken from the Literal, Verse by Verse interpretation of the Bible.

Contrary to the opinions of the world, our own Two Minute Warning can come at any time! Oswald Chambers lived only 43 years. His 4th Quarter would have been in his 30's!

No matter how young or old we are, when the Roll is called up yonder and the Master signals it is time to come home, we should be prepared to go like our hero, the Apostle Paul. In 2 Timothy 4:7 ("I have fought the good fight, I have finished the course, I have kept the faith).

From the moment we are born, we begin the Journey back home. The book rests on three pillars: Life Lessons, Leadership and Legacy. The Head Coach in this Book is the Lord Jesus Christ. The Bible is the Game Plan. Either we are suited up and ready to go on the field or we sit on the bench or worse, in the stands.

You will notice Effective Christianity is the foundation of the entire premise of our Faith, so it is with "Two Minute Warning". Effective Faith will give us the Power to live the true best life now according to God's authentic purposes.

It is this Power that was with me as I began writing this book. I started and stumbled, having writer's block for 4 months. After 3 people confronted me (including my wife) with a prophetic message of "either I write this book or not", the Lord opened the floodgates!

I sat for over two months, three or four times per week, sometimes until 4am or 5am without moving (even though I had to be at work at 7:30am, which I accomplished as the Lord was in this project all the way!)The sounds of Messianic music from a Christian Jewish station from Jerusalem would be playing on Sky Angel radio.

In those intense weeks of driven writing, inspired by the Holy Spirit, the Lord poured it out of me! I would stop and read a section after a couple of hours and humbly ask in wonder "did I just write that?" The answer was NO! I did not; I was just the writing instrument. Now I know how the Scripture writers may have felt, even as I used THEIR written inspired words myself!

There are lessons learnt from other Bible teachers and wise men over time without fear or favor. I share anything I consider helpful from years of being under the teachings of these wise men and women; things which have helped me over the years. Most of all, these lessons are from the Lord, the King of Kings and the Lord of Hosts. When He returns and reinstitutes the Feast of Tabernacles and other such worship, we will glorify Him together and marvel in His Goodness. His Goodness is as rich as the fertile black moist soil of Central Illinois; the same soil I ran through my fingers after tilling the garden for this season's vegetables. Glory to His Name!!

The Teachings He gave me as I wrote about His Word, verse by verse, are to be passed on to His people and I do so humbly. I am and will always remain His bondservant, until the day I graduate into Glory. Amen.

There is nothing new under the sun. Nothing has changed in 6000 years of human civilization; therefore we have all learnt basically a lot of the same lessons in our lives. How we apply them to the Full Counsel of the Word of God to live the abundant life Christ called His elect to be is what this book addresses.

Thank you for allowing me to bring these words from the Lord to you. You never know where He will lead you next. While obtaining permission to use material about the descendants of Obadiah

Holmes, the Puritan, the Lord led me to Ron Wightman. Who is Ron? Only the descendant of the last Martyr burnt at the stake in England AND a long distance relative of Abraham Lincoln!

May the Lord bless you and keep you. May the Lord lift up His Countenance upon you, and give you peace.

WHY WRITE THIS BOOK?

"Keep your fears to yourself and share your courage with others"
(Robert Louis Stevenson).

BACKGROUND

For over one decade, I was desirous of writing the book I had planned since the mid 1980's! At the time, I was a single, as well as a highflying newspaper journalist, business page editor and fashion photographer. A few years after graduating from college in Nova Scotia, Canada, I found myself in a lifestyle of 75 hour weeks, endless cocktail parties and total secularism.

Years of going to church, before becoming one of the lukewarm Christmas and Easter types, began to get to the very core of my soul.

I saw lives getting destroyed in the media, and I was part of it. I did not set out as a newspaper writer to do this. However just watching how battle-hardened "journalists" took delight in destroying reputations etc. really began taking a toll on my conscience.

The photos I shot at fashion shows and other places of young fashion models began to disgust me after seeing my name on the byline, or when I saw the proofs in the darkroom at the office. The office was a newspaper group in the Caribbean island of Trinidad, where I did a four year stint after college in Nova Scotia, Canada.

Finally in July 1988, the Lord knocked me down with an illness and fatigue for almost two weeks, which was sobering for a healthy young man of 32, who was going full bore day after day, month after month. Forced to be flat on my back, literally, all I could do was look upwards! So it was the conviction of my sin, as a single man, in transit in this wealthy, but spiritually poor island of Trinidad that finally turned me back to the Lord.

It was sad, looking back now. Having grown up in the church, preached my first sermon at age 14, and gone on mission trips, I knew all the songs of the faith and some psalms or favorite passages in the Bible while growing up.

Sin had corrupted me so much, along with the ways of the world, that I could not even remember Psalm 23. After many days of self-evaluation, and no "fellow Christian" evangelizing me (since I knew none!), I spoke to God myself.

How would a man, with no prompting know from where his strength cometh forth? Scripture says in Romans 2: 14-16 "*For when Gentiles who do not have the Law do instinctively the things of the Law, these, not having the Law, are a law to themselves, in that they show the work of the Law* ***written in their hearts***, *their conscience bearing witness and their thoughts alternately accusing or else defending them, on the day when, according to my gospel, God will judge the secrets of men through Christ Jesus.*"

The Lord writes His Law on our hearts and I was one messed up Gentile! My conscience bore witness to what a degenerate sinner I was.

The Law accused me and if I were to die right then, I would be in hell with the rest of the world of unregenerate sinners! I lusted in more than my heart. I sometimes had to use any means to get a story (just like the Mainstream American Media) and then use the information to nail someone in print.

Most of those written about deserved exposure on their corruption, but knowing this does not make it any better. I used the Lord's Name in vain…I can not think of too many more commandments I did not break, as James says in James 2:10 says "*For whoever keeps the whole law and yet) stumbles in one point, he has become guilty of all.*"

Having not only stumbled on one point, but fallen flat on my face on about 6 or 7 of the Commandments, how would I be able to stand before a Holy, Righteous and Indignant God on Judgment Day as a lying, blaspheming, and lustful young man? I could not!

Like the rest of the world, which has fooled itself into thinking being "good enough" will get you into Heaven, I knew different! I was not a good person! I had begun to despise myself for the aggressive journalism and photography I was involved in.

ENCOUNTER WITH THE LIVING CHRIST

From July to August 16, 1988, there was a purpose in my step. I did not realize it until later, but the Lord was prepping me for the most important encounter I even had in my life!

In July 1988, I had chosen God over the carnal things of this world and promised Him, if He ever allowed me to have children; they would all be turned over to Him, from whence they came!

On August 16, 1988 at 4am (I know the time because I woke up right after it); I was asleep when I found myself drawn up very quickly up the side of a huge mountain covered with green trees.

In no time at all, which is just like Jesus, I heard the smooth deep Voice of Him – the Lord – speaking to me. I could not see Him but heard His gentle, powerful masculine voice say to me "I have a plan for you"...then He made a joke, which up to this day I can not recall, due to the fact I was stunned!

I do remember asking Him "You? You are joking with me? He laughed and said "Who do you think invented a sense of humor?" With that He was done! I shot up in bed. I never said a word to anyone and since I was sometimes on my own schedule, just took off for four hours up to the mountain top century old stone monastery run by the Benedictine monks.

It was the only quiet, secluded place I wanted to lose myself in.

I sat for hours waiting for the Lord to reveal Himself and what He wanted me to do. I did not know how to really pray or communicate with Him and was too spiritually immature to know He does not work that way. It took a long time to work on a guy like me.

In 1990, while walking to work along the main streets of Hartford, Connecticut, He gave me Psalm 118 as my life meditation which I do daily for all these years.

The Lord had me do something which I thought someone like me could have never done – be a friend to and teach 2nd and 3rd Graders in Church School at Immanuel Congregational Church.

For almost three years my dear wife Vicki and I taught the same kids and watched them grow through their fears, lack of Knowledge of the Holy etc into well fertile soil, where the Word of God was planted. We did not agree with the philosophy of that liberal denomination which the conservative Pilgrims founded, but lived around the corner and felt a burden for those children.

Also there are not too many conservative churches in this city. So, my true spiritual journey began right there in Hartford, Ct. in the early 1990's! Later my spiritual walk moved into high gear after moving back to Illinois in 1993 to be closer to Vicki's family.

MEN'S MINISTRY

Men's Ministries became a passion for me in 1996, even though I did not have much of a clue what the concept was! I had come out of Catholic, Anglican and Presbyterian backgrounds.

All I knew about men is they thought they ran the church, but it was the women who took us to church and did everything else! Years of stops and starts; years of organizing retreats at a place called Camp Cilca, Athens, Illinois with a brother in Christ and church song leader, Harold Dameron and men's fellowship events at Springfield Bible Church were trials of fire.

The fires were testing ground of frustration, self-doubting and misdirected energies.

However, there have been opportunities for other things. Most folks who travel anywhere in the world are naturally curious about where all these Gideon Bibles come from in our hotel nightstands! I was one of the curious.

In January 1995, I took up the offer from brother Ted Lindquist, the new member coordinator of the Springfield, Illinois Gideon Bible folks and joined. This was more than an honor for me, having remembered receiving Gideon New Testaments as a little boy!

My appointment to Vice President of the Camp in 1996 was not a good move! I was totally out of my league in a position like this and resigned after one of my three expected years in that post.

The one thing the Gideons do best is to hand out the Word of God FREE to the public! We also speak in churches of all sizes creating awareness and any kind of support for an organization where there are no local overhead costs.

Something happens when the Word of God goes from a believer into the hands of a nonbeliever! What blessings and a privilege for a Copy of God's Word to pass from one hand to another! Even better with a prayer of "Lord, save that one!" My brother Gene Grman taught me this evangelistic prayer.

Over the years, we have gone into Nursing Homes where sometimes cranky old men have cussed us out. We have done certain public schools (which shall remain unnamed for a reason) where a huge administrator once even tried to intimidate me while I was standing on a legitimate public property)!

My favorite has been and will always be our annual August Bible Blitz on the Campus of Illinois State University, Normal, Illinois. Thousands of Scripture have been handed out over the years there to mostly the freshmen and women on this campus. We pray the Word of God continues to do its work as a two-edged sword – cutting to the quick and convicting sinners of their need for Christ!! AMEN!!

911 IMPACT

It was not until a Promise Keepers event on September 7, 2001 when Joe White brought the message of the Cross back to a dying Promise Keeper movement, did clarity, purpose and repentance refocus me on what was really important in Ministry.

After the single most visually striking illustrative "sermon" Joe or anyone has ever preached, where he hewed a Cross out of two massive telephone poles, I answered an altar call. There I put down some thoughts and sins on a piece of paper which brother Joe White nailed to the Cross.

Every single hammer stroke of every single nail felt as if I was driving it into Christ Himself. I never want to feel like that ever again.

Four days later, barbarians from the Middle East flew planes into the World Trade Center and the Pentagon. Brother in eternity Todd Beamer and his fellow martyrs caused Flight 93 to crash into a field in Shanksville, Pennsylvania.

The Terrorists' attacks of 911 burned something into the consciousness of every American, especially Christians. The 'event' brought us back to our churches and the other religions to their temples.

All over the country attendance skyrocketed, even in so-called 'Interfaith' services. I remember praying a three page Spiritual Warfare prayer as God gave me such an inner peace and rest, even amongst the angst of this horror.

One major problem was this renewed interest in God and the church was a short-lived and an illusion. These were professing Christians who had never experienced rebirth. Eventually those who sought refuge from the horror of 911 turned their backs on the Lord as soon as things normalized.

They became like those in John 6:65-66. They proved the Words of Jesus to be absolutely correct: *And He said, "Therefore I have said to you that no one can come to Me unless it has been granted to him by My Father." From that time many of His disciples went back and walked with Him no more.*

I did not want any of this, either for my family or myself.

The Celebrity Culture of America chose to go with Oprah Winfrey, the High priestess of the 21st century Baals – the New Age movement. Oprah's "insight" to her gullible followers was that each of the 3000 people who died on 911 went straight to Heaven, according to her own book of "theology".

She described them all as angels…never mind what Jesus actually said in the above verses from John 6:65-66! These sort of battles for promoting the Absolute Truth of the Gospel drove me to the point we are today in our ministry.

BUSINESS MEN IN CHRIST

After years of serving with humility with my sons Bernie and Sam, in preparing Men's Breakfasts etc at our home church, the Lord led me away in March 2004 to a new group of about 18-20 men called Business Men in Christ. This complimented my service at Springfield Bible Church.

The B.M.I.C. was nothing I have ever seen in a Christian Men's Group! First of all, it was not about businessmen! There were men from the street, insurance guys, construction workers and guys like myself there.

The group was started by former U.S. Marines Tom Cheshire, David Rosche as well as Doug Ryherd, the only businessman in the group! Springfield, Illinois and its suburbs has never seen such a committed group of men who are passionate about Jesus.

In less than a few months, I was graciously invited into the executive leadership team as the Communications Director and promptly set out to get the word out about our group and our mission.

The three pillars were simple but profound: Discipleship, Outreach and Service. To that end, we have a different pastor or ministry leader monthly come to speak at our monthly breakfast meetings on Biblical matters with practical application.

All speakers were and are, carefully chosen according to a very closely aligned Biblical Statement of Faith. This had to be reinforced after a former U.S. Marine Chaplain caused uproar by stating "all religions" go up different sides of the same mountain of God and began promoting unbiblical mysticism.

This kind of talk may be required in the land of political correctness, but not here with men who are His remnant and are serious about seeking Him, and Him alone, daily!

The wonderful thing about our group of sold out men in our red shirts is the involvement of wonderful wives and children! The support we receive from them encourages us to be bold in our witness anywhere He sends us.

We outgrew 2 locations in one year and with our 1955 American La France Classic Fire Engine Pumper have become identifiable in parades all over Sangamon County, Illinois where we distribute Gospel Tracts instead of candy.

We pray continually for those multiple thousands of tracts over the past 3 years to reach the person God had intended them for.

Of all the golf outing fundraisers for the Inner City Mission (a Christian homeless family residence where we serve; www.inner-citymission.net); or Couples' dinners etc we are involved with, nothing compares to the exchange of a Gospel tract from one hand to another, in the Service of the King.

However, two major events in Springfield during the fall of 2005 established Business Men in Christ as the premier Evangelistic Men's Ministry in the Capitol city of Illinois.

The Illinois Baptist State Association (IBSA) brought Christian Illusionist Brock Gill to town in mid October for a three day youth revival which the B.M.I.C. promoted across the region. Over two hundred youth were saved over those nights and from counseling at least four of them, I knew these kids were serious.

The very next week was the huge Casting Crowns concert which represented the first major Christian concert in Springfield in a large venue in over a decade. This in itself was a leap of faith and a testimony to how the Lord moves in mysterious ways for His Own Purposes!

In January 2005, two of our members – Calvin Miller and Brian Oaks - started emailing each other and us about bringing the Crowns to Springfield. Mark Hall and the Casting Crowns, a church worship band who had their start at the First Baptist Church, Daytona Beach, had stormed Christian music and brought serious evangelism back to the stage.

When a date opened up for the Springfield concert on October 27, 2005, we signed a contract in April with just $29 in the bank! To make matters more interesting, we had to make a down payment of $12,500 in two weeks and none of us had this kind of a resource!

I approached my brother in Christ, Rob Isringhausen, the late founder of one of the premier BMW dealers in the United States (Isringhausen Imports) to see if he would back this project. To my utter surprise and only because the Lord had His Hand on it, Rob spoke to his brother Geoff and they loaned me the $25,000 interest-free, with the pledge to repay them the day after the concert.

The entire early fall was spent behind the windshield driving up and down Interstates U.S. 55 and U.S. 72, speaking to churches, pastors, youth leaders, Sunday school classes etc. to promote both the Concert and Brock Gill for the IBSA. After all, we had to sell about 3500 tickets to pay our loans and bills!

To make a long story short, the reason the Lord allowed this concert to move forward was found in the urgent Gospel message by Evangelist Tony Nolan. Tony is a dynamic, popular youth speaker from Georgia. His altar call was the largest ever in Springfield.

Over 600 people answered the Altar Call, many of them older adults. I can not say they all accepted Christ as Savior, only He knows. But whatever it was, it was the biggest response to the Gospel ever seen in this city for many moons!

This event has set us on course as a ministry known not just for gospel tracts, golf fundraisers or a fire truck. The Lord has moved the leaders of B.M.I.C. into ministries where He wants to have an impact. From our local missionary Jim Cook, to our president Tom Cheshire, He has humbled us to His Service.

Tom is now spearheading a Men's Discipleship movement in Central Illinois, partnering us with Brian Doyle's Iron Sharpens Iron National Men's Conference. Brian was once the New England region manager for Promise Keepers. It was with humility and brokenness the Lord selected me to head up the prayer teams for the first National Men's conference ever to come to Springfield.

I salute my brothers in Business Men in Christ, especially my fellow executive leaders and the Co-Founders of the Group: Lt. David Rosche, USMC (retired); Tom Cheshire (USMC retired); Doug Ryherd and Roger Bucher.

STRENGTH THROUGH SUFFERING

"I will show him how much he must suffer for My name's sake." Acts 9:16

These are the Words of the Lord to Ananias about the newly converted Pharisee and well known Christian persecutor Saul. No one who is called to Ministry, at any level, escapes any level of suffering.

Saul, now Paul, recalled in 2 Corinthians 12:7-9 how he begged the Lord to remove the "thorn" in his flesh which a messenger from Satan had placed there to torment him and keep him from exalting himself. The Lord's response to him was *"My grace is sufficient for you, for power is perfected in weakness ".*

Oswald Chambers writes if you are going to be used by God, He will take you through a number of experiences that are not meant for you personally at all. They are designed to make you useful in His hands, and to enable you to understand what takes place in the lives of others. 1

What occurred in my life post-Casting Crowns celebrations sobered me up tremendously and has dramatically turned me from a Christian culture warrior on the edge to a full-fledged, Sold-out, 100% Crusader for Christ and prayer warrior!

Major physical problems in November 2005 and the following painful months at times had me thinking the end was not far off, and it was time to meet Sweet Jesus! It recalled the fall of 2000 when the Lord took me through a 30 day study by Luis Palau on death and dying out of His Own Purposes.

I never comprehended that until my own youngest brother Dinesh Earl, a physician from Chicago died in January 2001 at the age of 36 and I had to deliver the Eulogy and comfort the family. The Lord prepared me for the tragedy months in advance through His Word.

This time it was the most intense personal time of my life, borne completely with a smile. I knew something was wrong. The pain, the tests, the blood tests, X-rays, upper and lower GI's etc....all found nothing except the normal things associated with Upper GI problems (Acid reflux etc). I will never know what the Lord saved me from until Glory. I could feel the prayer of hundreds of the saints in four states on my behalf.

There was no questioning of the Lord. Life went on as normal. Through it all, I never turned from the Scriptures. In fact I plunged deeper into the Word studying the Prophets and obsessing about

Isaiah and Ezekiel and the Millennial Kingdom found from Ezekiel Chapter 34 onwards.

For any serious Christian, a Daily Bible is a must. Not just any Daily Bible, but the John MacArthur New King James Version Daily Bible. Its notes would make you want to go out and read all MacArthur's books and commentaries!!

One is able to read the entire Bible in one year and it is enriches you beyond your wildest hope! However, one of my most precious possessions is a Dramatized Version of the Bible. That resource was and still is my hope and comfort.

No commercial promotion here, but Zondervan did an excellent job selecting the voices who read the Bible as God Almighty, Jesus, the Prophets etc. It made the Bible come alive and reveals so many things to you, the more you listen to the same book or chapter, over and over again.

It makes you look in the printed book to see what you have missed. Daily listening to the Word, reading, researching were my escape from pain. What finally broke a looming depression over the pain and not knowing what it was my mother, wife Vicki and our dear friends Peter and Toni Martin laying hands on me one night!

My mom, a prayer warrior who spends hours on her knees for decades praying for her children, prayed the Blood of Christ down on me and from then on, I felt as if the bonds were broken off me.

Hallelujah! Christ had freed my suffering from an inward looking self- concern, to an upward looking fiery test which confirmed everything Oswald Chambers wrote.

To paraphrase Oswald, "it is not about me!" Another revelation was confirmed later in a reading from 1 Peter 2: 20, "*For what credit is there if, when you sin and are harshly treated, you endure it with patience?* ***But if when you do what is right and suffer for it you patiently endure it, this finds favor with God.***" (Emphasis mine) What the Spirit of God revealed this to me "endure this now, so you won't have to go through the same trial and testing twice!"

Praise the Lord as He reminds me of His Sovereignty and Testimony of Him before the world!

NATIONAL DAY OF PRAYER 2006

During the National Day of Prayer 2005, Marshall Brown, Dave Rosche and I showed up at the East Steps of the Illinois State Capitol, as many have done in the past, to attend the Annual Noon Rally. Except, there was none! It was cancelled.

We swore there and then to bring it back. In the spring of 2006, I obtained permission to hold the Rally there under the auspices of B.M.I.C. and WLUJ 89.7FM, the Springfield-based affiliate of the Moody Bible Institute Broadcasting network.

The run-up to May 4, 2006 held some special challenges. I ran into several obstacles as I discovered how real Spiritual warfare is! I sought out the officials at the National Day of Prayer Task Force, based at Shirley Dobson's office in Colorado Springs, Colorado and was certified as their coordinator in Springfield. (Dr. Henry Blackaby was the Chairman of the year's event.)

The Lord provided Prayer cover, as I head up this Event, from some of the most powerful prayer warriors I ever met in my life. I met a brother at the Springfield, Illinois-based International House of Prayer by the name of James Nesbit. Scott Beauchamp, director of the Springfield International House of Prayer and Dr. Earl Powell surrounded me with prayer.

James has to be the most unforgettable person I have met in 2006! He runs a ministry called Prepare the Way Ministry (www.preparethewaymin.com). It is a prayer and prophetic ministry. In the winter and spring of 2006, he and his team began a 40 day/40 city Prayer Tour around the state of Illinois. They stopped at all corners of the state, worshipping and holding Intercessory prayer meetings statewide.

What this has spurred is the renewal of a vital and critical Prayer ministry in Central Illinois. James became our lead Prayer leader at the Event. He, along with several other prayer warriors on our collective knees brought off this Prayer Rally. The Lord claimed His territory from the devil in victory on Thursday May 4, 2006.

It was not without controversy. A local newspaper had a reporter interview me about the NDP Rally's return to the State Capitol. In the story there was a comment against us from Americans United for the Separation of Church and State! The reason? We, Business Men in **CHRIST**, said the Rally was about **Christ** alone!

We were simply exercising our Freedom of Religion rights to have a Prayer Rally in America, which honors Jesus Christ!! Americans United is led by Barry Lynn, whom America sees all over television each Christmas trying to remove Nativity scenes from public squares. What Americans United did was to call into question all the good men, women and children who were participating in our rally with the intention of honoring God.

They ranged from children's choirs and the Fleming Violin Academy to pastors of Springfield largest "mega-churches" and African-American congregations. Despite receiving nasty hate e-mail etc. the Lord continues to move to accomplish His purposes. It is not everyday atheists email you to call you a Pharisee!! I thought they did not believe the Bible!

We are now expanding our prayer ministry county wide and into a nearby county. The Lord alone knows how He will use this movement to His Glory. Jesus instructed us to be as clever as foxes but pure as doves! We are compliant.

SUMMARY

This is the background for what follows here. In the pages ahead, there is the thread of Effective Christianity. I tried to fully and objectively examine various topics from every angle which could affect the life of a seeker and believer. Everything is fully based on the inerrant, literal Holy Scriptures - without apology.

In my own little way, I tried to put together a book which reads like a conversation between friends while holding up as a manual of teachings I have been blessed with over many years. It took many months, days and hours of reading, research and ringing on the e-doors of several ministry leaders to seek advice on several topics.

Many topics could not be examined in detail, except in personal intensive Bible and group study. The reason for even bringing them up is due to the absolute fact they have worked in my life. These steps to personal repentance, Holiness and sanctification have served to bring me ever so closer to the Holy God of the Universe who has been so good to us, and given so much joy and peace in my life, regardless of personal circumstance.

Life Lessons, Leadership and Legacy are the underlying theme-threads of the book.

You will like the story of Doug Mazza at the end of the penultimate chapter. Doug is the President of Joni Tada's ministry in Agoura Hills, California. My struggles pale in comparison to all past and present giants of the faith. Doug is a giant of the faith in his own right.

The Leadership chapters examine the qualities which made (and continue to make) certain Biblical and lay leaders the type of people they became as the Lord worked through them. We will look at Joshua and his leadership qualities. These attributes say certain things about his walk with Lord we can learn from.

The Legacy portion examines Biblical and historical examples of different types of legacies. The blessing of Jacob on his Twelve sons, soon to be the fathers of the Twelve Tribes of Israel is still the most stunning to me. You will be amazed at the Christian lineage of Abraham Lincoln and his current relatives in Salt Lake City, Utah!

In the dwindling minutes of the game of life, the Two Minute warning if you will, these three attributes are essential. Unlike a real football game, the Two Minute warning can come at any time!

This book is the result of a dream which began in June 2002 when the farewell message by outgoing President of the Southern Baptist Convention (SBC) Dr. James Merritt at the Edward Jones Dome in St. Louis, Missouri turned my life around.

The verse of the sermon responsible for this work is 2 Timothy 4:7 (KJV) "*I have fought a good fight, I have finished my course, I have kept the faith*".

Right around that time Dr. Jerry Falwell was talking about 4th Quarter winners in life and ministry. It crystallized in my mind. How can we live effectively the remaining days of our lives, so we can go home to Jesus as Paul did in the above Scripture?

For four years I collected research, clippings etc in a huge folder. Right before I was about to begin seriously writing, the entire folder disappeared!! Completely! Even after turning the house upside down Vicki and I could not find it! Simply put, the Lord wanted His story told FROM HIM, not a bunch of clipped materials. After a half year of looking for it, I still have not found that folder...and do not care to find it either!

Over the months of writer's block and then the final two months of intense outpouring of the Holy Ghost on my life, it was His Hand on my life which finally led to the following work.

I did have an opportunity to thank Dr. Merritt personally at the 2004 Indianapolis SBC for the message which put the rest of my life in perspective. He is a fine Southern gentleman and one of several big church preachers who are uncompromising in Biblical Truth! Glory to God!

Bryan McKenzie is now the pastor of Grace Bible Church in Lake Jackson, Texas. In 2002, he was the Central Illinois Director of the Fellowship of Christian Athletes and about to introduce a man named Dr. Robert Lewis and his Men's Fraternity to Springfield.

That winter, Men's Fraternity's Great Adventure moved men like Bryan, Tom Cheshire and I to the furtherance of the Lord's Kingdom. We have all come alive because what the world needs is men who HAVE come alive. It was a pleasure to finally meet Dr. Lewis in Greensboro, N.C. where he was doing a Men's Fraternity breakout session for the 2006 SBC. He took one look at me and said "you are living the Great Adventure, aren't you!!"

Indeed, we are, sir! We are indeed!

CHAPTER 1

EFFECTIVE CHRISTIANITY:

THE POWER OF GREAT FAITH

ON BEING A DISCIPLE........

Jesus promised His DISCIPLES three things: that they would be entirely fearless, absurdly happy, and that they would get into trouble.
W. Russell Maltby

"Quit playing, start praying. Quit feasting, start fasting. Talk less with men, talk more with God. Listen less to men; listen to the words of God. Skip travel, start travail."
Leonard Ravenhil (1)

DEFINING MOMENTS:

I once heard or saw this quote from the Prince of Preachers Charles Spurgeon *"Prayers are heard in heaven in proportion to our faith. Little faith gets very great mercies, but great faith still greater"*. I believe this because great faith comes from a vital, uncluttered relationship with an Almighty God!

Great faith is a sold out, solid, selfless, single-minded pure love for Almighty God and Jesus, through the Spirit.

Great faith is order, other-focused and obedience unto death.

Great faith is conscience, clarity, candor, charity and clinging to the Cross of Christ.

Great faith is purposeful practicality, perfected in prayer and if you have it you will know it.

It is a faith that is legendary as in the classic piece called "A Zimbabwean Martyr's Prayer". The testimony is well known in certain Christian churches for its power and commitment. According to Southern Nazarene University 2, their veteran African-American missionary Louise Robinson Chapman passed on this prayer which had been recovered from the Martyred African pastor's papers. It is not clear if his murder was by Islamic or other forces in this part of the world. However he did die because of his refusal to give up Christ!

After reading the entire prayer/statement, we will look at some famous last words of both believers and non-believers (at the end of this chapter). We report, you decide!

The question should then be asked, a la Joe White, "what it all comes down to, when it is all said and done, **WHICH SIDE OF THE CROSS ARE YOU ON**?"

Here is the famous statement by this young pastor who must have seen Heaven open up and Jesus standing next to the Throne applauding! I first heard this from Joe White at the Conseco Field house in Indianapolis on September 7, 2001, a night that changed my life's focus.

"I'm a part of the fellowship of the unashamed. The die has been cast. I have stepped over the line. The decision has been made. I'm a disciple of His and I won't look back, let up, slow down, back away, or be still.

My past is redeemed. My present makes sense. My future is secure. I'm done and finished with low living, sight walking, small planning, smooth knees, colorless dreams, tamed visions, mundane talking, cheap living, and dwarfed goals.

I no longer need preeminence, prosperity, position, promotions, plaudits, or popularity. I don't have to be right, or first, or tops, or recognized, or praised, or rewarded. I live by faith, lean on His presence, walk by patience, lift by prayer, and labor by Holy Spirit power.

My face is set. My gait is fast. My goal is heaven. My road may be narrow, my way rough, my companions few, but my guide is reliable and my mission is clear.

I will not be bought, compromised, detoured, lured away, turned back, deluded or delayed.

I will not flinch in the face of sacrifice or hesitate in the presence of the adversary. I will not negotiate at the table of the enemy, ponder at the pool of popularity, or meander in the maze of mediocrity.

I won't give up, shut up, or let up until I have stayed up, stored up, prayed up, paid up, and preached up for the cause of Christ.

I am a disciple of Jesus. I must give until I drop, preach until all know, and work until He comes. And when He does come for His own, He'll have no problems recognizing me. My colors will be clear!" 2

WOW!! AMEN AND AMEN!!

When it all comes down to this, choose Christ or DIE...do we have it in us? Do we have that kind of commitment and passion? Can we lay it all down when it is all said and done?

Here was this young man's defining moment. Here was his "Stephen" moment and he went home with all flags flying!

Speaking for myself, this is one thing I can stand on. When the roll is called up yonder and the demons of the Beast in their Nazi-like uniforms say "choose or die", I will Pledge Allegiance to the Lamb!

On April 20, 1999, two students in trench coats walked into Columbine High School and began shooting. Dylan Klebold and Eric Harris were both wearing Darwinist inspired T-shirts which said "NATURAL SELECTION" on them (how about that, evolutionists?)

The story of Cassie Bernall and how these two boys killed her is now historical legend. Her "YES" to the question of her belief in God right before these two thugs killed her has resounded world-wide and is stilled talked about.

That "YES" allowed Preacher Franklin Graham to speak to a grieving country bluntly about the Gospel of Jesus Christ He preached the Good News to untold millions at the Televised National funeral in Colorado. The killers meant it for evil but God used it for Good!!

That "YES" was Cassie's defining moment.

There comes a time in each person's life when there is a choice to be made.

The young Zimbabwean pastor's defining moment happened long before he penned those potent words in his final statement. His eventual sacrificial death for being a Christian was just the closing chapter for him.

My defining moment came on a sick bed in June 1988 when I was forced to slow down. I had a choice to make – a life of sin and alcohol or heaven! Then with no particular person in mind or no plans to marry, I dedicated all my future children to the Lord.

A defining moment can be described as the instant a life can be transformed due to a choice. This instant is the so called "jump the shark" moment when a person's Character is truly revealed.

For our purposes we have the Bible, the only Book sufficient enough for all life's issues. Please reflect on the consequences of each Biblical hero's choice to their contemporaries and thus, the Kingdom of Heaven.

Here are some defining moments throughout the Bible:

- Moses and the Burning Bush encounter with the Living God
- Ruth's decision to follow Naomi away from pagan Moab. Ruth later married Boaz. She is in the genealogy of the Lord Jesus Christ.
- King David's decision to break all the Commandments in order to have another man's wife, Bathsheba. After their son King Solomon dies, the Nation Israel followed a path to death.
- Elijah's confrontation with 450 pagan priests of Baal. Soon after, Elijah never tasted death as Chariots of Fire took him into Heaven! He was one of only two human beings in History who have never died.

- Nebuchadnezzar lifted his eyes up towards Heaven literally, after a long period of living with the beasts of the field, eating grass as the oxen. That specific act of the former pagan King of Babylon brought him into the Kingdom of God.
- The Roman Centurion's encounter with Christ (Matthew 8:5-11) was the first time Jesus remarked "Truly I say to you, I have not found such great faith with anyone in Israel." This moment was a precursor to the Time of the Gentiles.
- The Samaritan woman at Jacob's well (John 4: 4-30) moment came when Jesus asked her for some water. Little did she know His request was really an offer!
- Saul was knocked off a horse on the way to Damascus to kill Christians. Christ brought him up to the Third Heaven, made him Paul, the Apostle to the Gentiles.
- John Mark and Paul had a major disagreement. Paul sent him packing. John Mark continued to grow in the ways of the Lord...and wrote the Gospel of Mark.

One defining moment I wish to briefly examine is the story of the Rich Young Ruler. Here is the account from Mark 10: 17-25 (NKJV).

> *17 Now as He was going out on the road, one came running, knelt before Him, and asked Him, "Good Teacher, what shall I do that I may inherit eternal life?"*
>
> *18 So Jesus said to him, "Why do you call Me good? No one is good but One, that is, God. 19 You know the commandments: 'Do not commit adultery,' 'Do not murder,' 'Do not steal,' 'Do not bear false witness,' 'Do not defraud,' 'Honor your father and your mother."*
>
> *20 And he answered and said to Him, "Teacher, all these things I have kept from my youth."*
>
> *21 Then Jesus, looking at him, loved him, and said to him, "One thing you lack: Go your way, sell whatever you have and give to the poor, and you will have treasure in heaven; and come, take up the cross, and follow Me."*

22 But he was sad at this word, and went away sorrowful, for he had great possessions.

23 Then Jesus looked around and said to His disciples, "How hard it is for those who have riches to enter the kingdom of God!" 24 And the disciples were astonished at His words. But Jesus answered again and said to them, "Children, how hard it is for those who trust in riches[1] to enter the kingdom of God! 25 It is easier for a camel to go through the eye of a needle than for a rich man to enter the kingdom of Heaven.

The choice he made could not be starker in contrast to the Samaritan woman at the well. Both had powerful, face to face encounters with the Son of God Himself! Yet one chose the world, the other chose the master.

Here is what the rich young ruler experienced in his meeting with Christ:

- He asked about "inheriting" eternal life. As a rich ruler, he was accustomed to being an heir to wealth. Therefore knowing the Law and not being a Sadducee (who were so sad, you see, they did not believe in life after death), he knew and expected Heaven, as a son of Abraham.
- He told the Lord he kept all the Commandments from his youth. Notice the Scripture says "Jesus looked at him and loved him." This love is "agape"; a divine affection similar to the Love Jesus has for us!
- He got the command from the Commander in Chief in all active verbs: "**Go** your way, **sell** whatever you have and **give** it to the poor" The equation was Go, Sell and Give equals "have treasure in heaven".
- He was given three other commands: **Come**, **take up** the cross and **follow** Me!

HIS REQUIREMENTS:

Let us look again to the contrast with the Samaritan woman at the well.

By the way, Jesus used what the great Evangelist Ray Comfort calls the RCCR method. Ray is the first modern Bible teacher to return Evangelism to the days of Spurgeon and others when sin, repentance and hell were taught in order to show folks their need for a sinner.

The RCCR method is RELATE, CREATE, CONVICT AND REVEAL. 3

Jesus had her undivided attention. Here He was a "Jew" talking to the hated Samaritan people – outcasts from heaven as we once were!

He **related** to her situation by simply striking up a conversation. Jesus saw her worth as a potential child of His, even though He knew her outcast status as an adulterer and a woman living in sin.

By His evangelistic outreach therefore, He **created** the opportunity first by asking her for a cup of water to quench His thirst! This led right away into a discussion of Living Water. Jesus showed us the example here how to witness. We are to share the water which flows through us because the Spirit of God lives within us. SHARE YOUR JOY! Drink deeply of the Lord and tell the world Who has quenched our thirst!! AMEN!

Then Christ used the Law to **convict** her. Scripture says in Romans 7:7 "...I would not have known sin EXCEPT for the Law!" The Law is the schoolmaster which teaches us how we have fallen short of the Glory of God. What does this mean?

Simply, if a person has told a lie, even a little white lie, he/she is a liar. If a person has taken something without asking, he/she is a thief. If a person has lusted after another with impure sexual thoughts, he/she is an adulterer. As Ray Comfort says, that person is a lying, thieving adulterer at heart and has to face God on Judgment Day! Therefore such a person is in heap big trouble without a Mediator interceding for us to say "This one's Mine!" This is using the Law to Evangelize. It is the only meaningful way to bring a soul to the realization of the need for a Savior from the Wrath which is to come!

By her own admission the Samaritan woman convicted herself by admitting she had no husband. Jesus knew she had been divorced FIVE times...an ancient day Elizabeth Taylor! His Word, as He IS the WORD, pierced her to the quick and she was realized she was not talking to a mere mortal man!

Then He **revealed** Himself to her: *The woman said to Him, I know that Messiah is coming, He Who is called the Christ (the Anointed One); and when He arrives, He will tell us everything we need to know and make it clear to us. Jesus said to her, I Who now speak with you am He.* (John 4:25-26, Amplified)

This is what Ray Comfort calls RCCR. In all my years of reading books on the Bible, Theology etc…it was Ray's simple teaching found in Revival's GOLDEN KEY (redone in 2006 as "THE WAY OF THE MASTER") which changed my entire life and for the first time in 2002. The Gospel made sense to me as a tool for Evangelism! Before that I was just another "all heads bowed, eyes closed, and sing "Just as I am" 250 times kind of a guy"! Then it was actor Kirk Cameron (Growing Pains and ALL LEFT BEHIND movies) speaking at Calvary Temple in Springfield that year who then exposed me to the teaching of Hell's Best Kept Secret!

Now we know the approach Jesus used to evangelize on Himself to the Samaritan woman. He comes to each individual in a different way. Scripture says we do not seek the things of God; it is He who calls us to Himself. The thing to learn here is the method He used on two different types of individuals and how those of us in frontline evangelism can do the same.

But there is more. Jesus used clear instructions in both the Present AND Future Tense to both the Samaritan woman in John 4 and the rich young ruler in Mark 10: 17-25 AMP. Jesus' prophetic word was thus: "*A time will come, however, indeed it is already here, when the true (genuine) worshipers will worship the Father in spirit and in truth (reality); for the Father is seeking just such people as these as His worshipers"*… John 4: 23

He was predicting the end of temple worship and the coming Time of the Gentiles when the Gospel will be preached to the entire world before His Second Coming.

To the rich young ruler, whom the Gospel writer John Mark (Mark 10:21 NKJV) said "Jesus, looking at him, loved him…" Those words speak volumes to us and we need to go on our collective faces and thank Almighty God He loves us even before we loved Him! The young ruler was given simple, clear words: **GO, SELL, GIVE** and then **COME, TAKE UP** AND **FOLLOW.**

The man refused to Go; declined to Sell and would not Give. Therefore he could not Come, would not take Take up and would never Follow.

Are you that man or woman? What are your gods and worldly idols? What are the things which could cause even a maturing adult to say "not now, I am enjoying life? I never had it this good and want to grab it before it is gone. I will go to church on Sunday!" Do you know such a person?

The active verbs Go, Sell and Give are almost like a computer programming language; i.e**. if when you go and sell and give then come and take up and follow!** Jesus had used the same words – "come follow me" to some future fishers of men back in the rural, pristine Galilee region (namely the future Apostles Simon Peter, Andrew, James and John). That was all he needed to say!

These men were simple fishermen who had grown up under the usual rabbinical teaching, knew the Law, but could not make it past the genius stage to become a rabbi. So like most of their brethren, they went to work with their hands in humble toil. The rich man had a different calling because he had much more to give up.

Jesus calls us out exactly where He knows our loyalty lies. He went straight to the Samaritan woman's sin and the rich young ruler's (his love of his money). Is there something you are hanging on to which is preventing the Eternal Lord of Destiny from working in your life, or even bringing eternal salvation to your soul? If there is, let it go right now and turn to Him!

TAKE UP THE CROSS:

Something unusual jumped out at me in the passage about the young ruler, (whom Jesus also loved!). He said "take up your CROSS…. (and follow me)". Can you imagine the scholars and the teachers of the law, not to mention the ordinary man scratching his head and wondering "what does that mean"?

The Cross was already the chosen open method of execution to the Roman occupiers of the Holy Land. Everyone knew the horrible death one can experience there. The condemned person not only had to die on the two pieces of wood, but CARRY his own cross to the Execution site!

So why was the Great Rabbi telling certain people to "take up their cross and follow Him"? Was not this a cruel assertion? This is a fair question which Jesus will be happy to let the Holy Spirit explain to us! It is so completely required Jesus mentioned it five times in the Gospels (emphasis mine):

Matthew 10:38... *"And he who does not **take his cross and follow after Me is not worthy of Me."***

Matthew 16:34...*'Then Jesus said to His disciples, "If anyone wishes to come after Me, he must deny himself, and **take up his cross and follow Me."'***

Mark 8:34... *"And He summoned the crowd with His disciples, and said to them, "If anyone wishes to come after Me, **he must deny himself, and take up his cross and follow Me"***

Luke 9: 23... *"And He was saying to them all, "If anyone wishes to come after Me, **he must deny himself, and take up his cross daily and follow Me"**.*

Luke 14:27... "Whoever ***does not carry his own cross and come after Me cannot be My disciple"***.

We know the Cross is associated with brutal Roman death. We know the person about to die on the two pieces of wood carries one's own Cross. Therefore the theme of death runs through this absolutely CRITICAL message from the Lord to those who want to be His sheep!

Why death? Whose death? When should this death occur? To whom should this death occur? Jesus had not even gone to the Cross yet! No one on earth knew then He was to die on it! The religious authorities wanted to kill Him BY STONING! Jesus Himself had hinted about it many times, but NOTHING about any Cross. So why was He talking about this over and over, as written in these Gospels?

For us to die, means we have to come to the end of ourselves in a philosophical way in our entire being. Our self-sufficiency must end. Our independence must end. Our self-importance must end.

When He is all we have, He is all we need.

Hence we must totally and figuratively nail ourselves to the Cross. Again the following Scripture spells it out and tells us, why we are the ones of whom this death is required.

NOTE HERE: this death occurs ONLY when we finally submit to His Lordship in our lives and DECIDE we want to be HIS bond-servant and TOTALLY SOLD OUT TO HIM! There is NO other way! There is no formula, purpose-driven or otherwise.

There is only obedience (see next section). (Where there is disobedience, sometimes actual physical death follows for His elect or chosen children!!)

Romans 6: 3-11 (KJV)....why KJV? Happy you asked! Apart from the 'ye's and 'dieths and liveths'...the translation and its meaning simply could not be clearer!

3 Know ye not, that so many of us as were baptized into Jesus Christ were baptized into his death?

4 Therefore we are buried with him by baptism into death: that like as Christ was raised up from the dead by the glory of the Father, even so we also should walk in newness of life.

5 for if we have been planted together in the likeness of his death, we shall be also in the likeness of his resurrection:

6 Knowing this, that our old man is crucified with him, that the body of sin might be destroyed, that henceforth we should not serve sin.

7 For he that is dead is freed from sin.

8 Now if we be dead with Christ, we believe that we shall also live with him:

9 Knowing that Christ being raised from the dead dieth no more; death hath no more dominion over him.

10 For in that he died, he died unto sin once: but in that he liveth, he liveth unto God.

11 Likewise reckon ye also yourselves to be dead indeed unto sin, but alive unto God through Jesus Christ our Lord.

PERSONAL NOTE: I could have used one of those increasingly popular para-phrases in this book many times, but I do not wish to insult the intelligence of

the reader. The major translations, used entirely in this work, are as close to the original manuscript as you can get. Words mean things. As mature and aspiring mature believers, we value authenticity more than fad. We stand apart from the crowds of modern American pop Christianity because He has called us apart and set us apart (literal meaning of the word Holy means) for His own purposes. This is the reason for usage of all four historically accurate translations together with the Lockman Foundation's Amplified Bible. Therefore, the King James, New King James, New International and default translation of this book – the New American Standard Bible (most literal of all) – are the chosen Versions used within. The Amplified Version is produced by the same folks who did the NASB. It is the only text which explains both the meaning and context of the Scriptures.

So we see Christ was the only one who knew the Cross would be the instrument of his death. He laid the ground rules for being His Disciples. In the Romans 6 passage quoted above, the words 'death', 'dieith' and 'dead' appears 12 times in 9 verses! I think the Holy Spirit is giving us a hint of what we need to do! A sold out believer dies to self, period! Note the amount of times He says "dead WITH" Christ! If our 'old nature' is nailed to the Cross we 'took up and carried', we and our sin are DEAD with Christ!

Secondly, the word 'crucified' (or death on the cross) in Verse 6 is a guarantee. It assures us that by taking up our Cross and willingly submitting to this 'execution' our old man or old Adamic nature was nailed there with ALL our sins – past, present and future! Jesus became sin, died an excruciating death burdened by all the sin of mankind for all time, and if we wish to be part of this kingdom, we had better join Him on the Cross, PERIOD!!

Now as believers, we still sin, but we are not and SHOULD NOT be slaves to sin, my friends! Even when we sin, we are so convicted and torn up by it, due to the power of the Holy Spirit we HAVE to repent and confess it right away. After a while, we would want to avoid sin as much as we can, (and we can through His power).

Third, we see we have been nailed to our Cross with the example of Christ. We were crucified with Him. Then we are now 'buried' into 'the baptism of His death'. Here is what John Calvin says in his commentary on the Book of Romans: "*Christ's death was (necessary) to destroy and demolish the DEPRAVITY of our flesh and his resurrection, to effect the renovation of a better nature, and that by baptism we are admitted into a participation of this grace. This foundation being laid, Christians may very suitably be exhorted to strive to respond to their calling....In short, he (the Apostle Paul) teaches what the real character of baptism when rightly received is. So he testifies to the Galatians, that all who have been baptized into Christ 'have put on Christ'. (Galatians 3:27.)* 4

Verse 8 is conditional in saying "*if we be dead with Christ*", then "*we SHALL also live with Him*". Galatians 3:27 teaches this is a result of us 'putting on Christ'. We only put on Christ by being 'baptized into His death'. Now you see the progression here: take up the Cross; die on the Cross; baptize into His death on the Cross; be buried in this Baptism and then LIVE!!

Have you heard any better news than this? Can the world top this? It gets even better! Verse10 says because sin has no dominion over Christ, we who have now fulfilled the requirements of the previous paragraph are **with Him**. He, Christ, now lives in the Heavenly places or "unto God".

"CAN NOT BE MY DISCIPLE"

Anything worth anything comes with a cost...or 'there is no free lunch!' If we wish to renovate our kitchen, the first thing we would do is estimate the cost to see if it is affordable. So it is with following Christ with eyes wide open. We do not follow Christ blindly as opposed to the majority of mankind who is blindly heading straight to eternal separation from God!

When we follow all the directions from the Word of God about becoming a child of Christ we have made a rational decision. We, who are called by His Name, do not check our brains at the door to follow the onetime Nazarene Carpenter who shall return in Power and Glory!

We follow the dictates of ALMIGHTY FATHER in Isaiah 1:18 where GOD the Father says "Come let us reason together as men, says the Lord. Though you sins may be like scarlet, they shall be as white as snow. (AMP)"

Christ reasons in Luke 14: 26-27 (in the Amplified Bible version):

26 If anyone comes to Me and does not hate his [own] father and mother [in the sense of indifference to or relative disregard for them in comparison with his attitude toward God] and [likewise] his wife and children and brothers and sisters—[yes] and even his own life also—he cannot be My disciple.

27 Whoever does not persevere and carry his own cross and come after (follow) Me cannot be My disciple.

Is the Author of the Law telling us to 'hate our own father and mother'? NO! When the call of Christ comes, we are not to cling to them. The Greek word for hate "misco" does mean hatred. While the word "hate" seems almost "unChristlike", what Jesus meant in all honesty is this: YOU MUST PUT ASIDE ANY OTHER LOVE IN THIS WORLD, EVEN FAMILY, AND THEN PUT ME AS LORD OF YOUR LIFE OR YOU CAN NOT BE IN MY ELITE GUARD!

I have appropriated Psalm 27:4 as my life verse. It says *"One thing I have asked from the LORD, that I shall seek: that I may dwell in the house of the LORD all the days of my life, to behold the beauty of the LORD and to meditate in His temple."*

I want to be IN HIS Temple! I want the fullness of His Joy in my life. I want all He promised.

I don't want mediocrity. I don't want just sliding into heaven before the door closes. I don't want to almost live in Victory in Jesus. The only way I avoided this is by becoming His bondservant and disciple!

How about you?!!

<u>AT WHAT COST?</u>

"It is easier to find men who will volunteer to die, than to find those who are willing to endure pain with patience."[1]
— Julius Caesar

This is quite a quote by Caesar! Abraham Lincoln once said "I can make more generals, but horses cost money!!" None of these quotes have anything to with each other, except the underlying theme of "cost".

Being a soldier of Christ - whether you are an 18 year old girl, coming to grips with peer pressure as a senior in High School as a Christian in an anti-Christ world or a 40 year old man in a cubicle writing computer programs in a nameless, faceless bureaucracy of corporate America or any government office – is going to cost you something. Jesus said so!

It is easy to make this a cliché – no pain, no gain. It is easy to speak in platitudes because we live in the largest comfort zone known to Christians since the Cross. It is easy to even write this because we have the freedom, if not the time, to write prose on the topic.

What is not easy is to stand up as a modern Assyrian Christian in Iraq, one million of who have been abandoned to certain death and torture by hordes of Islamic terrorists who are now free to chase them out of their home of almost 2000 years and kill them.

What is not easy is standing firm on the promises of God and the Scriptures in Communist China, outside of the confines of their 'officially sanctioned' churches.

What is not easy is having your family and tribes wiped out in East Africa in bloody wars by the followers of Mohammed against the people of Christ. This is what costs to being a disciple of Christ can be.

But fear not, my friends. There is coming a time in America when those of us who are called by His Name will face the wrath of the prince of this world and his demons. Tribulation has already begun in many places, school districts, workplaces and even some liberal churches.

How do we stand up in times like these? How do we remained firmly planted in Truth while all around us, the world goes to hell – literally. We do not participate! Period!

FOCUS AND SAILING:

But for now, what should we do when faced with obstacles to our Faith. What should we do when the hucksters of heresy hurl hell's lies right at you? WE FOCUS! Focus on the Cross.

I am worse than an amateur sailor. In fact, the only time I went sailing with my friend, (former Rhode Island Street preacher Tommy Knox) 4 in Springfield, he had to tell me what a rudder, helm and other items on the boat were! But one thing became apparent on windy Lake Springfield – one should know how to sail before attempting it!

But I learnt several lessons while researching this section. They have led to several Scriptural life applications. Out on the lake Tommy handed me the controls and had me mark a certain house on the opposite shore of it. No matter what the wind did, I was to keep my hand on the tiller (the steering control) pointed at this arbitrary landmark house. At this point the old hymn by Horatio Spafford came to mind (It is Well with my Soul) 5:

Though Satan should buffet, though trials should come,
Let this blest assurance control,
That Christ has regarded my helpless estate,
And hath shed His own blood for my soul.

No matter what the strong lake winds did, it took a lot of concentration and strength to grip the tiller handle, though the wind 'buffeted' about. Keeping my eyes on the house through it all worked and it was an object lesson to me about never taking my eyes off the Cross! Read the words to the above hymn again then let it bless and encourage you as you face the winds of life beating down from every different direction. We battle principalities and powers of the air and no one knows where the next satanic attack is going to come from. Just know this: 'it is well with my soul' if you are a child of God.

Some of this may probably be old news to you folks who are used to sailing, but the 'center of balance' is important in a sail-boat....not unlike our center. How the sails are configured is important...not unlike our computer. If both are off, we are both off center and will crash into "Safe Mode"!

Both the configuration and the balance working together will determine how the boat will react to the gale force. If our lives are not grounded in Biblical Truth or centered on the Foundation of

Christ and configured by the Holy Spirit, Satan's winds will buffet us big time!

Next, the force of the wind coming onto the sail produces something calls "Center of Effort". In other words: "INCOMING"!! The resistance to this force from both the sailboat and the keel is called "Center of Lateral Resistance". The keel is significant here as it is the main structural beam around which the hull of the boat is built. If this beam or keel is not up to par, this boat is going to get beat up. We have often heard the words "even keel" meaning we are firmly grounded and balanced (at least most of the time!!Ha)

If the center of effort is moving forward to the center of lateral resistance, the sailboat turns away from the wind. This can cause something called heeling which can sometimes bring the Top Mast down as the sails succumb to the wind's angular turn against the force of resistance. If the winds are really strong, an accident may even occur. Extrapolate this to how Disciples of Christ can often lose our way if we not only take our eyes off the target on the shore (the Cross) but if we get so bogged down, we do not stay evenly keeled up in the Word of God! One day, the top mast of life could even come down on us and our boat is going to capsize. What then? Shall we sink or swim?

Then there is the other scenario. If the center of effort is behind the center of resistance, the boat turns into the wind. This can cause a "Weather Helm" or the tendency of the boat to steer itself and sometimes head right into the eye of the wind! Is this what we want: to go straight into trials and tribulations without the power and strength of Christ in us? If our boat of life is behind the winds of life, then we have not taken charge of our lives and are allowing the world to swallow us right into its vortex of oblivion.

Getting drawn in by the winds of the world is so dangerous because the weak amongst us leave themselves open to any EASY and great-sounding spiritual fad. It does seem also, some new movement comes along every decade or so. To correct this weather helm, a process called "Reefing" must be done. This reduces the actual sail area, so the boat will be easier to sail. However the reefing has to be in the main sail and not the jib (the triangular one in the front). A capsized boat can be thus avoided, Lord willing!

Take a look at this 'reefing' maneuver again. There are sometimes two sails on a sail boat (called a schooner or ketch). Some have three or more sails and they are called 'barques' and /or fully rigged ships. The tallest sail is always called the main mast or main sail and is the one which must be shortened when 'reefing'. To reduce the sail area of the main mast when a 'weather helm' is upon us ensures the boat moves straight ahead, most times. This is indicative of how a disciple of Christ should operate – shorten the sail; ***shorten the field***!!

Let us jump from sailing to football. Every coach knows the importance of shortening the field. This is crucial in the Red Zone (twenty yards from the end zone and a touchdown)! Shortening the field brings up the best in the entire team – on the line in the trenches, the running backs, the receivers and the quarterback. I am not talking about the defense here because a Disciple of Christ should not play defense! We are warriors! When Christ calls us as His, He calls us to a fight! I am not one of those Christians who will sit there and let the devil drag me into living in defeat and sacked back at the 40 yard line with first and 30 to go!

Shortening the field brings out honesty. Shortening the field brings out integrity. Shortening the field brings out just pure guts! However shortening the field means harder hits from the other side. Shortening the field requires more concentration for accomplishment and the rewards are almost, well, heavenly!!

This is crunch time for believers, whether we are 'reefing' (shortening the main mast on the sailboat) or shortening the field to advance and score on the enemy. Two things are happening in the life of a true disciple and they both demand one thing for victory – Focus! The first thing is know against whom you are playing and secondly, know Who has called the play! This could be your Two-Minute Warning!

By the way, did you ever wonder where the term "three sheets to the wind" came from?! It is a nautical term which originated around 1821. The sheet is not the sail but the rope on a sailboat. If a sailor has one sheet lose, he is look at as a rank amateur!! If he has all three sheets or ropes are loose, the boat tends to lurch about like 'a drunken sailor'. This is where that term came from!

FOCUS ON CHANGE:

O victory in Jesus,
My Savior, forever.
He sought me and bought me
With His redeeming blood;
He loved me ere I knew Him,
And all my love is due Him,
He plunged me to victory,
Beneath the cleansing flood 8

If anyone knows of any sweeter worship music than the old hymns, I am open to listening. This is from a fan of my brother in Christ Pastor Ross Parsley, the number one worship minister in America from the New Life Church in Colorado Springs and Australian Darlene Zschech of Hillsong. It brings up the following passage from Mark 4:35-41 and Mark 5:1(NKJV):

> *"On the same day, when evening had come, He said to them, "Let us cross over to the other side." Now when they had left the multitude, they took Him along in the boat as He was. And other little boats were also with Him. And a great wind-storm arose, and the waves beat into the boat, so that it was already filling. But He was in the stern, asleep on a pillow. And they awoke Him and said to Him, "Teacher, do You not care that we are perishing?" Then He arose and rebuked the wind, and said to the sea, "Peace, be still!" And the wind ceased and there was a great calm. But He said to them, "Why are you so fearful? How is it that you have no faith?" And they feared exceedingly, and said to one another, "Who can this be, that even the wind and the sea obey Him!" Then they came to the other side of the sea, to the country of the Gadarenes."*

There is no profound expository lesson to teach from the above passage at this point. I like this testimony about the Disciples and Jesus in a boat because it can be a metaphor for those of who are

His disciples and are called for this Trip of a Lifetime in His boat. We were saved and got signed up for a trip to the Golden Shores. When life's storms hit, let us not forget who is in the boat with us, my friends!! He is at the Helm, even when the waves start hitting high and hard. Just at the moment your boat starts taking on water, CRY OUT TO HIM! Why? If we don't go over, we will go under! AMEN?

We have talked a lot about sailing and the requirements of being His disciple. The thread running through all this discussion is Change. This is when the surrendered rubber meets the Road to Glory and we went from zero to Heaven in the wink of an eye! This is true change - the kind which takes us over troubled waves to the Golden Shores which we fixed our eyes upon, while holding the tiller on the sailboat.

The underlying principle is Change. Do not be like St. Augustine who once prayed "Lord, deliver me from Lust....but not just yet!!!" Do not start bargaining with God, telling Him "You ready God? NOW, I am going to change.....if....." The number one definition of change in Webster's Dictionary is 'an event that occurs when something passes from one state of phase to another'. This describes our conversion into Christ perfectly.

With a change like this, our Focus needs to change. He is now the Be-all and End- all; the Alpha and the Omega. The journey into being a true disciple who has paid one's dues comes from realizing life is a daily walk with the One True God and His Son Jesus Christ. Pinpointing this Truth and keeping our eyes fixed on Jesus.

Mike Breaux was a pastor at Southland Christian Church in Lexington, Kentucky the 1990's. In fact he was once a pastor at one of our local churches many years ago – Rochester Christian Church, where a number of my friends are members. A graduate of Lincoln Christian Seminary where a lot of our friends graduated from, Pastor Mike once did a sermon series during the winter of 1997 at Southland called Recovery (from any situation: alcoholism, divorce etc) 9. I think these seven main points he used are practical steps anyone can apply to prepare ourselves for the Growth Christ wish to achieve in us. *I added all the commentary to his seven bullet points in order to drive them home.*

Focus on the goals and not the garbage. This world is so full of noise, distraction and a lot of nothing. The prince of this world has so corrupted the information system that we have 500 TV channels and complain we have nothing to watch; we have a closet full of clothes and say we have nothing to wear and a fridge full of food with nothing to eat. Nothing, nothing, nothing. This is what our world is full of and why we need to follow the Scriptures as true Disciples: *"I press on toward the goal for the prize of the upward call of God in Christ Jesus" (Philippians 3:14)*

Focus on doing good, not feeling good. Too much of modern Christianity has merged with the cheap worldly pop psychology of "Feeling Good". There are so many doctor Feelgoods preaching, writing books and drawing multiple thousands to their mega churches, Biblical truth has gone out the door. Missions are down but giving is up! Why is that? James 2:20 says explicitly *"faith without works is useless!"* Put another way, whatever you have done for the 'least of these' you have done for Him. Charles Spurgeon, the Prince of Preachers once said, "Brothers, do something, do something, do something!" AMEN and AMEN! So the moral of the story: DO SOMETHING!

Focus on people who help, not hinder. Proverbs 17:22 (NIV) says *"A cheerful heart is good medicine, but a crushed spirit dries up the bones"*. As the great talk radio raconteur Rush Limbaugh once said he has never seen any books written about "How to fail". If one wants to be good at something, would one go to someone who has done it terribly? NO! So why listen to folks who say you can not accomplish a task, especially when it involves Kingdom word. God is the Designer behind all our plans and He will provide, if it is HIS will. Also, unless a righteous person is specifically sent by the Lord, under inspiration from the Holy Spirit, to encourage you to change direction on a specific project, seek counsel on your knees as the primary course of action.

Focus on progress, not perfection. When we were saved from the pit by the Blood of the Lamb, our behavior was less than desirable. Through a period of mentoring, study, worship, fellowship and prayer, we grow and mature as Christians. (Notice I did not say disciples because that definition has specific requirements as discussed.) There has never been a perfect man, save One – the God who became Man to save us. So quit trying to be perfect and concentrate on doing what we are assigned as honestly and God-inspired as we can, to the best of His Ability. We are also not in a sprint, but a marathon. Jesus said 'my yoke is easy and my burden light'. This is absolutely true. Do not let false doctrine, guilt-laden pop psychology or the secular world make your daily walk with the Lord harder than it should be. To the maturing believer, it gets easier and easier! Look at the words to this song "Just a Closer Walk with Thee" (Public domain). It describes the kind of walk we desire with the Lord.

Through this world of toil and snares,
If I falter, Lord, who cares?
Who with me my burden shares?
None but Thee, dear Lord, none but Thee.
Just a closer walk with Thee,
Precious Jesus, hear my plea,
Daily walking close to Thee,
Let it be, dear Lord, let it be. [10]

Focus on changing one defect at a time. Do not miss the forest, for the trees. Here is a famous verse from Jesus in Matthew 6:34 "*So do not worry about tomorrow; for tomorrow will care for itself. Each day has enough trouble of its own*". For most of my life, I would take the long view about matters of family, finances, fellowship and even personal responsibility. It was not until I was truly saved and sealed by the Holy Spirit until the Day of Redemption that I really began seeing my own faults and trying to correct them. In the interim, everyone else saw them because I was too busy with my head in the sand or thinking time would take care of everything. What has made a huge difference in my prayer life is praying Psalm 139: 23-24 almost daily – *"Search me, O God, and know my heart; try me and know my anxious thoughts; and see if there be any hurtful way in me, and lead me in the everlasting way*". The Lord has used this passage to root things out of me which had been long forgotten. I obviously needed to repent of and verbally renounce them while begging forgiveness! These were things in my past which Satan had covered up enough in order to throw against me one day but the Lord used for good. Please use this Scripture because no Disciple of Christ should have hidden blemishes. Satan revels in being able to sift the saints like sand.

Focus on victory, one day at a time....or start small. This is almost the flip side of the previous point. We have already won as children of Christ. Let us act like it. The late great British Prime Minister Winston Churchill has had some of the greatest quotes in Modern History. Here he is again *"Victory at all costs, victory in spite of all terror, victory however long and hard the road may be; for without victory there is no survival."* [11] When facing the trials of life, adopt the words of the great Winnie as your own and transfer Christ into every fiber of your being. Without Him, all is terror. Without Him, all is lost. Without Him, all roads are hard. Without Him, we will not survive – not for one minute, on the other side of Glory. Start small moving towards Him or you will remain small if you start without Him.

Focus on God's Ability, not your own power. This is a tremendous point. We live in a dying world which operates in its arrogance. We are supposed to be different. Throughout the Bible, all our heroes, the men who changed the course of History, did it through the power of God. They are Abraham, Moses, Joshua, a little shepherd boy named David, Nehemiah,

Daniel, Mordecai and all the New Testament saints who planted the one True Church – the Body of Christ.

The great Puritan Stephen Charnock writes "*The power of God is that ability and strength whereby He can bring to pass whatsoever He pleases, whatsoever His infinite wisdom may direct, and whatsoever the infinite purity of His will may resolve*". [11] Absolutely! Why I am quoting the Puritans? Well, these folks had a fear and respect of Almighty God that one is hard-pressed to find anywhere in Christianity today.

Time has not diminished the fact God is Pure, Infinite, Almighty and all-Powerful. Time means nothing to the God of Eternity. Somehow the entire world has lost the concept of this God who demands obedience, respect, awe and submission to His Will. True Disciples of Christ must, MUST, ignore those around us, even stumbling blocks in the church, and submit our own will to His. This is a difficult proposition for mortal man. However, what God wants is our AVAILABILITY. He has the Ability to bring to pass what He has purposed. All He wants is our obedience. The sooner we acknowledge this fact, the easier His Yoke becomes!

FAMOUS LAST WORDS:

Here are some famous final words of both the famous and infamous, the Christian and the non-believer.

NON-BELIEVERS:

Saddam Hussein (Iraqi Dictator): "Is that what you call manhood?"[12]

Kurt Cobain (Grunge musician in a suicide note): "Frances and Courtney (Love), I'll be at your altar. Please keep going Courtney, for Frances. For her life will be so much happier without me. I love you. (Cobain was a follower of Satan-worshipper and the god of many in rock music – Aleister Crowley, *my note*.)

Ludwig Van Beethoven (composer): "Too bad, too bad, it is too late!!"

Anne Boleyn (whom King Henry VIII married after divorcing his first wife): "O God, have pity on my soul, O God, have pity on my soul."

Cardinal Borgia (later to become the corrupt Pope Alexander VI): "I have provided in the course of my life for everything except death, and now, alas, I am to die unprepared!"

Sigmund Freud (favorite psychologist to the secular world): "The meager satisfaction that man can extract from reality leaves him starving."

Luther Burbank (great American agricultural genius, creator of the Russet-Burbank potato): "I don't feel good!"

Karl Marx (founder of Communism): "Go on, get out! Last words are for fools who haven't said enough!"

Tolstoy (author of War and Peace): "Even in the Valley of the Shadow of death, two and two do not make six!"

H.G. Wells (author): "Go away, I am alright."

Bing Crosby (singer): "That was a great game of golf!"

Vincent Van Gogh (artist): "I shall never get rid of this depression."

James Dean (actor): "My fun days are over."

W.C. Fields (comedian/actor): "I am looking for a loophole."

Winston Churchill: "There is no hope, all is lost". 13

BELIEVERS:

Jonathan Edwards (great American revivalist): "Trust in God and you shall have nothing to fear."

Patrick Henry (U.S. Founding Father): "Doctor, I wish you to observe how real and beneficial the religion of Christ is to a man who is about to die."

D.L. Moody (great American Evangelist): "I see earth receding; heaven is opening. God is calling me!"

William Shakespeare (the Bard of Avon): I commend my soul into the Hands of God, my Creator, hoping and assuredly believing, through the merits of Jesus Christ my Savior, to be made partaker of life everlasting; and my body to the earth, whereof it was made."

Martin Luther (hero of the Protestant Reformation): "Into Thy Hands I commend my spirit! Thou hast redeemed me, O God of Truth."

Daniel Webster (great American statesman and senator 1800's): "Thank God, the gospel of Jesus Christ brought life and immortality to light…I still live."

David Livingstone (great British Missionary): "Build me a hut to die in, I am going home."

Charles Dickens (British author): "I commit my soul to the mercy of God, through our Lord and Savior Jesus Christ, and I exhort my dear children humbly to try and guide themselves by the teaching of the New Testament."

Andrew Jackson (U.S. President known as 'Old Hickory'): "My dear children do not grieve for me…. I am my God's. I belong to Him. I go but a short time before you, and …I hope and trust to meet you all in heaven."

Isaac Watts (hymn-writer, hymns like 'Joy to the World' and 'O God Our Help in Ages Past'): It is a great mercy that I have no manner of fear or dread of death. I could, if God please, lay my head back and die without terror this afternoon!" [13]

THE GREATEST LAST WORDS OF ALL TIME: "IT IS FINISHED" Jesus Christ, Son of God A.D. 33 (John 19:30)

CHAPTER 2

EFFECTIVE CHRISTIANITY

THE POWER OF THE BIBLE AND SIN

Another century and there will not be a Bible on earth!
Voltaire (1694-1778) [1]

Voltaire was a French author – philosopher of the Age of Enlightenment and was a huge influence on one of the heroes of the American Revolution and fellow Deist, Thomas Paine. He was very virulently anti-Christian and denied the Gospels, the existence of Jesus Christ and once boasted Christianity would not last 20 more years and he would destroy it with his 'single hand'!

(1) He once said of the Bible 'in 100 years this book will be forgotten, eliminated'. Yet his last words were "I am abandoned by God and man.....I shall go to hell, and you will go with me. O Christ! O Jesus Christ"*! Unfortunately most of today's world will take Voltaire up on this invitation into the everlasting flames "where the worm does not die".

Whether one is in the first quarter of life as a Christian, at 'half time', or even the fourth quarter (and it is my contention we are in the Fourth Quarter as no one knows when we will be called home), one thing is constant. The constant is the Eternal Word of God – His Bible (from the Greek word "biblios" or books).

ORIGINS OF THE BIBLE: 9

The 57 Chevy was created in Detroit. The Hershey's of Pennsylvania began an American chocolate institution in their home. Coca Cola Classic comes out of Atlanta....but the elitists of this world: some scientists, academics, liberals and secularists – all want us to believe you and I came from a monkey AND we should also believe the world started with a bang because the Bible is just a 'collection of fictional stories'!

The argument against the Bible by secularists and even worse, their liberal Christian allies is that the Bible was written by a bunch of men (religious, political and military) whose only purpose was to promote their own ideals, causes and beliefs. They search the Scriptures to find numerous examples of murder, mass murder, adultery, homosexuality, torture, slavery.

They pull out stories of rape, abuse of women, harsh judgment of pagan and other cultic cultures. They quote kings and princes with multiple wives, concubines and prostitutes...etc thereby proving a massive failure to properly interpret the Bible. The only reason there is so much murder and mayhem in the Bible, is due to SIN and the fallen nature of man/woman. The Holy God of the Universe abhors this conduct yet does not shield us from knowledge of it, for our own illumination.

The only way to interpret the Bible is **LITERALLY.** God knows exactly what He says!! There is another type of interpretation called **ALLEGORICAL.** The majority of seminaries and too many preachers/teachers use this method. This teaching implies that God did not really mean what He had written. In fact His Words are 'symbolism for something else'! This is heresy because if one believes Allegorical teaching, one places the responsibility of interpreting the Bible on failed humans rather than God.

The Bible's authority relies on two categories: **Internal Evidence**, meaning that which is found in the Bible itself and

External Evidence or evidence found outside the Bible through science, archaeology and ancient manuscripts.

How did God write the Bible? He used ordinary men! God could have written, published and thrown down the Book from Heaven but He wanted to use flawed men whom He raised from their own cultures and even weaknesses. Under the inspiration of the Holy Spirit, 40 authors wrote the 66 books of the Bible over a period of 1600 years.

These authors came from all walks of life. Moses (the first five books of the Bible or the Pentateuch) was a shepherd and formerly the Prince of Egypt. Joshua was God's own general. Samuel was a priest. Kings David (Psalms) and Solomon (Proverbs, Ecclesiastes, and Song of Solomon) committed many moral lapses and even atrocities against a Holy God, yet He forgave them and used their experiences to show His Grace, justice and mercy!

Isaiah, Jeremiah, Ezekiel and Daniel were in a class by themselves as prophets of the Most Holy One who had face to face encounters with Jesus Christ numerous times. All of these men prophesied not only God's coming wrath against the pagan abominations of Israel and Judah, but the end times and the Second Coming of Christ, who was not even born the first time yet! Peter said in *2 Peter1:20-21: "Above all, you must understand that no prophecy of Scripture came about by the prophet's own interpretation. For prophecy never had its origin in the will of man, but men spoke from God as they were carried along by the Holy Spirit." (NIV)*

Amos was a shepherd. Jonah was a disobedient biased man, who did not want the Gentile Assyrians in Nineveh to be saved. Matthew was a corrupt Tax Collector. Luke was a doctor. Peter was a tempestuous fisherman who never went to seminary or Pharisee school, but brought more people to the Lord in one day after Pentecost, than every Pharisee put together. The Apostle Paul was one of those Pharisees who spent his non-believing days hunting and killing Christians!!

These authors wrote the Bible in three different continents over those 1600 years. These continents were Africa, Asia and Europe. The authors were eyewitnesses to the events and in the case where only God was present (as in Genesis); the Holy Spirit moved the pens of these men, using their own language and style. **ONE THING TO NOTE: MOST OF THESE AUTHORS, EXCEPT FOR THE NEW TESTAMENT WRITERS, NEVER KNEW EACH OTHER!!!**

The Book was written in three different languages: Hebrew, Aramaic and Greek by, in all cases of the New Testament, EYEWITNESSES! The Old Testament is an accurate historical record as well as Prophetic and Revealing of the Voice of God, the Father, Son and Holy Spirit. I recommend a lot of books and websites but the best teachers on Apologetics are Norman Geisler (**www.normangeisler.com**); Ravi Zacharias (**www.rzim.org**) and Dr. Voddie Baucham (**www.voddiebaucham.com**). Visit these websites and read their books and articles or listen to them when you can.

Moses wrote the Pentateuch (Genesis, Exodus, Numbers, Leviticus and Deuteronomy) in Hebrew and so did most of the Old Testament writers, but by 300 BC or so, the original writings and Language had begun to fade. So the Lord placed into the heart of 72 Jewish Scholars, under the reign of Ptolemy Philadephus in Alexandria, Egypt, to translate the entire Jewish or Old Testament into Greek. By that time, God had closed the Old Testament. (There was a 400 period of silence from the Malachi to Matthew. The final Old Testament prophet was John the Baptist).

These 72 Scholars translated the entire Scroll from Hebrew to Greek for two reasons: to preserve it and to reach Hellenistic Jews. They wrote in separate rooms and NOT ONE JOT OR TITTLE was different in their Translations! This body of work became known as the **Septuagint** or the LXX (meaning 70)! Many of the New Testament heroes relied on the LXX and quoted it regularly.

The New Testament was written or translated entirely into Greek. Jesus spoke Aramaic, a language still used in parts of Iraq (home of the Garden of Eden), Syria and Lebanon by Arab Christians and Chaldeans (of UR of the Chaldeans fame, the original tribe of the Patriarch Abraham). A flavor of this language can be seen and heard in the movie "The Passion of the Christ". It was a language, believe it or not, which descended from ARAM, the 5th son of Shem, the son of Noah, right after the Great Flood.

The Apostle Peter wrote in *2 Peter 1:16 "For we did not follow cleverly devised tales when we made known to you the power and coming of Our Lord Jesus Christ BUT we were EYEWITNESSES of His Majesty"*. Dr. Luke who wrote the Books of Luke and Acts and also ministered to our Apostle Paul gave an even longer defense in *Luke 1:1-4* when he writes about being handed down An Account from *"those who from the beginning were eyewitnesses and servants of the Word!"*

The Bible is **THE ONLY** Book of **ANY** religion with this much historical proof and data to support our Faith and contentions

Dr Voddie Baucham says in ***"The Ever-loving Truth"*** 2 there are Five main arguments to support the historicity of the Bible:

1. The Bible comes from varied, yet consistent sources
2. There are an abundance of early copies of the Biblical Text
3. The Bible was translated into other languages very soon after compiled.
4. The writings of the early church fathers contain massive quotes from the Text.
5. The Bible is corroborated by archeological evidence.

It has been estimated there are over 24,000 manuscripts (including ancient original portions) which contain all or most of the New Testament! These can be found under strict care and security all over Christendom. When compared to Jewish Antiquity and Writings, they have stood the test of time. The earliest copies currently surviving today, almost 2000 years later are from before 150 AD!!

When the **Dead Sea Scrolls** were found in Qumran between 1947 and 1956, it included all kinds of authentic fragments of original and ancient Jewish Scripture (the Old Testament), plus a guide on how to live in the current Messianic (or Christian) age! The first thing the orthodox Rabbis did when they found out there was a commentary on the Book of Isaiah was to turn to Isaiah 53 to find out what it said about our Messiah, according to tradition.

There has never been a Book of History with this much accuracy as the Bible. There are still books written about President Abraham

Lincoln....over 140 yrs after he died. The Disciple John wrote in *1 John 1: 1-3 used these active verbs: SEEN WITH OUR OWN EYES; HEARD, LOOKED AT, TOUCHED WITH OUR OWN HAND.* The GALLIC Wars of Julius Caesar and Aristotle's Classic "POETICS" were written 1000 yrs and 1400 yrs after their deaths. None of these secular classics were written by eyewitnesses to the events!

More can be said in major detail about the Origins of the Bible. We are encouraged to search out the Scriptures ourselves for more historical proof which can be cross-referenced with books by Historians like Eusebius and Hegesippus, the latter who lived less than 100 years after Christ died on April 3, 33 AD and rose on April 5, 33 AD. How do I know this date?

The secular historian Flavius Josephus, the son of a Jewish Pharisee was alive at this same time! After Jerusalem was destroyed by Titus in AD 70 and over 1 million killed at Masada, Josephus was taken to Rome by Vaspasian who later became Emperor of Rome. Vaspasian commissioned Josephus to write the History of the Jewish people.

Here is what he wrote about Jesus: *About this time there was Jesus, a wise man, if indeed one ought to call him a man. For he was one who performed surprising deeds and was a teacher of such people as accept the truth gladly. He won over many Jews and many of the Greeks. He was the Christ. And when, upon an accusation by the principal men among us, Pilate had condemned him to a cross, those who had in the first place come to love him did not give up their affection for him. He appeared to them spending a third day restored to life, for the prophets of God had prophesied these things and countless other marvels about him. And the tribe of the Christians, so called after him, has still to this day not disappeared.* *(Antiquities 18.63) FLAVIUS JOSEPHUS* 3.

So why did God give us the Bible? He did so to show us WHO HE IS – His True Character of Unbridled Holiness, Grace, Love, Justice, Wrath and Mercy. He also gave us the Bible as a Daily "OWNERS OPERATING MANUAL". It has the guidelines to live the good and upright life of decency, love and integrity.

THE PROBLEM OF SIN

DEADLY SINS

The word Repentance is used over 100 times in the Bible. The most famous practitioner of the word is John the Baptist. The cousin of the Lord Himself did not seem to be very well acquainted with his more Heavenly kin, Jesus, later on in life. This indicated a separate upbringing. As the Voice Crying in the Wilderness, he lived in caves and ate locusts and honey.

This final Old Testament Prophet brought the simple message to the Jews. He was emphatic, loud and clear: *"REPENT, repent for the Kingdom of God is at hand!"* Many repented and were baptized. Webster's dictionary describes 'repent' as "remorse for past conduct". The original Greek word 'metamelomai' is even clearer as it indicates a change of mind or remorse for sin.

No one who hopes to live a fruitful life at any point in time can achieve that point of vital communication with the Lord without addressing the matter of sin. In the long, hard road of development and discipline, the Lord has put me to the test many times and each time it involved one of the so-called Seven Deadly Sins. Each time, He showed me a way to grow out of it, repent of it and become dead to it.

Sometimes repenting of a sin and asking forgiveness is easier said than done. In many prayer meetings, personal prayer time, corporate prayer time as well, I would repent, seek His Face and go away feeling good about things. Soon after, another sin or a strange thought completely out of left field would be thrown right before my eyes. You see the devil knows how to not only mess with us but to destroy the peace of Forgiveness we get from the Lord. He can not take away our forgiveness because no one or nothing can snatch us out of His Hands, but he can really try to take our joy**, if we let him.**

I once heard a story about Martin Luther, the father of our Protestant Reformation. Martin Luther said that one night he awoke to find Satan at the foot of his bed with a huge scroll. Satan, who is called the Accuser of the Brethren (amongst other things in the Bible!!) started reading off Luther's sins one by one off the scroll.

After each sin, the Accuser would say, "do you remember this sin, Martin"...and Luther would say "yes!"

This went on for what Luther said felt like an eternity. The Scroll of Sins listed so many sins that he committed. Satan accused and Martin acknowledged. After a while Luther said he felt guilty, unworthy and heading straight for hell!!

Just as Luther began feeling that way, Almighty God spoke up and said:" Martin, tell the devil to unroll the scroll all the way to the end!!

Martin said, "Devil, unroll the scroll all the way to the end!" The devil said "shut up, Martin!!"

He said it again. Same result. Finally Martin firmly told Satan, "Devil, in the Name of Jesus, I command you to unroll the scroll all the way to the end!"

Reluctantly, the devil slowly unrolled it to the end and there at the bottom of the scroll WRITTEN IN BLOOD were these words:" THIS ENTIRE SIN ACCOUNT OF MARTIN LUTHER HAS BEEN PAID IN FULL!!"

How about that? The first thing to notice is even the devil submits to the Name of Jesus and secondly, our sins HAVE been paid in full for all time!! Hallelujah!!

What remains unfinished is the power of sin over human kind. This will never be over until we go to be with the Lord or He returns to claim His own.

GANDHI'S SEVEN DEADLY SINS:

Mahatma Gandhi is an interesting study. He was once turned away from a 'Christian' church in South Africa where he went to hear his friend preach, because of his skin color! While he allegedly admired Christ after the incident, Gandhi was a Hindu and led them to their Independence from Britain in 1947. He had his own list of seven deadly sins. These have been known for years as well as the story of Gandhi being turned away from the church in South Africa. The latter should not have been a deterrent to seeking to know the True Christ. As an aside, no one has an excuse once he/she has the Knowledge of the Holy!

Here are the Mahatma's so-called Seven Deadly Sins.

- Wealth without work
- Pleasure without conscience
- Science without humanity
- Knowledge without character
- Politics without principle
- Commerce without morality
- Worship without sacrifice

Everything about Gandhi's seven deadly sins is correct as straightforward maxims for life. We see an outbreak of gambling, lottery and get-rich-quick methods as people try to 'get it all' right now instead of working for it. The media, Hollywood and the culture says anyone can go ahead and have fun, 'as long as you do not hurt anyone'.

Modern science claims sovereignty over knowledge, something which belongs only to the Holy One. They claim man can change the climate and weather. This directly violates Scripture from Genesis to Revelation. He who created the world holds it in His Hands.

Knowledge without character is obvious in the elite colleges and institutes of higher learning in America. College campuses and classrooms, as well as the Federal judiciary are controlled by men and women who are as despicable in the Eyes of a Holy God as those "hypocrites and teachers of the Law (NIV)"

Modern politics and principle are an oxymoron. However, commerce and immorality do not necessarily have to go hand in hand. There are men and women of Christ in business who honor His Name.

David Green owns the Hobby Lobby chain of stores and the best outlet for anything pertaining to arts and crafts in America. When he started the company in 1972, he decided to follow Biblical principles. When he went through a financial crisis in 1986, he felt God's prompting on his spirit "you don't have the answers, I have a million of them...[6]" Green and Hobby Lobby is well known for standing alone among businesses in the U.S. and closing on Sundays to honor the Lord's Day. Each Christmas they do full page ads honoring the birth of Christ in every U.S. newspaper. Some Christian businesses are Chick-a-Fil and Domino's Pizza among others.

One thing Gandhi was correct on is Worship being sacrifice. Due to the sacrifice on the Cross (which the Mahatma did not mean), we have no other option but to sacrifice self so we can assign Him all the Worth, Power and Glory. The world has lost its awe and respect for Almighty God, just like both the Northern and Southern Kingdoms described in Chronicles, Jeremiah and Ezekiel. True worship is a rare thing these days!

As a point of humor, here is what George Bernard Shaw called the Seven Deadly Sins (7) – "food, clothing, rent, firing (?), taxes, respectability and children! Nothing can lift those millstones from man's neck but money; and the spirit can not soar until those millstones are lifted!!" Some may agree with this definition!

GOD'S DEFINITION OF THE SEVEN SINS:

Some time will be spent explaining all Seven Deadly sins for a reason. A true disciple of Christ can not have a vibrant, two- way, fruitful relationship with the Lord if any of these sins has a stronghold on him or her. I have experienced this first hand and it took many years of confusion, prayer, repentance and humbling myself to realize the fact. There is a prayer of confession after each sin is discussed along the lines of the same prayer(s) which have helped me overcome these sins.

The worst of the seven deadly sins is Pride. People in ministry should be the last to strut around boastfully and pat ourselves on the back for what "awesome Christians" we are. Yet this is exactly what we do. Every single person in the Kingdom of God from the lowest of the low, like me to mega- church pastor Rick Warren has been guilty of this sin. During the Christmas season of 2006, Fox News Channel did a special called "Can Rick Warren Save the World?" As a preacher of the Gospel, he should have shot that title down, as Christ is the Only One who saves, yet he participated in it.

James 4:16 (NKJV) says *"But you boast in your arrogance. All such boasting is evil."* If we must boast, do so only in the Lord, so people will see the Jesus we claim and glorify Him in heaven.

Pride is the opposite of humility. Don't be like the Kris Kristofferson song of the 1970's (O God, it's hard to be humble, when you're perfect in every way). *God resists the proud, but gives grace to the humble (James 4:6). The humble He guides in justice and the humble He teaches His way (Psalm 25:9).* All quotations are NKJV. Why am I quoting James? He is the half-brother of Jesus, the head of the church in the Holy City of Jerusalem and the author of the First Book of the New Testament, approximately 20 years after the Crucifixion. He was later clubbed to death by the Pharisees.

One more thing about pride. If we see the pride in others and become offended, this is vanity as well. Let us see ourselves as we are and humble ourselves before Holy God.

PRAYER: Father, in the Name of Jesus, I confess I have sought the praise of men and women even while saying I am doing Your perfect Will. I confess my sin before you, oh Most Holy Lord. I have made you my Co Pilot, instead of the Navigator of my life. I have created stone idols, put my name to it, and claimed it was all for you. Forgive me Lord, have mercy on me. I repent. Wash me with hyssop and I shall be clean, cleanse me and make me white as snow and I shall sing only of Your Glory and testify to Your Goodness. I humble myself before you. I bow before Your Throne. Father, in Heaven, I come on my face seeking You and You alone. I take up residence daily at the Foot of The Cross. Have mercy on me. In the Name of Jesus, Amen and Amen.

Meditate on: Psalm 40:4; Romans 12:6.

Envy is being resentful of the good things another person receives and trying to find ways to get them either from that person or being bullheaded enough to set out and pursue them for oneself, with a vengeance. It contains a certain amount of pride, but at the same time, it is entirely human nature to look at a successful person with some admiration. If the look has even a trace of resentment which says "what makes that no good person so much better than me?" you have committed the sin of envy. The opposite of envy is love. If the look towards a happy successful person is to congratulate them and share their joy, you are honoring the God who has blessed your brother or sister in Christ. Do not even be envious of those who are rich in worldly things but do not belong to Christ. They have their reward right now. Ours reside in the Kingdom of Heaven. Solomon writes in *Ecclesiastes 4: 4(NKJV): Again, I saw that for all toil and every skillful work a man is envied by his neighbor. This also is vanity and grasping for the wind.*

PRAYER: Father, in the Name of Jesus, I come to you in shame at violating Your Commandment. Lord, I realize I have sinned by being envious of the blessings You have bestowed upon others who are Your people. Lord let me not be a carnal Christian, but to seek wisdom first, like Solomon. Let me desire wisdom and discernment so that I may be able to accomplish the mission you have given me to, in my own life, rather than be envious of another. I fully repent and seek your forgiveness, in the Mighty, Mighty Name of Jesus, I pray, Amen.

Meditate on: 1 Peter 2: 1-2

Anger is something we all battle. We get varying degrees of road rage on the way to work, even us defensive drivers. We become upset at our children for not cleaning their rooms or doing their chores. Even the wife whom the Lord chose for us before the foundation of the world at times causes us anxious moments (imagine what we guys do to our wives…but that are another story ha)! Anger is often our first reaction, even at a mature age when we should know better. It shows almost an immature lack of patience when even the worse situation actually calls for a Christ-like dose of kindness! The great philosopher Yoda (!!) from Star Wars put it succinctly as he told the Jedi "anger leads to fear, fear leads to hate, hate leads to suffering"! How prescient! *Do not hasten in your spirit to be angry, for anger rests in the bosom of fools (Ecclesiastes 7:9). But now you yourselves are to put off all these: anger, wrath, malice, blasphemy, filthy language out of your mouth. (Colossians 3:8; all NKJV).*

PRAYER: Father, in the Name of Jesus, you said to not let the sun go down on my anger. Lord, first of all, take this burden away from me. I realize that if I continue to harbor hate and anger in my heart, I come close to breaking Your commandment to love. Forgive me Lord, for I have sinned against You. Take away my propensity to fly off the handle all the time, to react and lose my temper. Lord have mercy on me, I do not want to do this, but continue to get impatient. Father, I am concerned that if I do not surrender this sin, and You do not take it from me, it will continue to fester within me until it is out of control. So Jesus take this, make me dead to this sin. In Your Holy and Precious Name, Amen.

Meditate on: Psalm 37:8; Ephesians 4:26.

Sloth is not an animal on Sesame Street! It is what the famous Theologian Thomas Aquinas calls "sluggishness of the mind which neglects to begin good... [it] is evil in its effect, if it so oppresses man as to draw him away entirely from good deeds. As a ***former*** Catholic school boy, Aquinas' Summa Theologica was almost required reading! Hebrews 6:12 (KJV) says *"that ye be not slothful, but followers of them who through faith and patience inherit the promises.* Sloth is not something you do when your publisher gives you a deadline or the boss wants that job done right now!

PRAYER: Father, in the Name of Jesus, You did not put us here to bury Your talent under a rock. You did not put us here to sit on a couch and watch life go by while waiting to die. You did not place us with Your Law written on our hearts to be warts on the dead log of life. Wake us from our slumber oh Lord. Give us the fire that burns within us, even those of us who do not know you as Lord and Savior that we may turn from our wicked ways and seek your Holy Face. Only then would we awaken from the sleep of the dead into the promise of Eternal Life and find the Zeal to sing Your Name across the Land. In Thy Holy and Precious Name, I pray. Amen

Meditate on Proverbs 6:6-11; Proverbs 13:4

Greed is NOT good, no matter what the character Gordon Gecko says in the 1980's era movie Wall Street. Over the millennia it has caused murder, hatred, adultery, thievery and all else. Greed has led ordinary men to do evil things to obtain and hold power. Greed has caused the driven lust for more and more things, STUFF, things which shall perish on the Day of Wrath. Greed leads ordinary men and women to place their kids all day long in daycare, while pursuing careers designed to purchase the nicest SUV's; houses in the subdivision with vacations in Disneyworld while pushing their older kids into every imaginable activity every single night of the week! This Greed is not liberating, it is enslaving. It has shackles on your ankles so you can not run and handcuffs your wrists which are not fun.

One of the Ten Commandments can be found in Exodus 20:17 *"You shall not covet your neighbor's house; you shall not covet your neighbor's wife or his male servant or his female servant or his ox or his donkey or anything that belongs to your neighbor."* In his greed King David not only coveted Bathsheba, the wife of Uriah, but it led him to lie, cheat and murder the man. Here was the greatest king who ever lived on earth yet he was a bad example to his playboy son Solomon. Three HUNDRED (as in hundreds) wives were not enough for Solomon, so he needed seven hundred concubines. In the end both had to face the man in the mirror. Is this greed destroying you from within, even though you appear normal and happy on the outside? Look at King Solomon again! He went from the author of the beautiful tome to his virgin and first bride in Song of Songs, to the man with many wives who wrote in Proverbs 25:24 (NIV) *"better to live in a corner of the roof than share a house with a contentious wife*; to the defeated author of Ecclesiastes declaring "all is vanity"!

Greed also affects Legacy. Solomon was also known as the richest man whoever lived. Bill Gates with all his billions has nothing on Solomon. (Read 1 Kings in its entirety). His riches were known throughout the entire known world at the time and people came to bow at his feet just to see the Temple he had built Almighty God! However, in 1 Kings 12: 1-24, you will see the Kingdom of Israel split for one reason, under the Judgment of God – Greed! The people of Israel begged Solomon's son Rehoboam to please ease the heavy yoke of oppressive taxation and control his father Solomon had placed on them, so that he could indulge his and his family's decadent lifestyles. Instead of heeding the advice of the elders of

Israel, the youthful Rehoboam took the advice of the young friends and swore to make the burden even heavier!!

When the British tried this in 1775, there was a Boston Tea Party. The equivalent happened as Israel split in two – the Northern Kingdom of pagan Israel with no good king ever and the Southern Kingdom of Judah with some good, some bad kings. So we see the effects of Greed- split families, corruption and a hardening of the heart towards the God who gave the riches in the first place!

PRAYER: *Heavenly Father, in the Wonderful Name of Jesus, the one True King, the Son of God, who when He walked this earth had nowhere to lay His Head, no home or possessions, saved the clothes on His back; Father, that Jesus is my example of how to live humbly submitted and totally at one with You. Lord, lead me, convict me, discipline me, focus me and let me be the person whom You designed. Let me realize each day, each breath, everything I have, everything You have loaned me for a time, every child You allowed me to raise, is a temporary gift from You and those are what are most important. Lord, let me value my relationship with you over the world's relationship with its 'stuff'; let me turn away from it and place my priorities right where they should be. In You and You alone. In Jesus' Precious and Holy Name. Amen*

Meditate on Proverbs 11:28; Philippians 3: 12-21

Gluttony is deadly sin number six. Here is what Scripture says about it in 1 Corinthians 15:32-34 (AMP):

> *"What do I gain if, merely from the human point of view, I fought with [wild] beasts at Ephesus? If the dead are not raised [at all], let us eat and drink, for tomorrow we will be dead. Do not be so deceived and misled! Evil companionships (communion, associations) corrupt and deprave good manners and morals and character. Awake [from your drunken stupor and return] to sober sense and your right minds, and sin no more. For some of you have not the knowledge of God [you are utterly and willfully and disgracefully ignorant, and continue to be so, lacking the sense of God's*

presence and all true knowledge of Him]. I say this to your shame"

Jesus said "*the Son of Man came eating and drinking and you say 'here is a glutton and a drunkard...' Luke 7:34 (NIV).*

Of course, Jesus was not a glutton or a drunkard but a lot of us are at least gluttonous! Gluttony is really a form of self indulgence which if not reigned in can lead to addiction. Any kind of addiction from chocolate, to diet drinks to southern fried chicken at Po' Folks is not a good thing. Fried chicken at Po' Folks is worth storming the beaches of Normandy for, but over-indulgence of that, with down home biscuits and fried corn on the cob DAILY, can lead to a little weight problem! Once every other day is not bad though, and don't forget to throw in the chicken and dumplings! Whoa Nellie!

PRAYER: *Father in the Mighty Name of Jesus, I confess my sin of overindulgence in Your bounty and goodness. Lord, You have made all things good. Help me not only control my appetite but the tendency to let my eyes deceive me into thinking my stomach is not full. Lord we, as Americans, suffer from that delusion with food so readily available. Strengthen our determination and resolve and make us a healthy people once again. In the Name of Jesus, Amen.* **Meditate on Romans 13: 13-14; Peter 4:3.**

Finally lust....this sin weighs heavily on all humanity. For most of recorded history, men were the chief culprits of not just lust of the eyes, but full-blown active sinning through physical or sexual lust, lust for money, power and position. Things have shifted in the past generation as more and more women are up there competing with men in all of the above! You can blame MTV, and you will be right. You can blame Hollywood and you will be correct. You can blame books, magazines, music and on and on...all would deserve the highest indictment ever. But the problem is sin.

The Bible describes sin as rebellion against God. You know the universal quip in church about a guy who accidentally sees a gorgeous woman go by: "the first look's free and the second one is sin, so most guys take a longer first look!" This sounds funny but Jesus said in Matthew 5:28 (NKJV) "*But I say to you that whoever looks at a woman to lust for her has already committed adultery with her in his heart.*"

Everywhere we go and look, we find ourselves under assault by the god of this world – sin, sex and Satan. Not sex in the pure marital sense, as required by God, but in the worldly lustful, even perverted sense. Even an innocent billboard for a fitness club can cause some guys to drive off the road! I have seen things like this almost happen. Why is pornography, both internet –based and glossy magazines, so popular? Why is gangster rap with dancing half naked women now the rage of the land? You know why? Because we have no standards left!

However it is not just lust of the flesh which holds us down from living in Victory in Jesus. Anything or object which diverts our attention away from what was intended is lust or "emotional indulgence" and should cease immediately!! These "lustful" issues need to be addressed fully TO HIS SATISFACTION, before we can even come close to renewing our place near the Foot of the Cross.

PRAYER: *Father in the Mighty Name of Jesus, I confess the sins of my eyes. Father they have strayed from honoring you to looking, even if sometimes accidentally, looking with too much of a lingering on fleshly things I have ABSOLUTELY NO RIGHT to look at! Lord, make me dead to that particular sin of the flesh. Take from me the propensity to dishonor my dear spouse by looking at another. Father when I am tempted, let me see the dear face of my wife in front of my eyes, so I will not sin against thee. Lord, also take from me the desire to lust for material things and again be content with what You have given me. Lord, I desire purity and to honor You and You alone. To that end, I come again to the Foot of the Cross and see Your Holy Face, in the Mighty Name of Jesus. Amen*

Meditate on Matthew 5:27-30; 1 Corinthians 6:17-19 and Hebrews 13:4-6.

THE GOLIATH OF LUST

Lust is one of the giants we all face and age does not matter! A sixty year old man is just as apt to commit adultery with an increasingly permissive generation of women in their twenties as is a disturbing growth of female teachers abusing teenage male students. The correlation is stunning. There seems to be no line drawn whether it is the 'happily' married bank manager who is a stalwart at church or the principal's wife in Colorado now under trial for giving alcohol to a teen, amongst other illicit crimes.

In my entire life, I have found the best way to defeat the giant is not to run and hide like the armies of Saul in the Old Testament book of 1 Samuel, but to pick up the rocks and go after it! Why?

Well, lust will take you out! You are at its mercy.

Lust desensitizes you. The more you give in, the more it takes you in.

Lust demeans others. The more you ogle; you cheapen that person's humanity.

Lust corrupts your mind. The more you look; the Devil gets a foothold in you.

Lust breaks fellowship with God. The more the Devil gets in, the less room there is for God. Look at what David said in Psalm 51: 12 (KJV)"*Restore unto me the joy of Thy salvation; and uphold me with Thy free spirit*" David knew his relationship with the Holy One was ruptured after his evil adultery/murder adventure with Bathsheba and her poor husband Uriah the Hittite. In the verse 11, David who had known closeness with God unknown since Moses, begged for God NOT to take away His Holy Spirit.

We who are His elect already possess His Holy Spirit who lives in us and sealed us until the Day of Redemption. We are His and no one can snatch us out of His Hands. This does not mean we are not capable of the same vile sins David committed against God - sins of lust with Bathsheba and every other commandment he broke to get her as his own. We are more blessed as some of the old ancient heroes of the Faith in that we are given instruction by Jesus Himself how to defeat this giant.

Matthew 5:27-30 AMP says:

27 You have heard that it was said, You shall not commit adultery.

28 But I say to you that everyone who so much as looks at a woman with evil desire for her has already committed adultery with her in his heart.

29 If your right eye serves as a trap to ensnare you or is an occasion for you to stumble and sin, pluck it out and throw it away. It is better that you lose one of your members than that your whole body be cast into hell (Gehenna).

30 And if your right hand serves as a trap to ensnare you or is an occasion for you to stumble and sin, cut it off and cast it from you. It is better that you lose one of your members than that your entire body should be cast into hell (Gehenna).

Believe it or not, this giant can be defeated! The goliath of lust can be taken down and you do not have to literally pluck our own right eyes out to do so. Temptation bangs on the front door forever, so face it down and slam the door in its face! Everything we need to live in this world can be found in the Bible. We have the Creator of the World Himself praying for us here in John 17: 15-19 AMP:

15 I do not ask that You will take them out of the world, but that You will keep and protect them from the evil one. (Emphasis mine)

16 They are not of the world (worldly, belonging to the world), [just] as I am not of the world.

17 Sanctify them [purify, consecrate, separate them for Yourself, make them holy] by the Truth; Your Word is Truth.

18 Just as You sent Me into the world, I also have sent them into the world.

19 And so for their sake and on their behalf I sanctify (dedicate, consecrate) Myself, that they also may be sanctified (dedicated, consecrated, made holy) in the Truth.

We have been already prayed up to the Throne! The Holy Spirit is the Interpretator of our prayers and Jesus our Intercessor before the Father. We need nothing or nobody else. Go to Him, period! Just like that! As long as we are live we face temptation.

Paul gives the instructions in 1 Corinthians 6: 17-19 NKJV: "*But he who is joined to the Lord is one spirit with Him.* ***Flee sexual immorality****. Every sin that a man does is outside the body, but he who commits sexual immorality sins against his own body. Or do you not know that your body is the temple of the Holy Spirit who is in you, whom you have from God, and you are not your own?" (Emphasis mine)*

In other words: RUN!! When Miss America-wannabee bats her Revlon eyes and her $5000 Crest smile, RUN. When she asks for help to drive her to the mall to pick up a present for her mom, RUN. When he wants to talk about how his wife is not paying him much attention these days because they are so busy, RUN. When he says his wife does not understand him as you do, RUN!

And do not call it an indiscretion. It is SIN, pure and simple; if he or she takes offense... ***put another rock in the slingshot!***

Do not rationalize lust... ***wind up the slingshot!***

Do not make some kind of philosophical argument about it so you can lie to God and justify it to yourself...***raise the slingshot over your head!***

Do not see the passing pleasures of sin for a season but the guilt, shame and awful consequences of immorality....***start whirling the slingshot overhead!***

Go to the root of this desire. Confront it from whence it came. Pray Psalm 139:23-24. Ask the Lord to search you right now and find the wickedness, then grab it by the root and pull it out NOW. He will! He always does! He who is able always fulfills His promises to never leave or forsake us.....***feel the slingshot picking up speed now!***

Once He gets to the root and yanks, do not hold on by saying "oh, no one understands me, loves me, wants me, needs me"! Nonsense! Grab a hold of yourself, man....***LET THAT SLINGSHOT GO AND FIRE THE ROCK IN IT! WATCH IT HIT THE GIANT RIGHT BETWEEN THE EYES! WATCH HIM FALL!***

Do you think our God is a weakling? Do you think He who called the earth out of the darkness and told the waves "only this far you may come and no more" will sit on His Throne and watch His own servant fall to wickedness when the same servant cries out to Him for help from sin? NO!! He is faithful to complete it, my friends. Do not buy the line from a dying world. We are not of this world; we are in-transit back home. Do not put a stain on your white robe.

CHAPTER 3

EFFECTIVE CHRISTIANITY

THE POWER OF PRAYER

"You must pray with all your might. That does not mean saying your prayers, or sitting gazing about in church or chapel with eyes wide open while someone else says them for you. It means fervent, effectual, untiring wrestling with God...This kind of prayer be sure the devil and the world and your own indolent, unbelieving nature will oppose. They will pour water on this flame."
(General William Booth, founder of the Salvation Army) [1]

The good General Booth was a visionary. He was talking about the kind of communication with our Heavenly Father not the soft repetitive mantras we mumble in church once per week or as we sit around the kitchen table saying grace. General Booth is talking about the kind of wrestling Jacob did with the Lord in Genesis 32:24-32. Jacob refused to let the Lord go in their marathon wrestling match, until the Lord blessed him! This is the intensity and passion we should bring to our constant prayer before Our Lord.

In this chapter, we plunge below the surface of superficial supplications into the sound methods of Prayer and its Biblical foundations and applications for us.

Prayer caused the Mighty Hand of God to hold off destroying the pagan rebellion at the foot of Mt Sinai when Moses begged the Lord to spare them, so His Name will be lifted up amongst the Egyptians. Here is the prayer from Exodus 32: 10-14 (AMP):

> *10 Now therefore let Me alone, that My wrath may burn hot against them and that I may destroy them; but I will make of you a great nation.*
>
> *11 But Moses besought the Lord his God, and said, Lord, why does Your wrath blaze hot against Your people, whom You have brought forth out of the land of Egypt with great power and a mighty hand?*
>
> *12 Why should the Egyptians say, for evil He brought them forth, to slay them in the mountains and consume them from the face of the earth? Turn from Your fierce wrath, and change Your mind concerning this evil against Your people.*
>
> *13 [Earnestly] remember Abraham, Isaac, and Israel, Your servants, to whom You swore by Your own self and said to them, I will multiply your seed as the stars of the heavens, and all this land that I have spoken of will I give to your seed, and they shall inherit it forever.*

God did not destroy Israel at THAT time, but He is long-suffering and whatsoever a man sows, so shall he reap. Every soul, except Joshua and Caleb, who came out of Israel, died in the desert, not far from the actual Promised Land.

Abraham's request for God to hold off from destroying Sodom and Gomorrah was not answered because there not even ten righteous men in the city (Genesis 18: 16-33)

Other great prayers in the Bible should inspire us. Why? *"Aren't these superhuman people from the Bible from a time we can not even fathom and we are modern day Americans on the go?"* Well, yes and yes! Well, how about a motherless Hannah praying for the Lord because she was childless. There were people actually making fun of her for not being able to bear a child! How many women do we know in similar circumstances? Do they or we stop praying for them because the Bible stories are old-fashioned?

Look at Hannah's prayer in 1 Samuel 1:11 (NIV): '*And she made a vow, saying, "O LORD Almighty, if you will only look upon your servant's misery and remember me, and not forget your servant but give her a son, then I will give him to the LORD for all the days of his life, and no razor will ever be used on his head"'*. And He did!

Now let us relate Hannah's situation to modern times! From verse 11:

- She made a vow
- She made a request (look on YOUR servant's misery)
- She made a plea (remember and not forget)
- She made a bold demand (give me a son)
- She made a promise (I will give him to the Lord forever)
- She made a covenant (no razor will ever be used on his head).

Hannah did not fall off a kosher turnip truck and start demanding things of Almighty God. She made the Lord her Delight and her entire Being and while she wept bitterly at the temple year after year. She had a vital, living relationship with her Creator only a child of God can have! It takes a lot of courage to make bold prayers as listed in the six points above. Can we still pray like Hannah today and the God of Hannah, Samuel and the church today will still hear and bless?

You bet!! It happened to me! In July 1988 I was 32 years old, burnt out on a 75 hours per week fast past decadent journalist job. The Lord blessed me with a severe case of the mumps. I am not about to get into the medical details of this, but sufficing it to say mumps is one of the causes of infertility in men! I knew this even then and was worried. I wanted to have a Bernie the Third for a decade and now that was about to go the way of the Brooklyn Dodgers.

I said the Lord blessed me with this disease because it was the only way He could get my attention! I spent two weeks flat in bed recovering from a lifetime of living for the world. The rest of the story was already told in the introduction. I approached the Lord the same way Hannah prayed in 1 Samuel 1:11...and I did not even know the verse! A man who grew up in church, went to confirmation classes, preached my first sermon at age 14, did youth group and missions trips like all good young "Christian" men…did not know the Lord to whom he cried out!

I prayed this verbatim "Lord, if you give me children, I will turn them all back to you!" That was it! Nothing fancy. The rest of my confession, initial repentance and turning to the Lord have already been described. After much difficulty (as the Lord wanted me to really appreciate His gifts!) our first child was born almost four years to the day of the prayer in 1988!! Vicki and I have since had two other kids.

I dedicated them all to the Lord as I showed up in the delivery room, all three times dressed in a Rush Limbaugh T-shirt, ditto each time! Even our second child's near death experience was a gift from God. Just as Hannah called her son Samuel, our second – Samuel Eli – was delivered incorrectly by the doctor. He was blue in the face with an Apgar score of one! Five nurses spent what seemed like a long time trying to revive him as we stood turning green (a big feat since I am all brown all the time!).

Finally he coughed up the blood he swallowed in the way out and began the joyful noise he has been making since. Sam is our musician par excellence. He can pick up an instrument, learn two or three things about it, and then almost master it. He now plays with the Fleming Violin Academy. His biggest gig so far with them – the National Anthem at the 2006 World Series Champ St Louis Cardinals/Brewers game the same year.

My oldest son Bernie is walking with the Lord in a super way and now a student of Biblical Truth. He has been a percussionist with The Sangamon Valley Youth Symphony in Springfield and they get to play with their 'elders' in the Illinois Symphony yearly at the annual Christmas program. Sarah is our little eight year old going on eighteen but knows the Word more than some grown ups. All three are saved and then baptized at First Baptist Church in Petersburg, Illinois by preacher Pastor Dwayne Turley.

We only baptized them immediately after getting their own testimonies about their beliefs. Some churches wait until the kid is a teen or older and can speak fluently. That call is not up to me, it is up to the Lord. It is always more prudent to baptize again, if the first profession was not real, and to err in this direction. To paraphrase Scripture: you get saved to know it and baptized to show it.

None of this would be possible without the most Godly, loving wife in the world! Of course, every man thinks about his wife in like manner...as it should be!! Hannah had her husband Elkanah, an obedient observant worshipper of the Lord and so it with Vicki and I.

There are some other very powerful prayers in the Bible. They stand out so much the Lord included them in the Canon of Scripture according to His Divine Intervention. Only once in the Bible is it recorded God extended the life of anyone after a prayer! Look at this amazing story from 2 Kings 29: 1-7 (NKJV):

> *1 In those days Hezekiah was sick and near death. And Isaiah the prophet, the son of Amoz, went to him and said to him, "Thus says the LORD: 'Set your house in order, for you shall die, and not live.'"*
>
> *2 Then he turned his face toward the wall, and prayed to the LORD, saying, 3 "Remember now, O LORD, I pray, how I have walked before You in truth and with a loyal heart, and have done what was good in Your sight." And Hezekiah wept bitterly.*
>
> *4 And it happened, before Isaiah had gone out into the middle court, that the word of the LORD came to him, saying,*
>
> *5 "Return and tell Hezekiah the leader of My people, 'Thus says the LORD, the God of David your father: "I have heard your prayer, I have seen your tears; surely I will heal you. On the third day you shall go up to the house of the LORD. 6 And I will add to your days fifteen years. I will deliver you and this city from the hand of the king of Assyria; and I will defend this city for My own sake, and for the sake of My servant David."'"*
>
> *7 Then Isaiah said, "Take a lump of figs." So they took and laid it on the boil, and he recovered.*

King Hezekiah was one of the very few good kings of the Southern Kingdom of Judah. The Lord blessed Hezekiah with fifteen more years of life. You have heard the stories of people walking out of car crashes unscratched or falling off buildings and living. We all know why, the Keeper of the Stars has our lives in His Hands! Recently I almost drove in front of an Amtrak train without seeing the flashing red lights. It was one of those crossings which have no warning arms! Five seconds later, I would have been history! I know who let me live!

What a real dynamic Prayer is! It is the only way to communicate directly with the God who created us and whom we love, honor and obey until death do us part, in this phase of life! I have always prayed and knew He answered me. Sometimes the answer was 'yes', 'no' or 'no and wait'!

The thing is, from boyhood until 1988, I do not think I prayed effectively as a true warrior at all. Sure I had a huge number of phases made up of several worshipful months of intense fellowship. I think those times were the foundational pillars of an intense prayer life as I went, eyes wide open, seeking him for endless hours per day for months on end. This is huge, as my prayer life was already very good for a decade up until 2004, but not as prophetic and full of revelation as it is now. I can not believe what I had been missing! It was the Discipline of Fasting which changed everything.

During my single days, I spent countless hours sitting on a park bench 3 feet from Lake Ontario in the cold wintry months, late into the night praying over my future spouse Vicki. She was over 1000 miles away in the Chicago suburb of Lockport. The fellowship with my Savior on those nights, where the cold lake winds south of my job at Toronto's Eaton Center bounced off my overcoat, is something I can never forget. Night after night I sat on that bench and prayed as the seagulls landed and wintry couples zoomed by to the Queen's Quay malls. At all times, my eyes were fixed upward.

The months of prayer led into summers spent reading and praying for hours at my window looking into the Heavens. The Lord never left me or forsook me. He laid His Countenance upon me. Yet even those countless hours of prayer where I knew the Father was listening, I never had the Holy Ghost power of a prayer life which the Lord has allowed me to experience now! WOW!! Looking back now, I evaluate those precious times as moments of fear and trembling about Who God really is!

I remember considering fasting as a form of worship about 4 year ago and did nothing about it. In January 2004, I was in Wal-Mart reaching for a box of pop tarts when the Voice of the Lord could not be clearer to me: "I thought you said you were going to fast!" I put that thing back on the shelf faster than one can say "Jackie Robinson". All kinds of fasts have been tried from no lunch for one week, bread and water for two days to the only one which brings me closer to Him in Spirit for prayer – no food for 24 hours.

For someone who has never fasted, I recommend this one. Skipping one supper would not harm you, but check with your doctor first! I cook luscious meals for my wife and kids while fasting without desiring to taste. It IS a discipline. A night's sleep, no breakfast and lunch with an occasional sip of water and a day goes by quickly if you do not think about food and instead read the Word, pray, sing the Hymns from your childhood etc. Try it soon! You have no idea what the Lord has revealed to me in prayer and through His Word....things no preacher has ever spoken of, I guarantee it!

The insights the Lord have given during those years of fasting are invaluable and could never be had in the normal routine of life. This discipline was important when a significant turn in my life happened in May 2006 after the National Day of Prayer Noon Rally in Springfield. My prayer life just took off into the stratosphere as I sought out fellow warriors for intercession and found a home at the Springfield International House of Prayer.

BROKENNESS:

Christianity is the only relationship where the Creator has to smash us to pieces in order to put us together in His Image! If this sounds harsh, then reexamine your love relationship with the Father, through Jesus Christ! Sorry! It is only when we come to the end of our weak, dying mortal self that we can reach up and out to a Holy God who will bless repair us, remold us and restore us to Him.

You have heard the analogy of the potter who refused to sell the jar he made because he was not satisfied with it. The potential buyer could not find a flaw in the beautiful piece of work as he looked on at the potter molding and shaping with his skilled hands. Imagine his surprise when the potter refused to sell the piece to him and then proceeded to smash it to pieces in the fire.

You see, in Divine terms, we can not see ourselves and our flaws, but the Maker can. If we do not have His Eyes, ever seeing and ever knowing, we will die in our own sin and face a judgment of being dashed to pieces where there will be weeping and gnashing of teeth.

As the potter destroys his 'masterpiece' to remake it, so must He break His chosen children in Christ to make us more in the image of His Son? So what is this thing called Brokenness?

It is the shattering of my entire image of myself

It is the surrendering every inch of 'my' territory to Him who owns it.

It is the sidelining, permanently, of my rights to myself to Him.

It is the submission to His Complete discipline (Hebrews 12: 3-11)

It is the singular, focused, deliberate and conscious act of our will joined to His.

Unless a grain of wheat falls to the earth and dies, it remains alone (John 12:24). This means the grain has to come of its self-sustaining stalk, take a hard fall to the ground, be split open so that which the Lord created – the earth – can swallow it up. He then nurtures it with rain and nutrients, causing it to bear more fruit (or grain). This is what the Lord does.

He breaks us in many ways. Man is made up of mind, body and soul. Unfortunately all three elements are not aligned to the Lord all the time, or we would not need discipline!

He breaks us in the mind. As humans we worry about our children, our marriages, our homes, our bills, our parents, our safety, our community, our government etc. This is a lot of worry! This may be preaching to the choir (or not) but what are we doing with all this worry?

You say "why not?!!" Look at the perverted culture. In schools they are handing out condoms and teaching homosexuality to first graders. Teachers are getting arrested for molesting students. This is the result of another thing – the media. For a generation MTV, NBC's Friends, ABC's Desperate Housewives, anything on regular FOX TV have taken the 1960's Sex Revolution to the newest low ever. The same people – the boomers and their kids – who indulged themselves to extremes in the 1960's are now running TV/movie studios and magazines.

Disrespect for women is the worst ever, thanks to these same people who supported burning bras in the 1960's and 1970's for Women's Liberation. They glorify gangster rappers calling their women all kinds of dirty names. They do reality shows encouraging nudity and free reign on pre-marital sex between any gender...and on and on. On Judgment Day will not be enough millstones to put around these necks of those who have corrupted an entire generation! *("Whoever causes one of these little ones who believe in Me to stumble, it would be better for him to have a heavy millstone hung around his neck, and to be drowned in the depth of the sea". Matthew 18:6)*

Our marriages are under attack by the same people who pour illicit sex images at us day in and day out, even in commercials while we are watching something as innocent as Andy Griffith on TV Land!

Financial worries are at the worst these days as bills overwhelm us and we struggle with the high cost of living and education. Even the most modest living of folks feel the pain.

God is the real Therapist. He knows how to cure the patient. How does He do it? He goes straight at the biggest worry we have and brings what looks like disaster right into our lives! I have seen it first hand from finances to children to family crises. We are the potato and He is the masher! To make fluffy, hot buttered mashed potatoes, you got to crush the boiled tater!

God breaks us in the body as well as the mind. In 1997, my dear mother in law Joyce had a brain aneurism. It was the night before I was due to go to a Promise Keepers event, aptly called "Making of a Godly Man" in St Louis. Instead the family was called up to Silver

Cross Hospital in Joliet, Illinois for what doctors thought was the end. She had prayer chains in five states from Illinois to hometown Ardmore, Alabama.

Joyce was in a coma for over 24 hours by the time I was able to get in to visit late in the night. Her pastor Bert Baker was in there. We prayed and the discussion swung to Promise Keepers. Glory of Glory, she spoke out of her coma "aren't you supposed to be at Promise Keepers?!!" The dear woman now runs a Nursing home ministry with my father in law Verlin and Ben Tan. Dozens of people have come to the Lord so close to meeting Him because of this dear woman.

The best example of brokenness is again found in the Bible! The Old Testament book of Job has every attribute of Brokenness. The process that God used to take him through is a shining example of Faith buttressed by fiery trial. Can you imagine this conversation in heaven between Holy God and the scoundrel Devil? God said "have you considered my servant Job"...and then allows the devil to afflict Job with every imaginable disease. God gave Satan just one command – "do not kill him (Job)" This was quite a situation!

Remember the wager between God and Satan was Job will stay faithful to God no matter what. Satan said Job was only faithful because things were going his way! Sure, Job was the Christian Donald Trump of the time (estimated to be around the time of Moses) but then he lost every physical thing. He was a broken man as all his children died. He lost his wealth. He was bodily afflicted with painful sores and boils so bad, he just wanted to die.

He was a broken man in body and mind. The only thing left for Satan to attack and cause harm to was Job's soul. What was Job's reaction? One of the most famous verses in the Bible Job 1:21 "*naked from my mother's womb have I come, and naked I shall return: THE LORD GIVETH AND THE LORD TAKETH AWAY*"....and here is the best part of this verse "blessed be the Name of the Lord!"

How many of us in our trials would make this huge statement? Would we listen to Job's wife who said "curse God and die"? NO!! Fast forward to Job 13:15 when he is now deep into self-doubt and debate with his two friends Eliphaz and Bildad. Job says "*though*

He slays me, I will hope in Him, nevertheless, I will argue my ways before Him."

Chapter after Chapter of this unique book of the Bible is full of intellectual red meat for theologians and laymen to ponder. Chapter after Chapter Job is not only fed untruths about the Nature of God, but He himself joins the conversation.

As we are going through times of testing and trial, our faith gets questioned most of all. Here is where the rubber meets the road. Are we going to "praise Him in the storm" where every tear we cry is already in His Hand or do we 'curse God and die'? Many of us are like Job in all those chapters from chapter 1 to 37. We stand strong for the most part but in our minds or with our closest ones concoct and say all kinds of things to justify why God is doing what He is. Sometimes we are outright incorrect in our assessments, as Job's three friends were as they tried to get him to agree with them.

There is a very crucial thing to note when we are going through a time of trial, testing or discipline. It is something I have learnt from experience and will teach my own children. For your own sake, complete the time of trial all the way. Just go with it OTHERWISE God will take you through it again, if you do not graduate from this one.

Do NOT short circuit the Lord. Otherwise the test which replaces this one will be even more trying than this one. Here is what God told Job in Chapter 38: 1-4 and 40: 7-9.

Chapter 38: 1-4 (NKJV)

> *1 Then the LORD answered Job out of the whirlwind, and said:*
>
> *2 "Who is this who darkens counsel by words without knowledge?*
>
> *3 Now prepare yourself like a man; I will question you, and you shall answer Me.*
>
> *4 "Where were you when I laid the foundations of the earth?*
>
> *Tell Me, if you have understanding.*

Chapter 40: 7-9 (NIV)

7 "Brace yourself like a man; I will question you, and you shall answer me.

8 "Would you discredit my justice? Would you condemn me to justify yourself?

9 Do you have an arm like God's, and can your voice thunder like his?

This was the reaction of Almighty God when He had had enough! How do you think our whining sounds to God! Job was a blessed man because he is one of the few in Scripture who got to have a face to face discussion with the Creator Jesus! My own living encounter with Jesus on the morning of August 16, 1988 only lasted a minute or so and He was gone! In my own face to face I could feel the Power and Love coming off His Face from His deep voice, even the humor. When He spoke to Job, there was a righteous tongue-lashing.

A few things should be noted here. God answered Job out of a whirlwind! Go back to Isaiah chapter 6 and see how even the Voice of God caused the temple's pillars to tremble. Next, twice God told Job to "brace or prepare yourself like a man, I will question you and you WILL answer ME!" WOW!

How many of us could stand up under the Thunder and Majesty of the Voice of God? In all the blasphemy we hear or even used to participate in, or still do now by our passivity, could we stand up under the cross-examination of the Great Judge of the Universe? If one can not withstand the heat now, one will have to later....when it is too late!

Then a very important statement by God: "would you discredit My justice? Would you condemn Me to justify yourself?" God is so Holy, He has to punish sin. His Justice is true and NONE of us want or can handle the full consequences of our sins. As the Apostle Peter says in one of the scariest passages in the Bible; 1 Peter 4:18 (KJV)

"A*nd if the righteous scarcely be saved, where shall the ungodly and the sinner appear?"*

What we should never do is assign a thing to God He is not! For many chapters on end, Job and his friends spent countless debates on why Job was in this predicament. Zophar and the other three friends went so far as to say suffering is the punishment for sin and prosperity is the reward for righteousness. The arguments got more ridiculous. The names of the other three friends are Eliphaz, Elihu and Bildad the Shuhite, all short on wisdom of who God really is.

When we are being broken through the many trials of life, one sure way to prolong the testing is to get philosophical and assign all kinds of blame, man-made theory and psychological attributes to God. As God says in verse 9 "do you have an Arm like God and can your voice thunder like His?" My friends God can not be put in a box.

At the end of the Book of Job, God was more than angry at the four "psychotherapists" friends of Job. If these guys were around today, they would be on Oprah trying to sell their new book on counseling and most likely doing well with the audience blaming God. Instead the LORD spared them by having Job pray for them after the appropriate sacrifice.

FORGIVENESS

It was obvious from Job chapter 42 the LORD had forgiven Job's mindless ranting while in the throes of his pain and suffering, as he stayed faithful. The rewards of brokenness were tremendous. Job's health was not only restored, but God made him the richest man in the territory. Scripture says he was restored twofold and was blessed with 10 more children! Nowhere there were women more beautiful than this daughters and he lived another 140 years. This tells the Bible scholars Job lived either around or earlier than the time of Moses.

We all seek forgiveness whether we know it or not. We can never enter the Kingdom of Heaven without it! When we reach the point of brokenness where the Lord has finally had enough and says "who is this who darkens my counsel with words without knowledge?" The Hebrew word for knowledge is **"teed"** a noun derived from **"YeDa"**. In the ancient language God is saying Job is speaking of things he does not **PERSONALLY** have any of which he has no intimate information! Now Job was believing man! YET, he had no intimate relationship with the Father.

This is what Christ brings to us. For the first time in History, the veil of the temple to the Holy of Holies is torn, and we can approach the Father – but only through Christ. We are only forgiven after we get to that point and acknowledge Him.

Two things to note here - first, Job had to acknowledge his sin and folly: "*I know that you can do all things; no plan of yours can be thwarted. You asked, 'Who is this that obscures my counsel without knowledge? Surely I spoke of things I did not understand, things too wonderful for me to know" Job 42: 1-2(NIV).*

Secondly, and this is important, it was only after Job acknowledged his lack of a personal relationship with God that the trial was over

Salvation is the most precious gift God has given us. Do not treat it lightly, but be humble and seek forgiveness like Job. I once heard one of my favorite preachers and personally a very nice man, who stands firmly on the truth – Dr. James Merritt (the former president of the Southern Baptist convention) tell this story about Prison Fellowship founder and former Watergate personality Chuck Colson.

Chuck Colson, the head of Prison Fellowship Ministries and BREAKPOINT (www.breakpoint.org) was once President Richard Nixon's hatchet man during the 1972 Presidential campaign which exploded into Watergate and Nixon's resignation as well as Colson going to prison. John Erhlichman, Nixon's top aide, always blamed Colson for him getting sent to prison in the Watergate Scandal.

Colson accepted Christ in Prison and spent the next 30 plus years working for the Lord while Erhlichman used the rest of his life to wallow in bitterness and anger. He was wasting away in a nursing home in Arizona when Colson tracked him down and found him, spending his own money and time to go visit and make peace with and witness to a lost Erhlichman about the Lord. In his hatred, the latter threw him out, telling him not to come back.

In 1999, Colson heard that his old "pal" was dying from cancer as alone as he lived. He flew to Ehrlichman's death bed, hugged him close to his huge chest and prayed with him. As he began to leave the room, he saw a tear in John's eye and he raised his bony hand, this time in a gesture of submission…to the Living Christ!! Friends, no one is too far gone to accept Christ and no one is beyond forgiveness.

Here is an awesome practical way to live and practice Forgiveness. It is something Brother Lawrence, the 17th Century monk, called "**Short Accounts**" (itself a variation of the Biblical exhortation about not letting the sun go down on your anger.) Almighty God has put away our sin because Jesus did what we could not do for ourselves – appease God's anger against sin (Hebrews 2:17) or the word **PROPITIATION.**

Therefore to keep a "short account" with God, use this Brother Lawrence inspired tool and confess your daily sins right before bed at prayer time. All of them!! Not just confess them but repent! Then begin each day anew, renewed by the Spirit of the Living God who lives inside each believer. The blessings of such a simple discipline brings so much joy and peace, it will lead you to want to fall in love anew each day in Him, through His Word. Not a day will go by when you would not want to delight yourself in Scripture and fellowship with HIM because He walks with you and He talks with you!!

Believers will then want to practice the same forgiveness to those who have done us wrong! God forgave us and truly loves us, so no matter what the person has done to us, forgive his/her debt just as Christ forgave us and remember when we got saved, The Lord Our God accepted us just the way we were! We do not have to be intimate friends with the person(s) who wronged us, but accepting and forgiving them, is living as Christ told us in Matthew 6:9-13 (the Lord's Prayer).

OBEDIENCE

In 1991, my wife Vicki and I were living in Connecticut and enjoying our part in the Kingdom teaching kids. We were going to visit her sister and husband in Fairfax County, VA. where my brother-in-law, now also a pastor, worked for the Department of Defense. Tithing was new to me, coming for a Catholic background, and a discipline that I apparently took too lightly.

I foolishly decided to take my tithe with me, in brand new $50 bills, and then would replace it when we got back from Washington DC. As the offering plate was passed the next Sunday morning at First Baptist Church, Herndon, VA., I pulled out the money to put what I thought was a $5 and a $1 bill in the plate. Later on that day at the roller skating rink, unable to find the remaining $50 bill, it occurred to me what had transpired! God always gets what is His! AMEN?

The "learning" never stops! In 1996, I was asked to teach a Sunday school class that I really did not want to do. Everything in our Christian life was just peachy, but this Saturday night on the way home, the Lord decided to teach me *Hebrews 12:6* – "*those whom the Lord loves, He chastens*!" On a road which I knew blindfolded, my instincts were blinded, my windshield wipers suddenly went dead and I could not steer the car!! My entire family was in the car with me.

It was not my time to go home or end up in a ditch in a bloody mess, because once I got through that heart-stopping experience, I knew exactly what had just happened! I felt Him speaking to me later, after I said "Lord, I will teach the class" His Word to me was simply - I PUT you here for a reason!

The WORD itself teaches that those who are faithful in little things will be put in charge of bigger things. I praise the Lord for His Discipline at these two instances and another harsh lesson He has since taught me. The larger question is "ARE WE WILLING TO ACCEPT THIS DISCIPLINE?"

Do not be like Israel in the desert (*Joshua 6:1*) who did so much evil in God's sight, EVEN AFTER THEY HAD SEEN HIM IN THE FIRE AND SMOKE OF MT SINAI!!! He despised them as an abomination, killing them in the desert and handing them over to their enemies.

In order to realize the blessing of a true Disciple, study the passage from *Hebrews 12: 5-12*. The righteous man will undergo discipline from God, but the *mamzer* (Heb. for illegitimate son) will not!! This is to enable us to share in His Holiness.

The misleading Christian doctrines of the day lead people to think that a true Child of Christ will have no problems. For instance, a man or woman can possibly go to a fancy American church; be entertained by drama and sing harmless modern choruses. Then he or she leaves in self-congratulation saying "man, I <u>feel</u> good today!" Is this proper? What value to the Kingdom is there in this type of lifestyle? More importantly, what are the eternal consequences of this to the person involved?

Biblical Christianity costs us something! It cost Christ everything: <u>His Life and Innocent Blood on the Cross</u>. A brother or sister <u>MUST ADMIT</u> that all have sinned, in the foulest way, and fallen short of the Glory of God (*Romans 3:23*). Unless one has subsequently repented of ALL sin AND begged His Forgiveness, certain "feel-good" American Christianity will burn up on the coming <u>Day of Wrath</u>! *Biblical Christianity* must lead us to His Holiness or it is not authentic Faith.

<u>DISOBEDIENCE</u>

There is a cost to disobeying not just God, but the call of God... as I personally know!! The story of mankind began in disobedience and will only end when Jesus comes back with His bloody sword of Righteousness....and friends, this is a real sword! Re-read the entire book of Revelation.

Uzzah is a name which symbolizes Disobedience in the Old Testament. In *2 Samuel 6:7*, we read of Uzzah disobeying God's command never to touch the Ark of the Covenant. Scripture says that he reached out to hold it as it was about to fall off the cart transporting it. The Lord Our God smote him dead!! Uzzah demonstrated a basic innate human quality of self importance, albeit a reaction.

In the New Testament, Ananias and Sapphira (*Acts 5: 1-11*) both lost their lives after lying to the Apostles about the money they had obtained from the sale of their land. Their broken promise, made under oath from God, cost them their lives immediately.

In both instance, God's punishment was swift and decisive. Disobedience led to death. Uzzah, Ananias and Sapphira were saved people, but their sin was so egregious that a Holy God, who punished His Own Son for our sins, would not tolerate it.

Imagine Judas Iscariot being interviewed by Oprah about why he betrayed the Son of God to be killed. He might have come up with the following excuses: he had a betrayal syndrome or the responsibility of being Disciple Treasurer was too much for him! How about this one*: the chief priests/the devil made him do it, he felt rejected because he was not one of Jesus' Inner Circle or when the woman wasted the expensive Spikenard Oil on the Lord...well "that was the last straw, Oprah!"* Oprah would wipe away a tear and the crowd would applaud!

The fall of many a major Christian leader resulted from their disobedience. Former preacher Ted Haggard and the Reverend Jimmy Swaggart both used their gifts to satisfy their illegitimate personal lust against the holy commands of God. He removed them from their position of influence. Friends, the price of disobedience is not just a lost of life but a loss of face.

In Eastern cultures, this can lead to Hari-kari (Japanese suicide). For the Christian our NAME means everything? Why, because we are under the preaching and teaching of He who holds The Name. When the religious Pharisees tried to stop Peter and John from preaching Christ they said *"But so that it spreads no further among the people, let us severely threaten them, that from now on they speak to no man in **THIS NAME**" (emphasis mine).*

DO NOT DO anything which will cause our Lord's Name to be stained. I have to pray and remind myself of this daily. Our co-workers and vast majority of those we interact with day in and day out are watching for us to stumble and fall flat on their face! This is not a joke. They are constantly watching to see if we are who we say we are. Unfortunately too many people give them the opportunity to prove the naysayer's right and call us hypocrites.

How many times have we heard people's excuses for not going to church or coming to Christ? We get things like "there are too many hypocrites in church!" TRUE! We have people walking around as church members, deacons, elders and even bi-vocational or full time pastors who share the same dirty jokes as their comrades at work. They may even be found at the ball park having a few beers with their friends!

Sure, they are hypocrites! If these people are truly saved, they are on a short leash and will be severely disciplined in due course. More likely than not, they are just like the culture they participate in and will answer for their sins on the Day of Wrath.

So how do we deal with this "Hypocrite" issue? When someone says "I don't ever want to go to church because all Christians are hypocrites". Well the answer is "you work with them...and if you see one bad cow, would you stop drinking milk?" There are many such retorts. Friends, we live in a disobedient world and the reason the church is so INEFFECTIVE in changing our corner of the world for Christ, is because our church leadership is too fat, lazy and comfortable.

(***Sidebar***: For some reason, Evangelical preachers and authors etc have decided it is better to become part of the culture and then try to change it from the inside out. Contemporary Christian music is just as guilty of this practice. I have been around promoters and/ or involved in several Christian concerts. A lot of them – not all - with their management and promoter agencies have some requests which, apart from the alcohol etc...one would be hard-pressed to tell the difference between them and Bryan Adams! One thing about these musicians, when they talk on stage about how it is not about the money...ha...you fills in the blanks! Part of the problem is the majority of Christian music is now being controlled by three major secular music companies! You can hardly hear the Name of Jesus anymore in some of these songs.)

Finally, God is the Only One who can change. The church or the Christian leader who compromises with the world to "change" it is driven by purposes of his own, not those of the Lord.

SO HOW DO I PRAY?

As kids we all taught the bedtime prayer "Now I lay me down to sleep, I pray the Lord my soul to keep. If I should die before I wake, I pray the Lord my soul to take." 1 Corinthians 13:11 says " *When I was a child, I used to speak like a child, think like a child, reason like a child; when I became a man, I did away with childish things.*"

Now there is nothing wrong with being like a child before Christ, but our prayer life should reflect our growing intimacy or Knowledge of the Holy. We should long for and live for that vital, daily, loving, conversation with our Creator. We should long for the kind of **"teed"** or personal acknowledgment of Him which caused Enoch to walk with God until he was no more; i.e. God took him home. (Enoch was one of only two men in history to NOT die! Elijah was the other one taken up into heaven. There is a common thought the Two Witnesses named in Revelation are Enoch and Elijah...who will eventually die for the first time! We shall see!)

As previously mentioned, fasting and just plain old time invested in going into His Presence are what developed me. Here are the disciplines which molded me:

- Constant crying out and asking for wisdom and discernment.
- Constant time on your literal and figurative face while asking for mercy and compassion.
- Constant listening in silence while His Spirit soars in you, interpreting your prayer and requests so they can approach Christ in the proper manner for presentation to the Throne of Heaven.

What is really amazing is the speed by which these prayers get from you and the Holy Spirit to the Lord and Our Father, who art in Heaven!

You and I know we sometimes get answers in an instant. Of course, some answers are years in coming....and we should wait. The truly wise man or woman of Christ listens, so "be still and know that I am God" (Psalm 46:10).

I like how my brother in Christ and true friend the Rev. Randy Heinsch,(a Moody Bible Institute family tradition graduate and fellow proponent of everything Dwight Lyman Moody) puts in his acrostic **ACTS** (see below). I think it is proper to look at our prayer life with a structure like this, with your own tweaking and variation as the Holy Spirit leads us as individuals, yet with the same purpose. 3

A – Adoration (voicing praise to God)
C – Confession (voicing sins to God)
T - Thanksgiving (voicing gratitude to God)
S - Supplication (voicing requests to God)

PRAY LIKE JESUS PART 1:

The Lord Jesus Christ taught us how to pray. Before that, He taught us how NOT to pray – like the hypocrites (standing and praying to themselves, basically. Matthew 6: 8-13 (NKJV) is the Living Example from the Master about how to pray.

Our Father in heaven,
Hallowed be Your name.
Your kingdom come.
Your will be done
On earth as it is in heaven.
Give us this day our daily bread.
And forgive us our debts,
As we forgive our debtors.
And do not lead us into temptation,
But deliver us from the evil one.
For Yours is the kingdom and the power and the glory forever. Amen.

The Lord's Prayer should be the guide for us, from Prayer Warrior to new Christian, about how to approach His throne. The following through Jesus' Lord's Prayer is taken from my prayer journal, but only parts of each line are included here. It is meant simply as a guideline for the reader to do his/her own.

OUR FATHER: Oh Lord, You have known me since the Foundation of the Earth and chosen me as Your very own child. You knew me from my mother's womb, through the rotten years in the wilderness from whence You saved me. Thank you, my Father and God for bringing me to Jesus, Your Son in Heaven who created all things. Search me oh Lord and knew my ways. See if there is any wicked way in me, REMOVE it and lead me into Your everlasting Kingdom. In His Name above all Names, Jesus, Amen

IN HEAVEN: Father in Heaven, You have been around since the beginning of Time. No one can comprehend Your mighty Ways or Your purposes. The world speaks without knowledge of You. Teach me Your Ways here on earth as ordained in Heaven that I may come closer to You and seek after Your wisdom…until the day I join you in Heaven. In Jesus' Name. Amen

HALLOWED BE THY NAME: Heavenly Father Your Name is so Holy the ancients would call you YAHWEH, Jehovah God. Father every Name of Yours and Your Son in the Holy Oracles of Scripture has special meaning sent from You. Let me not disparage You, blaspheme You, disgrace You or stain Your Name at any time. Let me Honor Thee and bow at the Mention of Thy Name; Faithful and True and feed on Thy Word, the Precious Gift of the Spirit sent from Above all the days of my life. In Jesus' Name, Amen

YOUR KINGDOM COME: Lord, I am truly grateful and content in what little or much You have blessed our family with. However as You equip us for the work ahead, for the trials ahead, for the tribulation ahead, prepare us for Your Coming. We look and pray and stir with expectation at the seam in the Clouds coming apart, and the Trumpet sounds as you ride in Victory back to claim Your own. We who are sealed by You until the Day of Redemption long for Your coming! Even so, Come Quickly Lord Jesus. Amen

THY WILL BE DONE: Lord God Almighty, I pray for Your Sovereign Will in my life, to do Thy Will in thought, word and deed. I know I have not been as obedient as You demand, I know I have not always walked in Your Ways, I know I have not always worshipped You in Spirit and in Truth. For that I seek forgiveness. Turn to me and be Gracious unto me after the manner of those who love Your Word. Establish my footsteps in Thy Word and let no iniquity have dominion over me, so I will obey Thy Will for my life, In Jesus Name. Amen

ON EARTH AS IT IS IN HEAVEN: Father You said whatsoever we bind on earth will be bound in Heaven. We bind the enemy oh God. We bind sin. We bind our failings. We bind the stronghold of the prince of this world, Thy eternal enemy. Lord let Your Power over all rule all the earth. Let Your Power buttress us against those who rise up against us. Let Your Power and Your Word fill us. Oh God, have mercy upon Your people and reign in us in Grace, power and zeal for You. In Jesus' Name, Amen

GIVE US THIS DAY OUR DAILY BREAD: Lord, You said Your Grace is sufficient for us and it is. You have provided for us when we were at the end of our rope; when we did not know when our next meal was coming from; when we could not pay that utility bill; when we could not afford to take our kids to the doctor. Each time, dear Father, You brought that extra job, our overtime or long forgotten refund. You provide our jobs, our warm homes, our transport, our food, our entertainment, our churches....every good thing cometh from You, oh Father of Lights. Thank you Jehovah Jireh for Your mighty provision for us, Thy Servants. May we walk in Your Light to bring the Good news of the Gospel, in word AND DEED, at all times. In Jesus' Name, Amen.

AND FORGIVE US OUR DEBTS: Lord we have a sin debt we can not pay; from Your Holy Path did we stray and deserve judgment on THAT Day. But You sent Your Precious Son, Jesus Christ to die on the Cross for our sins, so that by us dying with Him, being baptized in His Death and then rising with Him, we have attained fullness of eternal life. For the sins committed in the body since our salvation, which are many, help us to keep short accounts with You and we sincerely and humbly seek Your forgiveness for all we have done to offend You. In Jesus' Name, Amen

AS WE FORGIVE OUR DEBTORS: Father, You said if we have something against our brother to go and make it right. You have forgiven us much so we must now forgive those who have offended us. We also pray for our enemies and those who have caused us harm, whether it is family, friend or foe; at home or at work, we pray for them to come to know You as Savior or if they do, that they be restored to You. We forgive those who cause us harm, like Stephen did to those who stoned him. Lord should they refuse our hand of friendship or the offer to do right or reciprocate, we put them completely in Your Mighty and Just Hands. In Jesus' Name, Amen

LEAD US NOT INTO TEMPTATION: Lord, Your Word says we will not be tempted beyond the ability to handle it. Your Word says resist the devil and he shall flee from us. Lord, we have the Power within us, the Power of the Holy Spirit, to say NO. To say GET THEE BEHIND ME SATAN. To be a man or woman of integrity like Joseph and to flee the adulterer, the briber, the thief, the kleptomaniac and more. Let us remember we wear You on our sleeves, so that we may never bring dishonor to You. Remove all temptation from our path, but when it comes oh Lord, You take over and turn our eyes away from it, so it may pass us by. In Jesus' Name, Amen.

BUT DELIVER US FROM THE EVIL ONE: Father deliver us from the evil one. He has many demons amongst us, many stumbling blocks, and many ways to bring confusion to our lives. He uses Your church to sow division, soft doctrine and shallow service. He has taken Your beautiful creation of this world and caused some to worship it, instead of You. He has taken the beautiful people You have created and perverted their images into raw pornography, MTV and various other idols of this world. Build a wall of fire around me. Build a wall of fire around my family and friends. Build a wall of fire around my marriage and my spouse. Build a wall of fire around my heart and my eyes so that when he sends his evil in beautiful packages and they get too close, they will burn up with the fire of Your Wrath because You are my shield and buckler, Oh Lord. Thank you, In Jesus' Name. Amen

FOR YOURS IS THE KINGDOM: Lord, You are Ruler of the Universe. At creation all the morning stars sang together and the Angels shouted for joy, even Satan before he tried to take over in Heaven. Father, he is the prince of this world and what a sick, perverted, evil and corrupt world it is. But his time is coming. You said to my Lord "sit at My Right Hand and I shall make Your enemies a footstool" When Your Son returns in righteous power and majesty, every knee will bow and every tongue confess that Jesus Christ is Lord. Thank you Father, for Your Majesty for You alone are Holy, Holy, Holy, oh Lord God Almighty. The whole world is full of Your Glory, through Jesus Christ our Lord, Amen.

THE POWER AND THE GLORY, AMEN: Lord All Power, Glory and Honor are Yours. The entire creation story in Job 38-41 reveals just how full of Awe and Might You really are. No one has an Arm like You. No one thunders His Voice like you. At the sound of Your Voices, the pillars of the Temple shook, the thunder reports to You and the seas remain still. Truly, truly, truly, Oh Lord of Hosts You slay mighty rulers, You bring down kingdoms, give grace to the humble and resist the proud. Thank You for who You are; for saving me; for allowing me into Your Presence and one day – Your Kingdom forever. All glory, laud and honor be to Thee Redeemer King, In Jesus' Name, let it be done. Amen

PRAY LIKE JESUS PART 2:

As Randy pointed out in his ACTS acrostic, there is a process in approaching prayer. Since the underlying theme of this book is Effective Christianity, we can not be effective without a solid prayer life. By all means follow the ACTS system to begin your prayer life, but then go deep. Go deep in the button hook or post of fly pattern, but go deep! In other words, dig deep into your relationship with Him and find the true Gold therein from His Glorious Face.

We all agree the best time to renew our minds and souls daily is when we rise daily. This is after the Lord has had time during our stillness in sleep to either speak to us or give us wisdom in our rest. Many times, I am positive you have been like me and woken up with major insight to an issue which was unresolved the night before. Scripture says the Lord gives to His beloved even in their sleep (Psalm 127:2b).

So how do we relate and have this Knowledge of the Holy One of Israel - the Jehovah God who grafted us into His Chosen people? We begin our day in prayerful reverence, no matter how awful our circumstances are.

Prayer is our lifeline to the Father. We must approach Him in reverent submission. Even Jesus learnt obedience to His Father, as the God/Man! Yes, Jesus!! Hebrews 5:7-9 AMP:

> *"In the days of His flesh [Jesus] offered up definite, special petitions [for that which He not only wanted but needed] and supplications with strong crying and tears to Him Who was [always] able to save Him [out] from death, and He was heard because of His reverence toward God [His godly fear,*

*His piety, in that He shrank from the horrors of separation from the bright presence of the Father]. **Although He was a Son, He learned [active, special] obedience through what He suffered and, [His completed experience] making Him perfectly [equipped], He became the Author and Source of eternal salvation to all those who give heed and obey Him**"*

HE, JESUS, is our example in our prayer life, from start to finish. Here is the Creator of the World (John 1:1) who has always existed from Time past, learning obedience as a Man. It was this perfect obedience we saw in Gethsemane when He asked for the bitter cup of the coming death on the Cross to be taken away, but then said "not My Will but Thine be done". If the Son of Man was so perfect in obedience, how much more so is expected of us, as children of the Light?

I encourage you to read the entire chapter of John 17 for the Priestly Prayer of King Jesus and how He loved His disciples as well as those whom the Father had given Him. See in this chapter how by extension, He prayed for us. John says in John 21: 25 (NIV) *"Jesus did many other things as well. If every one of them were written down, I suppose that even the whole world would not have room for the books that would be written."* This tells me some of the Prayer meetings Jesus was involved in; ESPECIALLY the last big one at Gethsemane may have gone all night....or at least hours on end. I say this because His disciples kept falling asleep on Him!

The Gospels only contain a fraction of Jesus' ministry because this is only what God wanted. We know Jesus spent long hours praying because it was His Nature being One with the Father! It is also the perfect role model for wannabe all pro moms and dads! If we wish to be honored by our children, we need to honor our Heavenly Father first! It is as easy as pie! This can all be encapsulated in one verse. John 15: 7 says *"If you abide in Me, and My words abide in you, ask whatever you wish, and it will be done for you."*

Webster's great Dictionary says the word 'abide' means to dwell in, remain or continue in. Jesus' statement is huge! "If you stay in Me (or remain True to be and have me as your Savior) AND My

Words (the teachings of the Gospel and the entire Full Counsel of the Word of God – the Bible), then you may ask and receive. This is real power for living, friends!

This is what the world does not want us to have. In fact most churches today do not even have this teaching. Prayer meetings? You would be hard-pressed to find a church which prays anymore. I am not talking "Lord bless this worship service, bless the pastor, Sunday school teachers, our building project, our missionaries, our families and Betty who is having surgery in two days...."

This is a sort of a laundry list of requests in the form of a prayer. Gone are the days of prayer vigils and intercession, except for a few hardy remaining churches left. James 4:3 says we asks and do not receive because we ask with wrong motives. Also be very wary what you ask for, because you may get it and the Lord will wait to see how you get out of this one before He disciplines you.

So we have the model of obedience for Prayer. Now how about intercession? It took me many years of hearing the words 'prayer intercessors" before I knew what it meant. It was not until the winter of 2006 when I sought out the best prayer warriors in Illinois, led by Brother James Nesbit that I knew how to intercede for others as Christ did for us. It was the anointed prayer of righteous men, washed in the Blood of the Lamb which availeth much. Then it came back to me! I had seen or heard about my mother doing this for most of her life (after my dad died leaving her with six young kids alone, with myself being the oldest at 11 years of age).

<u>INTERCESSORY PRAYER:</u>

Intercessory prayer is effective, critical, urgent prayer on behalf of others. Christ is our Intercessor before the Father, as our High Priest! Hebrews 5:7 this about Jesus *"who, in the days of His flesh, when He had offered up prayers and supplications, with vehement cries and tears to Him who was able to save Him from death, and was heard because of His godly fear."* This verse has a completely different flavor than anything in the Gospels! It reveals as well the depth of love Jesus had (has) for us His people!

We see earlier on in John 17 Jesus says "*I pray for them. I do not pray for the world but for those whom You have given Me, for they are Yours*". This is an amazing statement! Go back to John 6: 39 and Jesus says "*This is the will of the Father who sent Me, that of all He has given Me I should lose nothing, but should raise it up at the last day.*"

What is plain as day is God has called us to Himself (since no one seeketh after God, not one); He saves us then gives us to His Son! Then whomever the Father gives Jesus never leaves His Hands! We are secure in our salvation. We can now use this fact to be like our Savior and intercede in prayer for others.

Who gives us this Kingdom Authority? God! In the Old Testament, only the Levite priests were allowed to go before God to minister on behalf of the people. If we lived back then, we would be lined up week after week or month after month with all kinds of purchased animals to give to the priest to butcher and put on the fiery altar. There would be blood everywhere.

When precious blood was spilled on the Cross, the Holy Blood of Christ, the veil of the Temple was split all the way down and mankind did not need the blood of bulls and goats for some Levite priest to intercede and pray for our sins. We could go straight to the Father. We who are saved are now a Royal Priesthood (1 Peter 2:9) and a holy priesthood (1 Peter 2:5). THAT is our authority to pray for others, even non-believers. We can pray for opportunity and preparation, by the Spirit of God, of a hard heart for the Gospel.

We can pray for our family and especially our kids. We can pray for our spouse and with our spouse. We can intercede with heartfelt tears and petitions on their behalf seeking His Hand of Mercy upon our people. History is full of answered prayer for everything from unbelievable salvation of complete pagans to miraculous healing – all because of intercessory prayer. Sometimes intercessory prayer can become so fervent and powerful, you may come close to prophesying as you praise.

PRAY THE SCRIPTURES:

This is the easiest and most effective prayer as I seek just a closer walk with Him. While daily walking close to the Lord, there is nothing like praying back the Word of God to the One who wrote it! There is no better praise!

For instance take a Psalm or a verse of, for example, 1 Thessalonians, and place yourself in that verse to make intercession to God on your own behalf. Give thanks as you pray the psalm back to Him. This is a pure form of worship and adoration.

Some of my most rewarding times of growth in prayer life and on behalf of others came about after I prayed through every single verse of the Book of 1 Peter. Later on it took me three months to pray through the greatest (and longest) Psalm of all – Psalm 119. Oh but how I wish we all had the prayer and praise life of the writer(s) of that awesome Psalm 119. The indescribable blessing has driven me back to this Psalm 119 over and over again.

Solomon's great prayer at the dedication of the Temple was for wisdom. Read 2 Chronicles Chapter 6 for this prayer. It would take another book to examine this prayer by itself! Read this and pray for Wisdom like Solomon did. The Lord granted him his wish and as he did not do as most people and ask for riches, the Lord threw that in too!

The Power of the Word can transform and change any believer. This book is written for believers but if a non-believer has gotten this far, my prayer is the many Scripture passages used so far in the book will enter you heart and cause to inquire more about the only True God of Heaven whom we Christians serve. There is no other God, no other Bible and no other way than Christ, regardless of political correctness.

Since the Word of God is so powerful, praying it back to Him gives us some of that divine power! Do you ever notice when we pray on our own sometimes, unless we have been doing it for years and can address the Father as He truly wants to, we can sometimes drift off. When we drift off, Satan uses the slack time therein to get in the action. How many times have you been praying and all of a sudden a disgusting or distracting thought comes out of nowhere?! That is Satan.

If we pray the words of a Psalm or a passage of Scripture and cry out to God, especially Expository-style (as it is written) and if we glorify Him as HE alone is worthy, then we are truly engaged in real personal worship to the Father. This is what He wants. The prayer of a righteous man availeth much, especially when seen through the Eyes of the Full Counsel of God. This kind of true personal worship and devotion time focuses our minds on Him and Him alone, while taking ours off our problems.

Not only should we pray the Scriptures for ourselves but teach our children to do so. We pray for our kids all the time. When they see us reading and praying through His Word, it remains a solid example for a lifetime. Let us examine a living example of praying vital Scripture from Proverbs 22: 6 (the Amplified Version has the best English translation from the ACTUAL Hebrew).

The Hebrew is nothing like any English version and NONE does it justice. But here is what it says *"Train up a child in the way he should go [and in keeping with his individual gift or bent], and when he is old he will not depart from it."* Basically we are meant to monitor our child's **bent** to make sure he does not go off into it, in one sense. All mankind is bent to sin. If we should rein in that bent, only then "he will not depart from it"! (The Hebrew word is "bent" and NOT "the way he should go"!)

One way to correct the bent of our child is Family Worship and Bible Study. I have prayed with the kids while they were in the womb to present. We love reading to them in the hallway with all doors open as they lay in bed, so they last thing they hear is Christ. Even old English Pilgrim's Progress appeals to them after a lifetime of family prayer and worship. My wife Vicki is awesome with them on daily Bible study while I pick up the slack at night.

The next chapter will continue deeper into developing the proper disciplines necessary for an effective prayer life. We can not be ANYTHING God wants us to be without Repentance and renouncing every evil we have committed. Revival will be examined as well as how to handle the counter-attack by the enemy – Satan

CHAPTER 4

EFFECTIVE CHRISTIANITY

THE POWER OF REPENTANCE AND REVIVAL

Revival fire fall
Revival fire fall
Fall on us here
With the power of Your Spirit
Father let revival fire fall
Revival fire fall
Revival fire fall
Let the flame consume us
With hearts ablaze for Jesus
Father let revival fire fall
Paul Baloche [1]

You are now wondering what Revival has to do in a book with a title like Two Minute Warning! Before the reader puts this book down and takes off with head shaking, please afford me a moment. The very fact you are even holding this book is a testimony to your desire to be an Effective Christian. Many of us walk through our life's journey happily yet with a nagging "you know, I feel as if something is missing!"

For ever since I have been going to church, people keep praying and talking about Revival. The thing is, most do not have a clue what it is and if they did, they have no intention of doing what it takes to bring Revival! Every revival, from the Great Awakenings in American History to the Welsh Revival of 1904; from the small revival I witnessed in Virden, Illinois in 2002 to the great Walter Hill Revival brother Claude King talked about at Colorado Springs in October 2006 (at our National Day of Prayer Coordinator Conference) began with serious intercessory prayer and Repentance. Do you see that in ANY of today's church?

Even our more conservative churches do not seem to think they are in need of repentance! This is a sin. This is a lack of corporate repentance. (We shall examine personal repentance first because as a body of Christ we have absolutely NO power to effect corporate repentance ourselves, if we are not personally cleansed and reconciled to God.)

It is an acknowledged fact the Greatest Sermon ever preached was read in **monotone** voice by the great preacher Jonathan Edwards in Enfield, Connecticut on July 8, 1741. His chosen text was seven words "Their foot shall slip in due time" from Deuteronomy 32:35. What happened is legendary in the history of the American church and is called the First Great Awakening. 5

This most "fiery" of Fire and Brimstone sermons caused 500 conversions amidst the swooning, wailing and convulsions! Tradition has it he had to ask the congregation to pipe down so he can finish reading his sermon, "with eyes fixated on the church bell rope"! The truth of the Gospel and the reality of Hell, delivered with the uncompromising Calvinist theological precision of the time cut through to the assembled as the Power of the Word of God convicted and converted. There was repentance on a level never seen, before or since!

REPENTANCE:

One good reason to repent is to avoid being thrown into the burning Lake of Fire of hell! Repentance in the New Testament comes from the Greek word "metanoia" (*meta* - after and *noia* – the result of perceiving and observing). Therefore after thinking and observing our personal conduct, we agree with God we have rebelled against Him and committed serious sin. We then have a major change of heart, mind, body and soul and commit ourselves to change course. We confess and become mortified we even committed that sin. Then we resolve not to follow the same path anymore.

This is true repentance. Sometimes we do not even know we have sinned against a Holy and Angry God because the Power of Sin and weak preaching have so clouded our judgment. Here is where we ask the Spirit of God through praying this Scripture from Psalm 139:23-24 "Search me, O God, and know my heart; try me and know my anxious thoughts; and see if there be any hurtful (or wicked) way (sin) in me… (and remove it, root it out and expose it to me)….and lead me (to confess it) in the everlasting way."

This is a significant verse. Dr. Walter Zorn [3], professor of Psalms at Lincoln Christian Seminary (who had the editor of this book – John Woolridge – also edit the grammar in his textbook on the Psalms!) makes a powerful point about verse 24a *(see if there be any hurtful way in me).* Like most English translations as I have been finding out in researching this book, the actual Hebrew King David wrote means something else!!

The word "hurtful" (or "offensive" in the NIV) actually is from the Hebrew word **"eseb"**. What the original word in David's hand is **"oseb"** or false god or idol!! This is even more powerful, as we forgive the translators for this glaring error! Our God is a jealous God and the second commandment commands us to have no other gods but Him. Therefore in our prayer of self-examination, pray the Lord to remove any false god or pagan idol from you and me!

These can take the form of the false gods of work, TV, entertainment, leisure, alcohol, sex, gambling and so on. Just in case this is a perceived only as a counter- attack by the Vice Squad, there are the pagan gods of ministry and religiosity! Yes, sir, these too can be idols. When the things we think we are doing for Christ take away from His Majesty, His Glory and His Sovereignty, we are serving the false god of ministry, NOT the God of the Bible.

When our prayer and petitions as well as our actions, no matter how well intended, short circuits what God is doing right now in the life of someone else, we are serving the false god of good intentions, NOT the God of the Bible.

When our passivity in Kingdom work comes about because "those people are at a mission and I can't go there" then that stumbling block is a false god.

What are these false gods of today? How about when we think thus and such can help us solve a problem, instead of going to God? How about greed especially when we see someone prosper who hates Christ and all we stand for? How about allowing our relationship with another person to get us away from our first love – Jesus?

How about career, work, more degrees, more money, more cars, more clothes....more, more, more? How about that, folks? These are the new Baals. Could their gods stand up to the Elijah tests? NO! They are no different!

When a Christian starts moving about the community and fills his/her heart with the praise of others for 'doing good' in things like fundraising for the mission or a project to repair the home of the senior citizens down the way, he/she has taken the place of God. This conceit is vanity of vanities and now this Christian is a self-appointed god...even if this ministry was done in the Name of Jesus. Relent and repent of all of these things right now!

The last phrase of this verse 24 contains two words which are important to me. "Lead me" implies submission. For repentance to be real, we have to allow God to lead us out of our sin. There is no other way. We can not get caught in the cycle of sin and repentance because this is a result of 1. false repentance and 2. not allowing the Holy Spirit to do His Work.

Two passages of Scripture come to mind. Firstly Paul said in Romans 6:1-2 AMP *"WHAT SHALL we say [to all this]? Are we to remain in sin in order that God's grace (favor and mercy) may multiply and overflow? Certainly not! How can we who died to sin live in it any longer?"* In other words, can we repent, sin, repent, sin, repent, sin without any consequences? Not matter how small the sin is, as I can freely admit, the answer is NO!!

The other passage is known as "do-do" channel. Romans 7:14-24 NIV says

"We know that the law is spiritual; but I am unspiritual, sold as a slave to sin. I do not understand what I do. For what I want to do I do not do, but what I hate I do. And if I do what I do not want to do, I agree that the law is good. As it is, it is no longer I myself who do it, but it is sin living in me. I know that nothing good lives in me, that is, in my sinful nature. For I have the desire to do what is good, but I cannot carry it out. For what I do is not the good I want to do; no, the evil I do not want to do—this I keep on doing. Now if I do what I do not want to do, it is no longer I who do it, but it is sin living in me that does it.

So I find this law at work: When I want to do good, evil is right there with me .For in my inner being I delight in God's law; but I see another law at work in the members of my body, waging war against the law of my mind and making me a prisoner of the law of sin at work within my members. What a wretched man I am! Who will rescue me from this body of death?"

This passage was written by the man personally chosen by Jesus. He is the same man personally taken up into the Third Heaven. He is the same man entrusted with taking the Gospel to the entire Gentile world. Even this man faced the same cycle of sin! It is obvious he overcame it as he rejoiced in his suffering for the Savior.

The believer does not want to keep sinning but we will keep doing just that UNLESS we renounce it and stop immediately.

RENOUNCE YOUR SIN

Jesus said in Mark 8:34 *If anyone wishes to come after me, he must **renounce** himself, and take up his cross, and follow me"* How do you renounce yourself and by extension your sin?

The schools tell you "educate yourself".

The pleasure-seekers tell you "enjoy yourself".

The artists say "express yourself".

But Jesus tells you "renounce yourself"!! Huh? Yep, deny yourself in every sense of the word. The root Greek word is 'aparneomai" meaning a recoiling or removing of oneself from oneself! This is a tall order to mortals: "remove oneself from oneself"? Yet, we are called to doing exactly such a thing!

The next step in repentance is total renunciation or denial of self. In the process of personal cleansing, it is crucial. I will tell you why. Remember the story about Satan throwing up all Martin Luther's sins in an earlier chapter at his face. Martin felt so dirty he thought he was going to hell until God showed up and told Martin to have Satan roll the scroll all the way to the end. There written in blood, were these words "this sin account of Martin Luther has been paid in full".

I have been going through major personal cleansing since attending a few nights of the biggest revival in Illinois in decades back in 2002. Sins and past transgressions I thought had been forgotten and forgiven suddenly had to be dealt with. The Lord confronted me with them and had me ask forgiveness for each one of them. It was only then they were all washed away by the blood of the Lamb, as continued REAL repentance took place.

Over the years I kept praying Psalm 139:23-24 (search me oh Lord...). Then one day a sin I had totally forgotten over 20 years ago reared its head. I had thought it was dealt with because I was saved! From time to time, I still can not believe I used to live like the unredeemed sinner I was.

Friends, do not fall also for weak theology! To be born again is just the first step to reconciliation with God. The born-again experience can only be authentic if the Spirit of God brings rejuvenation after repentance. Do not take this lightly.

If you do not have the Holy Spirit search your heart and EVERY SINGLE NOOK AND CRANNY OF YOUR ENTIRE LIFE.; if you do not have the Spirit of the Living God then confront your sin one by one, until you verbally RENOUNCE, DENY, REPENT AND APOLOGIZE for them. You can never have true 100% blessed peace of the Assurance of your salvation without taking this prescription. Run from your sins and be redeemed! Renounce all your sins and live forever in Victory!

This message of audible, verbal renunciation of SPECIFIC sin is so important I could not emphasize it enough. This was a direct command to me from the Lord, via the Holy Spirit. The stain was gone right after! My goal is to share this teaching for as long as I live, as the body of Christ is in flux right now and living as if our God is some weakling up in Heaven and we have none of His Power down here.

The modern Evangelical church hardly, if ever, preaches about sin, hell, death. The message today is of a 'vacuum shaped void in your heart only God can fill', or 'come try Jesus, and all your troubles will be taken away.' This cheap Grace being preached in mega-churches and small, so that seekers will come and feel comfortable is blasphemy. The Law is not being preached anymore. The Holiness and Wrath of God are not either.

Even some of the modern Sunday school curricula are soft on the solving the difficult questions of sin and guilt. The curricula remain heavy on self-esteem, prosperity and feeling good. Emotionalism and Christian-sounding 'pop' psychology have replaced sound doctrine.

Do not let the modern church culture divert you from doing what is right in the Sight of God. Do not let your heart be turned away from Him. Do not let modern church philosophers tell you we are okay and all we need to do is 'take a phrase', chant it and meditate upon it. This contemplative prayer style has taken hold even in several conservative Christian quarters!

Beware of the Contemplative Prayer Movement. It is just another variation of Far Eastern mysticism and the Transcendental meditation frauds of the 1960's Hindu gurus who mystified the Beatles and other such types. Secular humanism, Hinduism, Buddhism etc cannot save you. Only Christ can and the only way to have the proper pure relationship to the Savior is to be free from the guilt of past sin. Only Christ can give you His Holy Ghost power and anointing from Above and He can only do it if you are truly saved and sealed for Heaven.

PUT ON THE ARMOR [4]

Nothing the Christian does exist in a vacuum. The enemy does not want us to have any measure of victory at all. When we renounce our past; when we deny ourselves; when we admit we have lived according to the world and then turn to Christ, he loses another one from the domain of darkness.

This can not stand as far as he is concerned and the battle is joined. Scripture in Ephesians 6:12 says *"For our struggle is not against flesh and blood, but against the rulers, against the powers, against the world forces of this darkness, against the spiritual forces of wickedness in the heavenly places".*

Friends, we are in a war. We are in a war against flesh, folly and the devil. We can not fight this battle alone, especially when we repent and turn to our Lord as Sustainer of all life.

The Bible encourages us to be outfitted for this battle. Ephesians 6: 11-18 (NKJV) describes the Armor of God. Each piece of the armor is briefly discussed so we can have maximum understanding of the tools He has given us. "*Put on the whole armor of God that you may be able to stand against the wiles of the devil. For we do not wrestle against flesh and blood, but against principalities, against powers, against the rulers of the darkness of this age, against spiritual hosts of wickedness in the heavenly places. Therefore take up the whole armor of God, that you may be able to withstand in the evil day, and having done all, to stand. Stand therefore, having* ***girded your waist with truth****, having put on the* ***breastplate of righteousness,*** *and having* ***shod your feet with the preparation of the gospel of peace****; above all, taking* ***the shield of faith*** *with which you will be able to quench all the fiery darts of the wicked one. And take* ***the helmet of salvation****, and the* ***sword of the Spirit,*** *which is the word of God". (Emphasis mine)*

THE BELT OF TRUTH (Gird your waist):

Each unit of the Armor of God has a specific function which, when put together, protects us in our daily battle against Satan. In a certain sense, the Belt of Truth may be most significant. If one does not know Biblical Truth and accepts it, there is no salvation and everything else is academic. Paul used the imagery of the Roman soldier's Cingulum belt as a showpiece as well as protection for a vulnerable area. The noise of the belt in motion intimidated opponents! The Truth of Christ does the same! We are to "gird our waists with Truth" (*Ephesians 6:14*). *Therefore, the Belt of Truth holds us up when we are under both enemy* and sometimes, friendly fire from the secular world and bogus liberal or apostate "Christianity".

Put on the Belt so we can stay in His Ways, because Jesus prayed that God will "Sanctify them in Truth, Your Word is Truth," (John 17:17). Put on the Belt so we know the Holy Spirit will use that Truth to guide us through any circumstance, (John 16:13). Put on the Belt so we can have wisdom and discernment to see the devil's lies from a mile away (Read Hebrews 4:12.). Put on the Belt so we can move with agility, fight effectively and be ready for Battle (1 Kings 18:46 and 2 Kings 4:29).

How does one put on the Belt daily, a belt which needs to be maintained in fighting condition like every piece of artillery in the United States Marine Corps? First of all, we speak it, i.e., Praise, pray and proselytize. Speak your beliefs; sing out loud in the car, say His Name with reverence and BE IN AWE about WHO He is! Then do not just say it but set aside a daily time to study IT!

Can an athlete run a marathon without training daily? Therefore develop this discipline. Jesus said "you will know the Truth and the truth will make you free (*John 8:32*). Speak study and seek! The Lord said "seek and ye shall find". Seek guidance from the Holy Spirit, the same Spirit of Truth (*John 14:17 and 15:26*) who will remind us of Truth and then guide us in the path we should go. Seek protection immediately as well.

In all things, we must not grow fat in the "pleasures" of this world. This will cause us to "loosen" our belt.

THE BREASTPLATE OF RIGHTEOUSNESS:

The next defensive weapon is the Breastplate of Righteousness. At the point of Salvation, the believer is clothed with the Righteousness of God. We are meant to live lives devoid of offence to Holy God. The Righteousness of Christ IS the Breastplate, the covering which covers the symbolic heart. This calls us to be a people of Integrity with no opening through which the devil's arrows can attack us.

Righteousness is also a state or condition acceptable to Holy God where there is virtue, purity of life, rightness and correctness of thinking. The call can be found in *1 Peter 1:13- 25*. The Word calls us to *"be Holy as I am Holy"; vs. 16, NKJV.*

Righteousness is twofold: imputed and imparted. It is imputed to us, meaning we are given the eternal cover (through the Blood) free of charge. It is imparted to us, meaning the Work Christ does in us through our obedience to His Teachings and His Word.

We put on the Breastplate each morning by SPEAKING IT. *Study the entire chapter 3 of Zechariah.* Here the Lord shows how our filthy garments of sin are replaced by His Righteousness (also see *Ephesians 4:24, 1 John 1:9*). Then we are to *a. Obey God's Commands for living which allows us to stayed plugged into His Power for Daily Struggle (Romans 8:11, 13) and b. Live in Love, thereby showing God's Righteousness to others (Galatians 5:14 and Colossians 3:12-14).* These allow us to grow in Holiness, the main objective!!

There are tremendous benefits to putting on the Breastplate or Holy Living. These are Protection (*Prov. 11:6*); Life and Honor (*Prov. 21:21*); Filling of the Fruits of the Spirit (*Matt. 5:6*); Everlasting confidence (*Isaiah 32:17*) and Renewal (*Eph. 4:22-24*). Putting on the Breastplate of Righteousness is a conscious act thus we become aware of stepping into His Presence each morning. He wants us to come boldly to Him (*see Hebrews 4:16*).

What manner of Love is this??!! We can never fathom the Gift of Grace and the Love He has for us, but we see His Holiness in *Isaiah 59:17, "For He put on Righteousness as a Breastplate"*. He is/was/ is Righteousness! He is our Model! I suggest the entire *chapter 59* be read, to see what happens to someone who is not clothed in His Righteousness, Salvation and Grace!

THE SANDALS OF PEACE:

What Roman Citizen Paul of Tarsus had in mind (***shod your feet with the preparation of the gospel of peace*** *OR the sandals of peace)* was metaphorical equivalent of the Roman CALIGAE or "combat boots". The fearsome 1st century Roman soldier was an armored carrier by himself. These boots were made for walking...over any kind of terrain, through all kinds of weather and were well ventilated. The key was the iron hobnails at the bottom in a pattern. Roman soldiers feared no one dressed like this, not even their pagan gods.

The Journey of Faith is not a Sprint, but has been described as a marathon or a WALK with the Lord. Briefly, Isaiah 52:7-12 shows us how to prepare for "shodding our feet" for our WALK through Satan's minefields. (Isaiah is actually Christ's advance PR man as we read throughout his Book.) Here in verse 7 he says *"How lovely on the mountains are the feet of him who brings GOOD NEWS"* (the Gospel!)

A Soldier of Christ is equipped to not only fight a war, but to bring the Message of the Prince of Peace. We should not be content to just have our own lives protected by Christ but to proclaim His Message of total freedom to earthly lives destroyed by sin and hopelessness. Just like the American soldier liberating millions around the world, we are not in a fighting for our own freedom but that of others. Satan is a defeated foe, but he is not going down without a fight. BE PREPARED!!

In verses. 8-9, the Prophet talks about the *"watchmen lifting up their voices"*. The Watchmen are us, Soldiers of the Cross, who whoop and yell because we have seen what the Lord has done to restore us to Himself!! Good news...huh! Watchmen of the Faith do not walk around barefooted thereby stubbing our toes on jagged rocks of sin or the traps of thorns in thickets everywhere.

Our family, friends and neighbors are hungry for true inner peace. If we are always prepared with our Gospel shoes, we can exhibit; in part, a reason Christ called us - to bring them the good news!

The Gospel never wears out; it is a roaring lion which can stand on its own. We HAVE to wear our Hobnail Sandals of the Gospel 24/7/365. Never take it off!! The Israelites wandered around in the Sinai desert for 40 years due to their evil disobedience. However their shoes never wore out (Deut 29:5) on the rugged terrain nor did their feet swell (Deut. 8:4)! God preserved their evil feet supernaturally.

If YAHWEH did that for them, how much more has He done for us through Christ?

Isaiah 52: 10-12 talks about the Holy Arm of the Lord, Him "going out before us" and being our "rear guard" (ALL AT THE SAME TIME)! All because we carry the *"vessels of the Lord"* vs. 11, i.e. we are His conquering Warriors, shod with the Gospel!

The exhortation is to return to the metaphor of the Roman Hobnails Sandals.

The Hobnails of the Gospel ensures we do not lose our footing.

The Hobnails of the Gospel endures through shifting sands, mud and dirt.

The Hobnails of the Gospel insulates and protects the soles (souls?) of the "feet" from the filth of the world.

The Hobnails of the Gospel gives us a firm grounding in HIM, less we fall!

THE SHIELD OF FAITH:

As we know by now, the Roman Soldier was the Epitome of the Ultimate Warrior!! Many times this soldier faced an enemy who used arrows with its tips wrapped with pitch. Pitch is a form of petroleum. It was lit and then shot at the warrior. As the flaming arrow hit the skin of the soldier, the burning pitch caused an infection which quickly spread through the body.

Death soon occurred because there was no medical care on the battlefield. This is the flaming arrow which the Apostle Paul warned about in vs. 16 above. The infection of sin from Satan's Poison Darts will kill us unless we are protected.

Roman Commanders used a tactic called "TESTUDO" or the Tortoise Formation. Twenty seven soldiers combined their shields on the outer edge of the platoon with six at the front and seven in three rows deep. The rows furthest in, formed a roof which was tested by a chariot running over it and could stop those fiery arrows which were coming out of the air!! The formation looked like a protective turtle shell, thereby frustrating Rome's enemies who were subsequently defeated!

The Roman shield was 4 ft. high and 2 ½ ft wide. It was a curved laminate fortress of three layers of wooden strips covered with leather with a bronze binding which blocked flaming arrows, javelins and spears.

Our Shield of Faith is fortress against the fiery darts of lust of the flesh and the eyes.

Our Shield of Faith in Tortoise Formation is a fortress against pornography, prostitution, homosexuality, internet adultery and chat rooms.

Our Shield of Faith is a fortress, only if we are clothed in the Righteousness of Christ and belong to Him!! A Mighty Fortress is Our God, Our Bulwark never fading!!

Faith is the gift God gives us because He has given us Salvation (Ephesians 2:8). The Gift is GRACE or as the old Baptist saying goes: GOD'S RICHES AT CHRIST'S EXPENSE. Paul ties Salvation closely to Faith in that order. Without a saving knowledge of Christ as Savior, we have Faith in NOTHING.

With Christ and the Shield of Faith, we discover the following:

- there is a saving Faith (Eph. 2:8, 9)
- there is a justifying Faith (Romans 5:1)
- there is a strengthening Faith (Phil 4:13)
- there is a praying Faith (Hebrews 7:25)
- there is a rejoicing Faith (Psalm 35:9).

We have just seen what the Gift of Faith can do for a True Believer. Christ's promises are true and not one of His Sheep has been lost through a fiery arrow from Satan!! Not one arrow has ever pierced a shield of true faith. Not one brother or sister has been lost who ever stood behind this protective shield.

However if we leave our flanks exposed, the enemy will drive his satanic slice of sin in like a Mack truck. Continued exposure to sin will lead to premature departure from this life. The person will be saved, but God's justice will be swift.

The life of a Biblical Christian is not easy. The Bible says in this life we will have many troubles, but our Hope is in Christ who conquered death and sin! So do not lose heart when the Shield of

Faith does not shield us from grief or the death of a loved one; when it does not shield us from losing earthly stuff through dire financial and economic circumstances or when it does not shield us from physical pain (read all the hardships Paul endured in 2 Cor. 11:24-27). Also, if Satan damages our shield, go to your knees at once and repent.

Therefore believe God, through Jesus and speak your beliefs. Let your shield protect you from the Temptations of Doubt, fear, helplessness, sin and surrender to the forces of the dark side. God is Absolute Truth. Believe His Promises. He has the Power to protect you more than the threats of the enemy.

THE HELMET OF SALVATION:

The helmet Paul mentions in Ephesians was like the one above for a reason. It was worn by Roman soldiers to protect every part of the head and neck without obstructing vision. Paul was/is talking to Christians. The closer we get in our relationship with the Lord, the more the attacks will come. Paul teaches that Satan wants us to doubt our salvation in the Lord as well as doubt the authenticity of Jesus! The evil one is not called the Accuser of the Brethren for nothing! His favorite one is "how can God forgive somebody like you? Look at all the bad things you have done".

If we do not wear our seat belts in the car, we are in mortal danger in the event of an accident. Similarly, if a biker owns a helmet, but does not wear it, chances are slim during a spill. Satan goes for our mind first. He plants the evil, tempting thought which comes out of nowhere, even while we are praying! If we want to avoid a blow to the head from him, PUT A HELMET ON!! (To quote Conservative Christian Comedian Brad Stine).

The Helmet of Salvation gives the Christian supreme confidence that we can battle the enemy of old and win, through Jesus Christ! (1 Thessalonians. 5:8). It can strengthen, embolden and give us courage so that in due time, our foot does not slip!! Too many of our fellow believers lose courage, give up, quit, and walk away... all because they own a helmet...*but it is in the closet!* Finally, the Helmet of Salvation, when used according to directions, enables us to put Eternity into context! The Battle has been engaged.

THE SWORD OF THE SPIRIT:

The Roman Gladius (or short sword) which Apostle Paul used as a visual in *Ephesians 6:17* was double-edged, short enough to handle with ease in close combat and extremely brutally effective. The Sword of the Spirit is such a weapon. The Sword of the Spirit IS the Word of God! God gave the Written Word by the Inspiration of the Holy Spirit to all the 44 men whose hands wrote the Bible (*see 2 Timothy 3:16-17* and *2 Peter 1:21*). Jesus is called the Word (logos) in *John 1:1, Luke 1:35, 1 John 1:1 and Hebrews 4:12.* In *Revelations 19:13* we see the future and the Return of the True King who is "*clothed in a Robe dipped in Blood and His Name is called the Word of God!*"

Jesus gave us the truth of the Gospel when He said in *John 6:63:"the Words (Rhema) that I have spoken to you are Spirit and are Life"*. Rhema means the Spoken Word or revealed truth. Friends, whether the world believes it or not, we have a direct Revelation from Heaven, eternity past, present or future! When we go into daily Spiritual Battle clothed in the Armor, we are literally fighting the enemy with Jesus Christ!!

There is no other more potent weapon against the forces of evil. NONE! *Hebrews 4:12* reveals just how powerful the Bible is: "*For the Word of God is a living and active and sharper than any two-edged sword").* The main reason Christians are constantly defeated in 21st Century western civilization is because they do NOT KNOW THE WORD OF GOD!!

We now go to the Source. Matthew 4 tells the account of our Lord in human form, being taken into the wilderness for 40 days and 40 nights to be tempted by Satan, without food or drink.

The devil told Him to turn these stones into bread? *Jesus replied "IT IS WRITTEN" (vs. 4).* The devil told Him to throw Himself off this mountain and see the angels come to save you. *Jesus replied "IT IS WRITTEN' (vs. 7).* The devil told Him to fall down and worship him to receive all the kingdoms of the world. *Jesus replied "IT IS WRITTEN" (vs. 10).*

Jesus is our ideal model of how to wield that penetrating Sword of the Spirit. Three times the devil attacked Him in His human weakness and each time Jesus replied from the Book of Deuteronomy.

Matt 4:4 is from Deut. 8:3; Matt 4:7 is from Deut. 6:16 and Matt 4:10 are from Deut 6:13. The devil turned and left a beaten man!! Know your Bible....READ your Bible!!

Be very vigilant at all times because Satan knows Scriptures too! He misquoted Psalm 91: 11-12...to JESUS...THE WORD of GOD in Matt 4: 6. He will do the same to us. At the risk of being called a fuddy-duddy fundamentalist, I strongly suggest reading an appropriate Version of the Bible which is **not** a paraphrase.

One can easily misread what Jesus is saying to us as too much liberty is taken with KEY doctrinal words from Jesus or Paul in these modern paraphrases. *Revelation 22:18-19* warns about the disaster to be visited upon anyone who adds to or takes away from the Holy Word of God. It is a fearful thing to fall into the Hands of the Living God.

Jesus is our Example. So what are the requirements necessary in moving to the frontlines of Spiritual combat? The number one requirement is Biblical training. Second *Timothy 2:15* says "**STUDY** to show thyself approved unto God, a workman that needeth not be ashamed, rightly dividing the Word of Truth!" (KJV).

Next we should **PRAY** the Word....read *Philippians 6:6-7.* Study diligently with prayer and fasting in true face down humility before the Throne. Our battle is not only on the frontlines but up close and personal. This is when our "gladius" or short Sword of the Spirit will protect our hearts and minds. "*God has said 'is not My Word like Fire...and like a hammer which shatters the rock in pieces?'" Jeremiah 23:29 (NKJV).*

Stand firm with complete Faith in the Promises of the Word God has given us when fighting off temptations or even more vile satanic attacks. Satan is the ultimate jihadist and fights dirty. We have been washed clean by the Blood of the Lamb, why put up with this?

Here are the rest of the requirements for Frontline Spiritual Battle:

Pray the Word (Hebrews 4:12).
Preach the Word (Mark 16:15).
Prove it with the Word (James 1:22).
Praise with the Word (Psalm 150).

There are specific Scriptures the Lord put in the Bible for every situation. All we have to do is be there with Him. The late Dr. Adrian Rogers, the great warrior of the Southern Baptist Convention, once said "God is not interested in our ability. God is interested in our Avail – ability"! Make yourself available to Jesus, fellow believer. Do not short change Him who sits upon the Throne of Grace! Do NOT!

Do not compromise with this world. This is a world in severe enmity with God and the battle is fierce. The great preacher Charles Spurgeon says "we must go to Heaven Sword in hand!" If we are truly His, we will use this Sword while acknowledging the worthiness and divine nature of it!

The Holy Spirit is only given to those who are truly converted through repentance and rejuvenation. He (the Spirit) rides in the Chariot of the Scriptures and not the wagon of modern thought (Spurgeon). AMEN! Do NOT go into battle with a weapon from the world like modern pop psychology. This is a doctrine from the pit of hell.

Spiritual warfare is not child's play. The devil means business and so do we! The devil aims at the heart or mind. A spear, 357 Magnum, bow and arrow or 500 lb bomb would not do in this hand to hand battle, where we are attacked even in our sleep. Only the Word of God speaks with the Authority necessary to deal a blow to Satan's head. *Ephesians 6:20* says we are all Ambassadors of Christ with the power and Authority to use His Words to achieve Sweet Victory in Jesus. Keep your short sword polished and sharper than anyone's on both edges. Stay on guard as the Watchmen on the Gate with the Sword of the Spirit.

REVIVAL:

THE THREE GREAT AWAKENINGS [5,6]

The entire process of Personal cleansing will lead to personal revival and Joy beyond measure in the life of the believer! Jesus said come to me all who are weary and heavy-laden because "His Yoke is light". His Yoke is light; the road to personal revival however is rough and narrow. Conversely, the road to hell is wide and a six lane highway!

People in American churches constantly ask for revival. Why does this not happen? There are steps and several criteria to be met. We have already seen how an individual must make himself right with God through prayer, repentance and renunciation of sin. But what about the church? Can a church repent? Yes, and it should. Also, what is this Revival Fire thing? Is not Fire reserved for bad people? Yes and no! The Lake of Fire awaits the wicked who do not know Christ. Revival fire is an unbridled passion when the Word of God is let loose by the dynamic preaching by Christ's ambassadors!

Fire is prominently featured all through the Bible! We see God appearing to Moses in the Burning Bush in Exodus 19:18. The Prophet Daniel describes the awe-filled sight of the ANCIENT OF DAYS, the one True God "whose throne was like the fiery flame and His wheels as burning fire…" (Daniel 7: 9, 10 KJV).

Fire consumes the animal sacrifices which the Law required from Israel for atonement of sin (Lev. 9:24). The Lord calls His Word FIRE in Jeremiah 23:29!!! The Holy Spirit appears to the First Believers in the Upper Room as tongues of Fire (Acts 2:3). Our God is called "a Consuming Fire" in Hebrews 12:29.

Fire cleanses (Isaiah 6:6, 7 and Psalm 104:4). Fire has Spiritual Power (Isaiah 33:14 and Matthew 3:11). The Lord led Israel out of Egypt in a pillar of Fire (Exodus13:21, 22) and the Lord will condemn all non-believers to the Fires of Hell (Matthew 18:8).

Remember an outraged Jesus cleansing the Temple of money-grubbing moneychangers, Starbucks coffee shops and bookstores…. no I just made the last two up…!! To get back on track, read Luke 19: 45-48 about Jesus driving out the money changers with these immortal words: *"It is written, '**My house shall be called a house of prayer**,' but you have made it a 'den of thieves'"* (Matthew 21:13 NKJV).

Isaiah 56:7 says *"Even those I will bring to My holy mountain and make them joyful in My house of prayer their burnt offerings and their sacrifices will be acceptable on My altar; for **My house will be called a house of prayer** for all the peoples."*

These Scripture passages are no accident! The church or the Modern incarnation of the Ancient Temple is supposed to be a house of prayer. Is it? You answer the question! Most churches in America are so comfortable looking inward at themselves they do not think they need prayer, far less Repentance as a body (or Corporate Repentance). Yet this is the only way Revival is going to come to the church.

So what is Revival? Webster's Dictionary describes it as "to restore from a depressed, inactive, or unused state; a restoration of force or validity". So what needs to be restored from an inactive, floundering, inward looking state? Beats me!

The history of Revival in America and around the world has been amazing in how God can move. To get the power behind Revival, please read this Revival verse: "*if My people who are called by My name will humble themselves, and pray and seek My face, and turn from their wicked ways, then I will hear from heaven, and will forgive their sin and heal their land". (2 Chronicles 7:14).*

When 500 people were saved at Enfield, Connecticut at the hearing of the Word by Jonathan Edwards in 1741 as he preached "Sinners in the Hands of An Angry God", **the First Great Awakening** was underway.

The Rev. H.C. Fish [2] said "*Revivals are seasons when Christians are waked to a more fervent prayer, and to more earnest endeavors to promote the cause of Christ and redemption; and consequent upon this, seasons when the impenitent are aroused to the concerns of the soul and the work of personal religion. They are times when the Spirit of the Lord again moves on the face of the waters and the freshness and beauty of the new creature comes forth. Nature itself seems fuller of God; the very words of Scripture seem thereby invested with a new light and glory and fullness and meaning.* ***As Jonathan Edwards says: "All things abroad — the sun, moon and stars, the heavens and the earth appear as it were with a cast of divine glory and sweetness upon them."(Emphasis mine as we marvel at the Workings of God!)***

The great Methodist evangelist preacher George Whitfield came visiting from England and preached fire and brimstone across the great colonies of America following on Edwards' heels. Not long after that, the American Revolution gave us the great United States of America! Are the two connected: Revival and Freedom? Your guess is as good as mine!

The Second Great Awakening is listed around the early 1800's (circa 1801) in the United States but did spread from England where it began in 1792. While England is now a godless, almost a majority Islamic country now, the great Christian societies were born out of this Revival. These included the Baptist Missionary, Religious Tract, London Missionary, British and Foreign Bible and Church Societies. These societies were pioneers because they were all responsible for the Word of God in all printed forms going around the World. Praise God for these good people. Think of the many millions of people saved through the novelty of gospel tracts and free bibles worldwide since this Great Revival!

We and our forefathers in the Western hemisphere at least, are Acts 1:8 people and I bless God for these societies. The great American revivalist preachers from this revival were the big three Calvinists Lyman Beecher, Timothy Dwight and Nathaniel Taylor. The Calvinists joined the Revival because they wanted to stop the spread of Armenianism (believers in the doctrine of Free Will) and revivalism! Charles Gradison Finney came in around the end of the 2nd Great Awakening and had a huge impact on New England.

It is amazing Beecher was a Congregationalist, now one of the most liberal mainline denominations. It was the free will revivalists led by Finney who brought Evangelical Protestantism to the majority of America who became professing and/or practicing Christians. The majority! Modern Calvinism (or belief in pre-destination) was later reconciled into this revival.

The Third Great Awakening is especially exciting and unique to me as it begun with one man praying! One man! In 1857, Jeremiah Lanphier (who was born wealthy but got converted at Revivalist Charles Finney's Broadway Tabernacle) was a missionary from a downtown New York City church. He felt the Spirit of the Lord burden him with the need for salvation of souls all around him. So he printed up flyers and invited *"merchants, mechanics, clerks, strangers and businessmen generally" to join him in "calling upon*

God" to come to a 1 hour prayer meeting during their lunch. They would be free to come and go as they wish.

On September 21, 1857, he opened his doors at noon on Fulton Street, NY and waited for half hour until the first person came. In due time 6 men showed up and they prayed. One week later, the 6 turned into 20. On the third week, 40 men showed up! After the third week, Lanphier made a decision to change the meeting times from weekly to daily!! The prayer meeting then grew to 100!! Almost every street in New York City now had its own prayer meeting! All because one man, a local missionary, was faithful and resourceful handing out flyers.

Briefly, less than one year later, the Fulton Street Lanphier meetings were so crowded that they had to hold prayer meetings simultaneously on three different floors! The newspapers began to sit up and take notice and to report on the happenings. It became front-page news that over 6,000 were attending various prayer meetings in New York, and 6,000 in Pittsburgh. Daily prayer meetings were held in Washington DC at 5 different times to accommodate the crowds.

Other cities followed the pattern. Soon, a common mid-day sign on business premises read, "We will re-open at the close of the prayer meeting". By May, 50,000 of New York's 800,000 people were new converts. Finney wrote of this revival, *"This winter of 1857-58 will be remembered as the time when a great revival prevailed. It swept across the land with such power that at the time it was estimated that not less than 50,000 conversions occurred weekly."*

PRAYER, PRAYER and PRAYER are the keys to Revival. Scripture says in 2 Chronicles 16:9 *"For the Eyes of the Lord run to and fro throughout the whole earth, to show Himself strong in the behalf of those whose heart is loyal to Him."* Jesus said in John 14:13 *"whatever you ask in My Name (consistent with everything I have taught you, that will I do..."* The Lord also says in James 5:16 *"The effective fervent prayer of a righteous man avails much". (All Scripture are from NKJV)*

Jeremiah Lanphier changed the course of America with Prayer!! ONE MAN!! He started the first **"Business Men in Christ"** prayer meeting that swept New York which then spread across the United States in less than one year.

The Cleansing fire of purity and holiness in the Tabernacle of the Most Holy in His Heaven, where Jesus is our Priest forever according to the Order of Melchizedek awaits those whose hearts burn for the knowledge of who He is and what His Ways are (**Isaiah 55:8**).

We, who have gone on our faces in front of a Holy God...who have seen revival in our own hearts and minds...who have allowed the Spirit of Christ, after repentance and rejuvenation, to restore us to a right relationship with Him...we have stored up for us a Crown of Righteousness. We need to share that passion in order to save others from the eternal fire of damnation. We need to pray for the deliverance of a wicked and soulless generation. We need to preach the Word to all for Reclamation.

There were only 120 people in the Upper Room when the Tongues of Fire, the Holy Spirit of the Creator of the World (Acts 1:15 and Acts 2:3) descended from Heaven. God used only 120 in the beginning of the modern church to eventually overturn the Pharisees and the Roman Empire. His Mercies endureth forever. His church will endure forever. God used one man, Jeremiah Lanphier and his flyers and 6 men in New York City in 1857 to start a brush fire across America. God can use you and me.

First we must tremble and fear Him and Fear Him ONLY! Solomon says in Ecclesiastes 12:13, 14 *"Fear God and keep His Commandments, for this is man's all. For God will bring every work into judgment, including every secret thing, whether good or evil." (NKJV).* It is said Fear is a motivating Factor. But the Fear of the Lord is not just an awesome, even scary thing. It is an acknowledgement of who He is. Scripture says in 2 Kings 22:11 that King Josiah *"when the king heard the Word of the Book of the Law, that he tore his clothes."(NIV)* Do we revere and tremble at the Word of God like this? WE SHOULD!

Next pray. Pray without ceasing and never cease to pray. Pray with urgency. Pray all day. Pray like there is no tomorrow, because one day the Father will say to the Son in Heaven, as the Trumpets line up to be sounded ***"Son, LET'S ROLL!"*** When the last trump sounds, when the roll is called up yonder, I will be there!

SMALL-TOWN MODERN AMERICAN REVIVALS:

There are pockets of America under the Power of the Holy Spirit where He has brought genuine revival. Life Actions Ministries is the Premier Revival Ministry in America. I was fortunate enough to be led by God in September 2002 to the small town of Virden, Illinois where Life Action was holding an 11 day revival at Grace Southern Baptist Church.

The few nights I was able to go, and even take my two sons with me, were the most powerful nights I had this decade. It was not because I really love old fashioned Baptist tent revivals. It was due to the fact God showed up and moved the entire town of Virden into what I call the Virden Revival of 2002. I had not seen anything like this before. The preaching was vital and firm; solidly Biblical. There was no fun, games or people jumping up and down in front of a praise band.

I saw the Holy Spirit cause something to happen I have not seen before or since – the senior pastor of Grace SB Church got up in front of all the people under the Armbruster tent and repented! He confessed to the major sin of pride and repented! I know of genuine conversions of a friend and several others. There was so much repentance and people getting saved through personal cleansing, they extended the revival to 15 days. In the end 250 decisions for Christ were made.

The good thing about an intense small town revival is follow up becomes relatively easy. From the power-prayer tent where the converted were counseled, they went out to various churches to begin their walk. However, this was not the typical Billy Graham type crusade altar call. When someone felt move to repent and make a decision, they were invited to go straight to the prayer tent. There was no walking the aisle because the preaching continued.

This Virden Revival was the transforming moment for me. The messages pierced right through and began the Spiritual cleansing in me which continues to this day. What began back in Virden then continues today as God brought a young pastor from Arkansas named Brent L. Williams who has turned that town upside down for Christ. He is the epitome of a fisher of men and women. Brent took over a small church and in less than three years has taken Christ to the streets of Virden to methamphetamine addicts and other lost in his town.

He has done outreach in the town square and is a living, breathing model of Jesus' kind of pastor. His church has more than doubled in attendance with baptisms off the charts with over 200 in the same time period of his stewardship.

Not just that, but brother Brent has lead in missions as well. In terms of percentages and the size of Virden, Pastor Brent Williams has had more of an impact on an entire town for his own church than most, comparably speaking, in the United States! In my humble opinion, the 2002 Virden Revival was the stage set by God to move His own man in, Brent, into this town!

There are countless small town stories like this told in books and seminars. I heard brother Claude King (co- author of Experiencing God with Dr. Blackaby) speak of a few in Colorado Springs, one of which stood out to me. It was the 1994 Walter Hill Revival in Lacassas, Tennessee where the entire church went through corporate repentance and the Lord did a work through His Holy Spirit to bring Personal repentance in the lives of His saints.

The Lord gave this church a praying pastor named Darryl Whaley who returned his small Baptist church to being a house of prayer. Once the pastor and his people began truly praying, God unleashed His Power in a Mighty Way! Long lost members started returning. Long hidden sin was dealt with. New people began coming to church. Six people got saved in one week (big for a small town).

Revival can happen in your own small little circle of influence. God is still involved with His remnant. He is not just about huge revivals like the 1904 Welsh Revival where 100,000 were saved, bars went out of business and police had no work to do as crime stopped! God is just waiting for His people. America will not be healed of its transgressions and return to the Lord until its people fall on their collective faces and cry out to the Lord.

GOD'S REQUIREMENTS

This brings us back to our Revival verse of 2 Chronicles 7:14 where the Father lays out His requirements for Revival ***"if My people who are called by My name <u>will humble themselves</u>, and <u>pray and seek My face</u>, and <u>turn from their wicked ways</u>, <u>then I will hear from heaven</u>, and <u>will forgive their sin and heal their land</u>. (2 Chronicles 7:14; emphasis mine)***

IF MY PEOPLE WHO ARE CALLED BY MY NAME: Revival is meant only for Christians and believers in the Lord Jesus Christ. ***Pray James 4: 6-10; 1 Peter 3:13-17; Ezra 9:6 and Psalm 51:16-17.***

WILL HUMBLE THEMSELVES: Revival is the result of true personal and corporate repentance, prayer, fasting and humility on our part. Time to go on our collective faces before the Throne. ***Pray 1 Peter 3: 7-15; Ezra 9:6 and Psalm 51:16-17.***

AND PRAY AND SEEK MY FACE: This is easy! Here is the command – pray and then pray some more! Seeking His Face is also easy as we have His Spirit in us, leading, teaching and guiding us to that closer relationship with Him. ***Pray 1 Timothy 2:1-4; Philippians 4:6-7; Psalm 27; Psalm 91; Hebrews 11:6 and Isaiah 58:6-12.***

AND TURN FROM THEIR WICKED WAYS: Revival depends on us repenting AND renouncing our personal and corporate sins. Let us resolve to reject our wicked ways! ***Pray Psalm 119: 8-1; Romans 2: 1-2; 2 Corinthians 7:9-10 and James 5:16.***

THEN I WILL HEAR FROM HEAVEN: the previous four phrases had the conditional "IF" as the prefix. Now God says ***"IF those conditions are met by Me, only "THEN I will listen to your prayer, from My Throne in Heaven!" Pray Isaiah 59:1 and Psalm 103. While praying Psalm 103, thank Him and even write them down, for everything He has given us, as written in that Psalm!***

AND WILL FORGIVE THEIR SINS AND HEAL THEIR LAND: God comes to us in our own unique personal and corporate fellowship revival AFTER sin has been confessed, dealt with and renounced successfully. He then forgives us and gives us restoration, reformation and transformation. As far as America is concerned, all we can do is to continue to pray for the country and for God to put His own people in office. ***Pray 1 John 1:9; Hosea 6:1 and Joel 2:25***

There is no one in National leadership in America now or for the foreseeable future, unless the Lord raises this person up, in the area of Christ's Ministry or national political scene who is calling America to repentance and renewal. No, not one. However this should not affect God's people. We are called by His Name; now let us act like it!

CHAPTER 5

EFFECTIVE CHRISTIANITY

THE POWER OF LEADERSHIP
PART ONE
THE ULTIMATE WARRIOR

Outstanding people have one thing in common: an absolute sense of mission.
Zig Ziglar [1]

"I thank my God, making mention of you always in my prayers, hearing of your love and faith which you have toward the Lord Jesus and toward all the saints, that the sharing of your faith may become ***effective*** *by the acknowledgment of every good thing which is in you in Christ Jesus". Philemon 4-6 NKJV (emphasis mine)*

What a victorious, encouraging verse by the Apostle Paul above to Philemon (a runaway slave)! Look at this key phrase: "the sharing of your faith may be come effective". What does Paul mean by "effective"?

The best definition of the word which I found is "productive; efficient; in operation; impressive or striking". If this is not the best definition of leadership, what is?

It is timely the word "effective" is used here. Look at this verse, in part, again:

> "BY THE ACKNOWLEDGMENT OF EVERY GOOD THING WHICH IS IN YOU IN JESUS CHRIST".

This means affirming, confessing and testifying to every benevolent and useful thing (agathos in the original Greek). To testify to something carries the connotation of Truth. Benevolence defines our Holy and Loving God who gives and gives from His bountiful Goodness! We testify to His benevolence or merciful kindness to us and admit He does this work IN US (reference the part of the verse which says "which is in you").

This entire phrase runs together ONLY on the foundation of the last three words of the verse:" IN CHRIST JESUS". We are nothing if we are NOT in Christ Jesus and He in us. If the reader does not have a personal relationship with Christ, I pray for you as you hold this book that the Spirit of the Living God works to draw you unto Him. This is the only way to experience the Joy we know so fully.

Therefore, having looked at this most instructive of verses, I wish to take a look at Effective Leadership, God's way! By the way, this verse was a prophetic word sent my way out of the blue just recently. Pastor Emeritus Donald Tabb is the man who started up the huge Chapel on the Campus of Louisiana State University thirty five years ago.

The former rodeo cowboy/US Army Ranger from Texas was once an advance pastor for Billy Graham's Crusades decades ago. As the mentor of Springfield Bible Church Pastor John Standard, Don is a regular visitor to us in the cornfields of Central Illinois. After church recently we were talking about this book and all it took was one word – effective – for him to pull out his King James and give me Philemon 6! God does speak through His Word!

In this unofficial handbook of Effective Christianity, we wish to examine four facets of Biblical leadership for the man or woman of God. Roles are clearly defined in the Bible and it is not the point of this dissertation to get into gender politics. What we will do is look at a few leaders in the Bible and see what made them great and then examine modern heroes of the faith and what makes THEM tick.

Four Facets of Leadership examined are: leadership in Evangelism and the church, in the Community, at work and home. To understand both men and women, we briefly touch on Stu Weber's Four Pillars of a man's heart and the Four Pillars of a woman's heart. What gives me the authority to write on a woman's heart? I am married to one!!

THE WARRIOR LEADER

There is an Arab proverb which says "an army of sheep led by a lion would defeat an army of lions led by a sheep". Exactly! Ultimately we Christians are the sheep of Our Shepherd, who is called the Lion of Judah!

As an army of sheep we are ultimately led by the Commander in Chief and Shepherd in Chief, the Lord Jesus Christ. However, He has ordained men and women on the earth to be His ambassadors in Jerusalem, Judea, and Samaria and even on to the ends of the earth. In modern terms, these could be Huntsville, Alabama; Lake Jackson, Texas and Brooklyn, New York or China, Calcutta or Cape Town, South Africa.

We can look at the Four aforementioned Facets of Leadership in a vacuum as an academic exercise and close the book or we can look at the underlying qualities necessary to create that leader. First of all we have to acknowledge leaders are generally not born. The old Vietnam hero Pastor Bobby Welsh is the most Evangelism-minded president of the Southern Baptist Convention ever. Dr. James Merritt is of course a hero of mine, but Bobby Welsh is cut from warrior cloth.

In his tenure as president of the largest protestant denomination, he took Evangelism and the Passion for Souls to a 21st century passion. I would liken him almost to the great Dwight Lyman Moody. Moody stands head and shoulders above all as America's Pioneer Evangelist. Bobby Welch's nationwide bus tour of churches in the U.S. and Canada is in that genre.

Welch's book "The Warrior Leader" made a huge impression on me because it is the kind of man I want to be, even if I never had the knowledge and experience President Welch had as an evangelist and doer of the Word. He mentioned the U.S. Army (which he served so well) has three legs in its leadership foundation – Be, Know and Do. 2

However the leadership model for the Foot soldier of Christ (FSOC- my term) is fourfold – Be, Do, Know and Die! Why die in the Christ model but not the Army model? Good question! While a member of the U.S. Military should be prepared to die in combat or in the line of duty, the follower of Christ is expected to DIE TO SELF upfront.

There are about fifty expectations which the Warrior Leader has in Brother Bobby's book with a few of them listed here:

- Leaders don't run things, they lead
- Leaders have a vision that is clear bold and specific.
- Leaders have vivid imagination and bold FAITH.
- Leaders get people to reach levels they do not think possible.
- Leaders get people out of their comfort zone.
- Leaders let people get loose, puts the best people in the best opportunity.
- Leaders are not interested in running things but building people.
- Leaders are interested in everyone understanding and running with the vision.
- Leaders draw out workers' energy and creativity.
- Leaders often have team members who are brighter than themselves
- Leaders learn how to swallow their egos, lose their identities and expend themselves for others and the good of the vision. 2

As leaders in our families, homes, churches (women's or men's ministries), community groups the first requirement is we know who we are. We should know ourselves as well as whom we are in Christ Jesus. This is all about Him. I know many a ministry leader who has deluded himself because of whatever good works he/she is involved in, but there is no evidence of the Love of Christ in it.

Truth is more important than deeds. What good is it to have the best community outreach in the town or feed the most homeless or run the best rehab drug center if the Revelation 2:4 Test can not be passed? This is where Christ warns the church at Ephesus about all they are doing YET He found them lacking in Truth – they had left their First Love, Christ.

So the FSOC, the Warrior leader, has to know him/herself completely. Such a person needs to be the most humble and broken before the Lord DAY AFTER DAY or the entire exercise is academic. If the doctrine is wrong, the deeds are wood, hay and stubble.

What do the people who are led by the Warrior leader expect from him or her? Here again, brother Bobby Welch has many sought-after characteristics from the leader and only is few are listed below:

- The leader leds a Spirit-filled life.
- The leader lives by core values.
- The leader follows the correct motivation, mind, mission and ministry
- The leader leads by example.
- The leader is trustworthy.
- The leader admits mistakes.
- The leader has humility.
- The leader expands the army....to accomplish the Great Commission
- The leader plans and prepares.
- The leader challenges others and him/herself. 2

As a grunt, a foot soldier most of my life, and a Warrior leader in other respects, I have been challenged to live all twenty some-thing of the above items. The older and more mature one becomes in Christ, the easier it gets. However, it requires stamina, energy, commitment and a daily walk with the Lord.

There is no better basic training for the ultimate Warrior leader than having your nose to the grindstone of truth. This is the best way to keep folks away from the proverbial millstone necklaces awaiting the unredeemed.

We have seen the expectations of a leader of him or herself and what the team expects of their leader, but what should a leader expect of his/her team? Here are a few items on the Bobby Welsh list:

- They try to lead a Spirit-filled life.
- They are committed to learn.
- They are teachable.
- They live core values.
- They care for others.
- They are trustworthy.
- They too equip themselves to be Warrior leaders and live the attributes.
- They are humble.
- They have confidence and are decisive.
- They accomplish the Great Commission. 2

All of this may sound a bit too militaristic for some folks. Even so, when Christ called us out to be in His Kingdom, He called us to a fight – the fight for souls and eternity. As we saw in previous chapters, He gave us the weapons – the Sword or the Good News of the Gospel.

Scripture did not say we should be in a kumbayah labyrinth of love of as some today's more liberal theology. The Bible says in Ephesians 6:11 NKJV "*For we do not wrestle against flesh and blood, but against principalities, against powers, against the rulers of the darkness of this age against spiritual hosts of wickedness in the heavenly places.*" We are in a war whether we like it or not, and only the strong in Christ will survive unto Glory.

JOSHUA, ULTIMARE WARRIOR LEADER

When I asked Dr. Steve Farrar how he would sum up how he would describe the leadership style of God's own General – Joshua, Dr. Farrar had a simply powerful answer. He said **"let the Lord go in front of you and fight your battles".** (Dr. Farrar is the men's ministry leader at the Chuck Swindoll's Stonebriar Community Church, Frisco, Texas. He is well known to Focus on the Family listeners and Promise Keepers Conferences during the 1990's.) 3

This is a most poignant description of the man's modus operandi; the same man who brought down the Walls of Jericho. Of all the millions who left Egypt led by Moses during the Exodus, Joshua and Caleb were the only two to make it into the Promised Land after 40 years in the desert. Both men where full of integrity, boldness and bravery. More importantly, they were obedient to the Lord and His commands.

Joshua was a man of faith.
Joshua was a man of courage.
Joshua was a man of vision.
Joshua was a man of loyalty.
Joshua was a man of prayer.
Joshua was a man of obedience.
Joshua was a man of dedication to God.

HAVE THE FAITH OF JOSHUA

We will briefly examine each one of these attributes and show what is expected of us as FSOC's –Foot Soldiers of Christ. Faith is the number one qualification. Moses had sent out twelve's spies to gauge the enemy in the land of Canaan. (Read the account in Numbers Chapters 13 and 14.) Ten came back whimpering. They said "sure the land is good and flowing with milk and honey BUT there are giants there…boo hoo (paraphrase!)"

Joshua and Caleb had a different spirit. These men of God remembered the promise Yahweh God made to Israel. Joshua's answer was "yep, there are giants – and we can take them"! Why? Read what Joshua said in from Numbers 14: 9-10 NIV: *"Only do not rebel against the LORD. And do not be afraid of the people of the land, because we will swallow them up. Their protection is gone, but the LORD is with us. Do not be afraid of them. But the whole assembly talked about stoning them. Then the glory of the LORD appeared at the Tent of Meeting to all the Israelites."*

Note Joshua said the giants could be beat. The Lord had removed their protection and the Lord was with them. This pure simple Faith in a Holy God by Joshua set him apart as the future leader of Israel. Sure the ungrateful former slaves of Egypt who were still slaves to their own sin wanted to stone the two Warriors of God, but the Lord Himself showed up in the Tent. Now when the Father shows up like this, it means trouble!!

All the characteristics of his faith give Joshua to both men and women as the ideal of faith. The giants we face today are enormous. They come at us with everything they have, straight from the pit of hell.

The giants are the judges of America who legislate their own morality. The giants are politicians who tell the unbelieving public anything they wish to hear. The giants are the media and Hollywood elite who feed our youth irresponsible pre-marital sex and drugs and rock 'n roll. The giants can even be found in the church where the Power of the Gospel has been replaced by the PowerPoint of Feelgood guru. But we who are sold out on Christ we can face them and take them out. Martin Luther said in "one little word shall fell him!" That word is Jesus.

HAVE THE COURAGE OF JOSHUA

Girded up by the Truth of Faith, we next need to have the same type of courage like Joshua. God told him in Joshua 1:7 "*Only be strong and very courageous; be careful to do according to all the law which Moses My servant commanded you; do not turn from it to the right or to the left, so that you may have success wherever you go*"

Strength and courage go together in leadership. Many times in the Book of Joshua, the Lord tells Joshua to be "strong and courageous". Remember what the mission was for him – go into a land of strange pagans, kill them and take it away! This was the Promised Land flowing with milk and honey.

So what is our mission? It remains the same! We are to go into a strange land, the highways and byways of our city and state, then America. To those whom God calls thus, they go into the ends of the earth. There will be no Second Coming of Christ until this occurs.

I once saw a parody by one of my favorite people in the world Ray Comfort. It describes the average church in America and their attitude towards Evangelism:

Backward Christian soldiers, fleeing from the fight
With the Cross of Jesus nearly out of sight.
Christ our rightful master, stands against the foe
But forward into battle, we are loathe to go.

Like a might tortoise moves the Church of God
Brothers we are treading where we've always trod.
We are much divided, many bodies we
having many doctrines, not much charity.

Crowns and thorns may perish, kingdoms rise and wane,
but the Church of Jesus hidden does remain.
Gates of Hell should never 'gains the Church prevail
we have Christ's own promise, but think that it will fail.

Sit here then ye people, join our useless throng
Blend with ours your voices in a feeble song
Blessings, ease and comfort, ask from Christ the King
With our modern thinking, we don't do a thing......
(Written by anonymous to the tune of
"Onward Christian Soldiers") 4

Now this can of military maneuver needs no courage! All one has to do is sit in the pew and think Evangelism is for those nuts on the street with the gospel tracts. Winston Churchill says 'courage is going from failure to failure without losing enthusiasm'. In Evangelism we will fail more times than win. I have been in many parades handing out Gospel tracts.

My favorite parade is the St. Patrick's Day parade in Springfield, Illinois. Our entire group is always decked out in Blood-red apparel to go with our 1955 American LaFrance fire engine affectionately known as ALF. Our fiery RED symbolizes the Blood of Christ and emblazoned on the truck is "ON FIRE FOR CHRIST".

It is amazing to see the eyes of people along the parade route as you attempt to hand them the good news on a tiny piece of paper, my friends!! You have never seen people recoil as they sometimes do. Another noticeable thing is the amount of dead eyes I have seen over the years looking back at me; eyes which do not know Christ at all. It is amazing the looks I get from all these bar patrons covered in Kelly green when a brown skinned dude dressed in red shows up in front of their bar to hand them a gospel tract!! That alone is priceless!

It takes courage sometimes to risk getting punched in the nose in front of those bars. But this is where the harvest is. It is not sitting in a church pew speaking to oneself saying "Lord, send revival" without first prayer and repentance, and secondly, Evangelism!

HAVE THE VISION OF JOSHUA

Thirdly, Leadership is Vision. We see Joshua's faith and courage. When you add vision, the uniform of the FSOC is starting to fill out. A visionary is one who has foresight and imagination. The foresight was provided by God. Joshua says "…. *And do not be afraid of the people of the land, because we will swallow them up. Their protection is gone, but the LORD is with us. Do not be afraid of them…*" Never mind the majority of Israel who now wanted to kill this "wacky optimist! Back to Dr. Farrar's definition of Joshua's leadership style – let God go before you and fight your battles.

Therefore, no leader in ministry, work, community or home can be successful without Christ preparing the way. Even in ministry, I have seen people with delusions of grandeur who appropriate the Lord's Name into every thing they plan, purchase or pontificate about, only to see the result as flat as a pancake! Be careful of this vision thing. It can only come from God. This happens in the office and at home as well. Every family has planned for different things with a goal in mind, only to see the Lord move in a different direction.

To the unredeemed, this is "bad luck". To those of us in the Will of Christ, God is saying "not so fast, bucko"! By the way, there is no such thing as luck. Luck implies chance and is associated with gambling. Nothing happens by chance. God is Sovereign and whether the world believes it or not, He is in control. So in order to have vision like Joshua, all we have to do is be still, know He is God and will make it clear. This type of discernment can only come from faithful prayer and fasting.

HAVE THE LOYALTY OF JOSHUA

Leaders are loyal, as well as faithful, courageous visionaries. At home parents are the leaders and we are loyal to our families to the nth degree. We are loyal to the United States of America. We are loyal to our favorite football team, the New York Jets!!!! Some Chicago Cubs fans..... (!!!) We are loyal to our employer or company. Are we this loyal to God?

There is no more act of Loyalty than Joshua's Farewell Address before he goes home to be with the Lord. Please read the entire chapters of Joshua 23 and 24. For this discussion, here are two verses from them. Joshua 24:14-15 NKJV says:

> *"Now therefore,* ***fear the LORD, serve Him in sincerity and in truth, and put away the gods which your fathers served*** *on the other side of the River and in Egypt. Serve the LORD! And if it seems evil to you to serve the LORD,* ***choose for yourselves this day whom you will serve****, whether the gods which your fathers served that were on the other side of the River, or the gods of the Amorites, in whose land you dwell.* ***But as for me and my house, we will serve the LORD****."* ***(Emphasis mine)***

The call is to serve God in sincerity and truth PUTTING AWAY THE GODS (which your fathers served). God knows if we are sincere or not. We are constantly tested to see if we are truly walking in the Light and if we fail, it is because we put the gods of this world before Him. These gods can appear to be good things as well as bad.

Modern gods are family, job, money, power, position, taking oaths to pagan gods in fraternal 'do-gooder' organizations etc. What? Family? Yes! If the Lord is not the Master of your house, someone else is! But "I do well at my job", is the cry. Unless we work as we would unto Christ, we are simply just working for a paycheck. This could take another book to develop on the other false gods of everyday life!

Suffice it to say things have not changed in 3400 years since Joshua. Human nature is still perverse and corrupt. No one seeks after God, not a single one. This is why the choice is now ours. We must decide, as leaders in one sphere or another, whom we are going to serve. The sooner this is settled, the better it would be!

Are we going to serve ourselves or our association with a select band of powerbrokers for the power base which some hunger? Are we going to be so base as to join some group of likeminded people which claim all gods are the same and then bow down to this universalistic false doctrine? Are we going to pour the world's values into our children and say all systems are okay, as long as you are sincere? OR are we going to recognize the One who caused us to be born in the first place and His intention was to have you become a worshipful child of His?

The choice is yours. One of the most famous verses in the Bible is Joshua 24:15 ***"AS FOR ME AND MY HOUSE, WE WILL SERVE THE LORD".*** This reads the same in almost every legitimate translation of the Bible. This is the true definition of Loyalty.

A loyal, faithful and courageous visionary leader is daily a person of prayer. There is an entire chapter in this book on the Power of Prayer. Without it, we are nothing. Without it we are whistling both Dixie and the Battle Hymn of the Republic. Without it, this entire thing is academic.

HAVE THE PRAYER LIFE OF JOSHUA

Prayer is the engine of our lives. Prayer is the spoke in our bike tire. Prayer is a symbol of our Love Relationship with our Creator. Be careful not to neglect it. There is a huge prayer in Joshua 7:2-15. I would like to focus just on a few verses. In part Joshua prays "*Alas, Lord GOD, why have You brought this people over the Jordan at all—to deliver us into the hand of the Amorites, to destroy us?" (verse 7a, NKJV)*

Now Joshua had just lost a battle at Ai (pronounced "eye") and the reason was the major sin of the Israel. God had turned His Holy Face away from them as certain of them committed abomination. The Lord demanded the "accursed" be removed physically and completely.

One thing to note here is we can not blame sin all the time for our defeats. In this instance though, and in others, it is obvious what brought disaster upon them – disobedience! For us, we need to seek the Lord for discernment and pray for wisdom. We can not heed the advice of Job's wife who told him to "curse God and die".

God said an interesting thing to Joshua which He has said to me recently, through my praying through a Scripture in a specific troubling situation. I have since shared this verse as prescient. The Lord said in verse 10, NKJV: "*So the LORD said to Joshua: **"Get up! Why do you lie thus on your face?"***

I will never forget that Friday in February 2007. It was like a bucket of cold water right in the face! You have no idea how refreshing this verse is to me! GET UP OF YOUR FACE, AND QUIT WHINING is what I heard! It worked for me! It also worked for Joshua. He was one who believed all the promises of God, but at the first major defeat, he was whining about the entire rationale of the Exodus.

First of all, I feel more than blessed amongst men, the Lord will even speak to one such as I! It confirms the Lord speaks through His Word, and uses His Holy Spirit who lives within us to interpret the Word in us! Secondly, there is however a controversy over whether God speaks today and HOW He does it.

SIDEBAR: GOD STILL SPEAKS TO HIS PEOPLE!

As we see, God speaks through His Word. Unless an unsaved, unredeemed person has a Road to Damascus experience and God speaks audibly to Him, God speaks through His Holy Spirit, *almost* exclusively. Why *almost*? Well, God can do what He wants with His Sovereignty, period. The dispute comes mainly from both conservative and liberal church leaders and theologians.

I am living proof the Lord spoke to me in a vision on August 16, 1988 and no one can take that away from me, OR tell me otherwise. It changed my life and I will never forget the powerful smooth Voice. No matter how brief it was, I can still hear the love coming out of it.

God speaks through the actions of others, even those who are not His elect. God speaks through circumstances. (By the way if you are under the circumstances, what are you doing there? Get out from there!) God speaks through revelation to other people in your life.

I can recall countless times my wife would either say or do something to change direction in a certain issue. I will never forget this one time two years ago when I was planning to write the monthly column for our website (www.businessmeninChrist.com). Out of the blue, at 11 o'clock in the night, my friend Gene Grman calls me and talks for over an hour.

Gene is a fervent Calvinist who reads and prays the Scriptures (the Bible, the ONE and ONLY True Scripture in the World) for up to 3-4 hours daily! He has become a mentor to me in many ways and still lifts pianos at 80 years old! I am 50 and can barely lift a Casio keyboard (just kidding, of course)!

His first question is "what are you planning to write on, Bernie"?!! No kidding! I told him "Hell"! He said "don't do it!" We got into an hour long discussion about the column. Then we switched to Jonathan Edwards and the greatest sermon ever in America "Sinners in the Hands of an Angry God". We then talked about hell and the misconceptions about it. All through this late night call, I got the impression something was up and I had better listen.

He kept saying I should write about something else. On and on. The Spirit put the idea of Spiritual Warfare in my head and I realized I was talking to the modern day equivalent of Isaiah! Remember Isaiah was sent by God to tell King Hezekiah He (God) had heard his plea and was extending his life by fifteen years. One thing I have learnt, lo these many years, when God tells me point blank to NOT do something, I better listen!

The last thing Gene said to me was something he has only said to me once. In all the many years and endless hours of theological discussion in person or on the phone, he has never repeated this.

After he got me to agree not to even go near that Topic of Hell, as he signed off he said "THIS IS FROM THE LORD!" I smiled inside because I had already willed to obey and knew exactly where the message came from! Sometimes even nail-heads like me do not need a hammer to fall on us!

While writing this book. I had a two month period of nothing but writers' block and too much Christmas fun going on. My brother and editor of this book, John Woolridge, a Godly and humble man, came seeking me out of nowhere one day. "When are you going to get back to the book? Either you finish it or you don't write it!" he said.

This followed on the heels of another solid brother, Heritage builder and author Jim Weidmann. Jim was once the Focus on the Family ministry director and had a popular radio segment - *Jim Weidmann the Family Night guy*. He told me in an email, "If God put it on your heart to write this book, He has an audience for it". Then my wife got on the case, unbeknownst to the other two mentions here! I got the message.

Does God still speak to His people? YOU BET! Acts 2:17 AMP says *"And it shall come to pass in the last days, God declares, that I will pour out of My Spirit upon all mankind, and your sons and your daughters shall prophesy [telling forth the divine counsels] and your young men shall see visions (divinely granted appearances), and your old men shall dream [divinely suggested] dreams."*

How do we know when God speaks? We must have wisdom and discernment. Not too many people I know take what someone says outside the Bible as Gospel. Solomon is the wisest man in the Bible (except with women!). I took from his majestic prayer at the dedication of the Temple of God, and have been praying daily for Wisdom and discernment above riches. It has worked! The Lord has blessed me with all three – *none of which is material or of this world*! Praise be to God for His indescribable gift!

Finally, this may be a controversial statement to my conservative Bible church brothers. I believe God can give a prophetic word to His people, and we understand what it means through His Holy Spirit. He gave us His Spirit as a Guidance Counselor. When brother Gene Grman to instruct me not to write a column on Hell, he had no idea I was planning to do such a thing! My brother who runs the Springfield branch of the International House of Prayer Scott Beauchamp has never known me before 2006. We do not move in the same circles. But he has prayed alongside me for about an hour per month at our intercessory prayer meetings.

We are pray the Full Counsel of God. We intercede. We worship. Scott has told me things about myself, after intense prayer, I had thought of, but hardly anyone knew about! Never discount the power of prayer as well as the power of intercession for someone else.

We are our Father's children. He says in Ephesians 4: 11 "*And He gave some as apostles, and some as* ***prophets****, and some as evangelists, and some as pastors and teachers"* This is the prophetic word. The crucial thing in discernment is "when in doubt", PRAY and then run it through the Full Counsel of the Word of God.

HAVE THE OBEDIENCE OF JOSHUA

Going back to Numbers 14: 10, we see "*the congregation said to stone them with stones*!!" The 'them' is Joshua and Caleb. Here is a 'congregation' willing to murder because someone dared to challenge their pessimistic view of God's promise! What this congregation did was to call God a liar! For that and other crimes against the Holy One of Israel, they would die in their sin in the desert.

Think about Dwight Lyman Moody. One person we all wish to meet in heaven is DL, as we Moody Bible Institute fans call him. We have all heard the story over our lifetimes about Moody being told he could not teach Sunday School. After all, who does this untrained, non-seminary schooled shoe salesman think he is? Well, DL had the answer for the conundrum.

He went out into the seamy streets of Chicago and convinced all the young boys to come to his own created Sunday School class. The very first week, he had 18 kids. He then first began teaching Sunday School to the unwanted children of Chicago on the shores of Lake Michigan! This led to his renting an old railroad boxcar as a classroom and an abandoned saloon. The drinking hall of sin and vice was converted to the Lord's use! From here Moody had such an impact; a former Windy city's mayor took notice. The ex-mayor donated an assembly hall. The rest was history! 5

D.L. refused to lay down in defeat. He was the ultimate prayer and preaching warrior of the 19th Century. He impacted the country from the 1850's up to this day. Here is a partial list of famous Moody Bible Institute (MBI) associates and graduates: Evangelist and prayer warrior R.A. Torrey; MBI Presidents Drs James Gray, George Sweeting and Joe Stowell. Alumni include authors Gary Chapman (Five Love Languages), Jerry B. Jenkins (Left Behind) and the great Baptist preacher/author Arthur W. Pink. 6

There are twenty one MBI alumni – men and women - who lost their lives in the cause of Christ, in countries at 'the ends of the earth'. 6

These "Stephens" walked in the obedience and were 'strong and courageous' as Joshua, God's General. They lived this verse from Joshua 23: 6-7 (NKJV): *Therefore be very courageous to keep and to do all that is written in the Book of the Law of Moses, lest you turn aside from it to the right hand or to the left and lest you go among these nations, these who remain among you. You shall not make mention of the name of their gods, nor cause anyone to swear by them; you shall not serve them nor bow down to them,*

Joshua warned the Twelve Tribes over and over in both Joshua Chapters 23 and 24 during his Farewell address. What we need to take away from this most stunning address is the consequences of disobedience as a people. Not only had God rescued them from slavery in Egypt but He wiped out completely huge pagan nations to give the Land flowing with milk and honey to His people, Israel.

The battle was not easy. The burden on Joshua and his army was tremendous as they led ungrateful, sometimes disobedient people into Canaan. God has done the same for this blessed country, America. In fact NO other country in western civilization has been so blessed by Almighty God. He seems to have a special place for America because of the Godly Principles of its founding. Just look at the lives of people like D. L. Moody and see the obedience of the Great Commission.

HAVE THE DEDICATION OF JOSHUA:

The man God chose as His General was as single focused, as any leader should be. That object of his complete focus was the Holy One of Israel. It was the Lord who brought Joshua through battle after battle.

It was the Lord who kept working on his behalf. It was the Lord who told him "be strong and courageous and do not be afraid". Through it all; through every bloody battle; through the miracles of the sun standing still for a day; through the miracle of the flooded Jordan River rolling back like a scroll; God was there for Joshua. How much more then would He be for you?

The encouragement is to be like Joshua and "take diligent heed to yourselves to love the Lord your God" (Joshua 23:11).

A great example of dedication to the Lord is Anna the prophetess. Now she was not prophesying like Isaiah or Jeremiah. Here is all the Bible says about her in Luke 2:36-38 (NIV): "*There was also a prophetess, Anna, the daughter of Phanuel, of the tribe of Asher. She was very old; she had lived with her husband seven years after her marriage, and then was a widow until she was eighty-four. She never left the temple but worshiped night and day, fasting and praying. Coming up to them at that very moment, she gave thanks to God and spoke about the child to all who were looking forward to the redemption of Jerusalem"*

If there was a picture of Dedication to the Lord, it was Anna. Note a major point here – "she never left the temple". My life verse of Scripture is Psalm 27:4 KJV (*One thing have I desired of the LORD, that will I seek after; that I may dwell in the house of the LORD all the days of my life, to behold the beauty of the LORD, and* ***to enquire in His temple****)*. The default translation of this book – the New American Standard Bible – translates the underlined phrase literally as "meditate in His Temple".

The Hebrew translation would apply to Anna in her mission in life – she continually sought the Presence of the Lord through the protection and security in His Temple. She found all that through prayer and fasting. She worshiped day and night. This is so powerful. Even in my own little time of a fraction of this kind of worship, the

Revelation of the Lord is so powerful. Can you just imagine Anna's dedication?

God the Father rewarded her faithfulness and dedication in worship with wisdom. Because of the intimacy with the Heart of God to one who fasts and prays, Anna could do things in this male dominant culture, most men could not do! This was also a culture where women were relegated to second class status. So what did Anna do?

This statement is very powerful and revealing: "*Coming up to them at that very moment, she gave thanks to God and spoke about the child to all who were looking forward to the redemption of Jerusalem.*" God gave her the unique and tremendous privilege of not only meeting the Infant Jesus, but to prophesy and speak about Him to the assembled.

This is huge. Luke tells the Bible reader a. Anna may have been the only woman to "preach" in the Temple and b. it was the first official presentation of Baby Jesus to those in the Temple who were eagerly awaiting the Messiah.

What awaits the dedicated man or woman of the Lord is Jesus! The One True Pearl of Great is His Name Price (among the other 177 Names of Christ).

What awaits the dedicated leader is Divine Revelation.

What awaits the dedicated leader is wisdom and discernment.

The woman or man God chooses to be His leader, in whatever capacity, needs to have all these seven attributes of Joshua. I can think of no better example of a completely Effective leader...right out of God's Word!

He was fearless from the beginning (sure there are giants, but we can take them!). He was obedient and faithful to the end. As he headed of to the bosom of Abraham, Joshua threw down the gauntlet to those he had led into the Promised Land of milk and honey.

It was now up to them to stay true to Holy God. The Bible actually affirms they did remain faithful....at least those who came into the Land with Joshua. This is the legacy of a strong leader. He not only inspired them to follow the Book of the Law, but to live it as he did. The fact they took him up on it for a time is a testimony to the power of his witness.

The next chapter briefly examines the Four Pillars of both a man's and woman's hearts as well as how we lead in four key aspects of life - family, church, community and work.

CHAPTER 6

EFFECTIVE CHRISTIANITY

THE POWER OF THE LEADER IN ACTION PART TWO

"Too bad that all the people who really know how to run the country are busy driving taxi cabs and cutting hair"
......George Burns (late comedian) [1]

The Good Lord has given us His model for Biblical Leadership – His General Joshua. How we apply it to various facets of life take experience and understanding roles. Over the past decade many books and seminars have been written to get both men and women to step up to various forms of leadership in all spheres of life.

The past two decades have seen all kinds of movements crop up which attempt to provide the basis for leadership in the home and the community for both men and women. Iron John was a book written in 1990 by author Robert Bly which decried the lack of masculine men, male mentors and the male spirit.

I remember the stories of guys going out in the woods to bang drums and discover their inner warrior self in the wilds of nature. The Promise Keeper (PK) movement began on more than a fast clip and soon had millions packing Football stadiums around America as well as the Washington D.C. Mall for Stand in the Gap. It has been responsible for at least 90% of men's ministries in the Churches of America. (The Seven Promises of the Promise Keepers are seen below.) 2

1. Honoring Jesus Christ through worship, prayer and obedience to God's word in the power of the Holy Spirit.
2. Pursuing vital relationships with a few other men, understanding that he needs brothers to help him keep his promises.
3. Practicing spiritual, moral, ethical and sexual purity
4. Building strong marriages and families through love, protection and biblical values
5. Supporting his church by honoring and praying for his pastor and by giving his time and resources.
6. Reaching beyond any racial and denominational barriers to demonstrate the power of biblical unity
7. Influencing his world, being obedient to the great commandment (see **Mark 12:30-31**), and the great commission (see **Matthew 28:19-20**).

Then the Men's Fraternity movement came out of Fellowship Bible Church in Little Rock, Arkansas. Developed by Dr. Robert Lewis in this once small church, Men's Fraternity has gone where PK left off. Dr. Lewis attracted a lot of non-believers to his early morning classes in Little Rock where over 1000 men would show up to his weekly leadership training classes.

What attracted them as well as our believing brothers was Dr. Lewis using the Word of God to pierce the darkness of men's heart and teach them how to live in victory. Several were saved and reconciled to families. Hundreds more discovered their hidden father or mother wound and vowed to not repeat these with their own kids.

Even more were set on a path for the Great Adventure – the Life abundantly promised by God for His people. A lot of us were already at peace with our God, but were not maximizing the gifts He gave us for His Glory. Men's Fraternity has now gone international, impacting men and families for Christ.

Women of Faith is the largest Evangelical Women's movement in the civilized world. Founded in 1996 by Stephen Arterburn (author Every Man's Battle; Every Young Man's Battle etc), this movement is run by such luminaries as Lucy Swindoll (Chuck's wife); Sheila Walsh and Patsy Clairmont among others. Over the past decade almost four million women have attended their national conferences. 3

So our evangelicals do not lack for anything. What do we do with all these pep rallies; books; seminars; even fads like the purpose driven life? How do we live the lives laid out in the PK 7 Promises listed earlier on in this chapter?

Again we go back to the Biblical definition of a leader – faith, humility, faithfulness, obedience, faithfulness....and did I mention faithfulness? Divorce amongst Evangelicals is rampant and just as bad as the secular world.

We dealt with the lust issue using Biblical teaching in the chapter on "The Bible and Sin". One of my heroes is Dr. Al Mohler, the dynamic and fearless leader of Southern Baptist Theological Seminary in Louisville, Kentucky. On June 11, 2006 he had eye surgery. He then showed up on June 12, on the first day of the 2006 Southern Baptist Convention in Greensboro, N.C. to debate another seminary president on Election of the Saints with his eyes bandaged up so he could not see his notes! He did not need his notes. A man of Christ needs only the Holy Spirit as his eyes!

His daily blog 4 of June 9 mentioned the waning credibility of us Evangelicals on marriage, as if we live in a parallel universe to the rest of the world. This is not good. We have the best God has given us in the abstinence movements. Let us be resolved to drum this into our children who are brainwashed daily into a sexualized culture while the church remains silent.

Some churches and youth group leaders, who really gave a hoot, have rediscovered the True Love Waits program (and similar ones). Cervical cancer is now afflicting so many teenage girls (of no faith as well as professing Christians), now is the time to teach purity and abstinence. Why do I say "give a hoot"? Well, a lot modern mega church and their wannabee clones are single focused on experimenting with too many modern fads in music, worship and style and are minimizing the basics. Gone are the true Biblical disciplines of Discipleship, Outreach and Service.

FOUR PILLARS OF A MAN'S HEART

One of the most unique books I ever attempted to read was "Men are like Waffles, Women like Spaghetti" by Bill and Pam Farrel (Harvest House Publishers, 2001). The entire premise of their book was understanding and enjoying the differences between men and women. The Farrels correctly say men are like those little boxes on waffles; namely men compartmentalize and can only do or focus on one thing at a time! They say women are like a strand of spaghetti wound all over the dish, as they multitask holding the baby while talking on the phone and kicking the door shut with their feet!

All of this is true. I readily acknowledge I am no expert on this kind of thing. Therefore I take comfort in the Bible and am careful about what I know, less I fall. So I look to the 'experts'. To get to the point of how a leader operates in community, work, church and home, we have to understand the individual.

Before we move on, one thing comes to mind. From biology days, we know the heart has **Four Chambers**. The two upper chambers are called the Atria. It is here the blood flows into and NOWHERE else. The lower two chambers are called the Ventricles. It is from here the blood leaves the heart and NOWHERE else I accentuated these because each level of chamber has its function which follows form. It works no other way.

One of the most famous works in the Christian Living book revival of the past 25 years is Stu Weber's "Four Pillars of a Man's Heart: Bringing Strength into Balance". In it, Weber presents a case for what every boy wants to grow up to be; what every man needs to develop in himself and even what every woman may want in a husband.

Weber uses the Bible as a basis for the model of the **Four Pillars of a Man's Heart** 5. You can almost see Weber the imagery of the Four Chambers of the Human heart here! *The commentary, after each definition, is my own.*

Pillar Number one is the Heart of a King! Here the man follows Biblical examples like Abraham, Isaac and Jacob by offering justice and mercy to others. So much so that even our family may think we are nicer to other people than to them. This is not necessarily correct but showing mercy at the Mission or other acts of community services brings out the True Leader in you. The Heart of a King is the noblest of all.

Pillar Number two is the Heart of a Warrior. I know of no man in my circle of Christian brothers, even co-workers, who would not lay down their lives for his loved ones. Jesus said in John 15:13 "Greater love hath no one that he would lay down his life for his friends". He was talking about Himself while giving us the example of the kind of leader we need to model – Him! My best friend is my wife, Vicki. I would do the same for her, or our kids.

We already examined the Warrior Leader and namely the Ultimate Warrior leader – Joshua. (In fact the Jewish name for Jesus is Yeshua or Joshua!) Well, men are called to be just like him, in order to be Christ like. What, you say? Christ is the Prince of Peace. God is Love. This is all true! Look at what Jesus said: ***"Do not think that I came to bring peace on the earth; I did not come to bring peace, but a sword".*** I underlined the entire sentence to show this Jesus is not a pushover. When He comes in Judgment, He will be swinging more than a cord of whips at moneychangers.

The entire Bible is full of military imagery. Paul did not tell us to put on the Velvet Vest of God, but the FULL ARMOR. We are in a war. We are in a war for the Kingdom, for our families and our freedom. Do not fall for the false idols of an increasingly Godless Western society which has diminished the role of the Biblical male. Evangelical Christianity is the last bastion of true manhood. Both pillars – the heart of a king extending Grace like King Jesus, and the Warrior heart must work in sync to defend this Fortress of masculine freedom.

Pillar Number three is the Heart of a Mentor. This is the chamber of a man's heart which leads him to want to pass on a legacy. In one of the final chapters this book on Legacy we will see an amazing story of two ordinary preachers from Salem, Massachusetts. Obadiah Holmes and Roger Williams were two mavericks who refused to along with Infant Baptism man-made traditions of the

Puritans (who got it from the Church of England and the Roman Catholics). For that they were tried as heretics and later banished.

After both men set up shop in Rhode Island, they became the foundation of the huge Baptist church of America. Generation after generation of pastors and preachers did not just happen. These men and their descendants poured their lives and the Word of God into their children who passed it along.

No one takes the time anymore to be a mentor and this is worse in the church, where it should be happening. For instance now I have an older, wiser brother in Christ Gene Grman who has taken an interest in making sure I have the correct Biblical view of theology for most of the past few years I have known him. Before that, there was another 80 year old now-deceased brother in church who literally groomed me to become a teacher of prophesy starting with the Book of Zechariah.

However, I have since found out, I am blessed amongst men in this regard. Not many people I know (who are not pastors) have a Godly elderly mentor. Of course, many may have a wise brother or sister of his/her age group they can call on for counsel. American Christianity is to blame. Legacy and discipleship is not preached anywhere. Therefore the leader whom God raises up needs to find him/her around Godly men and women who would pass on their wisdom.

Pillar Number Four is The Heart of a Friend. This defines the part of a man who is compassionate and loving. In the Bible we can think of best friends such as David and Jonathan or Paul and Timothy. What occurred between Paul and his former protégé John Mark really spoke to me at this point in the book. Here is a good lesson to learn on how to reconcile with a friend.

John Mark was not a disciple. It appears he was present at Jesus' arrest by the Temple soldiers in the Garden of Gethsemane. Mark 14:51-52 carries a noteworthy account of a man who escaped the arresting soldiers, running away naked when they grabbed the linen sheet he had around him! Most Bible scholars take this to be Mark himself, when he was just one of Jesus' followers. Later on, during the second stop of Paul and Barnabas' first Missionary Journey, guess who ran off again – this time to Jerusalem! He was taken on by Paul because he was one of the Lord's followers and his running off during serious evangelism did not sit well with the Apostle.

The next time they were preparing for another Evangelistic outreach or journey, Barnabas requested Mark be taken along with them. Paul, formerly Saul of Tarsus, said "absolutely not"! This caused a split in the Evangelistic team (read the account in Acts 13) as Paul took Silas and Barnabas went off on his own outreach with Mark.

Barnabas was a mentor to Mark as the elder of the two and shepherded him along the fierce paths of preaching in the Nazarene's Name. He encouraged him patiently and watched the growth. Being part of the same family also meant a lot to this relationship.

John Mark committed two errors in his life as a follower of Christ. He ran when Judas betrayed the King. So did His Disciples. He turned and ran back home to Jerusalem when his cousin Barnabas and Paul hit possibly a harsh new town to spread the gospel. So do we when the giant calls out our name.

Mark's restoration to Fellowship was complete. The Lord not only forgives youthful fears and actions. Paul heard of his elevation in the Eyes of the Lord and was so impressed that years after wanting nothing more to do with John Mark, he asked for Mark to come join him in 2 Timothy 4:9-12. This was near the end of his life as he awaited execution to go home to Jesus.

This same John Mark wrote the Gospel of Mark! It is only appropriate the half brother of Jesus – James – would write the first book of the New Testament. HOWEVER the very first Gospel ever written was by this young lion of the Faith – John Mark. It is the most easily comprehended of all Four Gems.

What does this have to do with the heart of a friend? Everything! In spite of all the inter-ministry friction between two Giants of the Faith – He who is a Friend of us all, and calls us friend, can do greater things with weak and wounded sinners we can ever imagine. It is quite possible Paul was preaching out of Mark's Gospel in his later years for background flavor. Mark learnt a lot of his Gospel from talking directly with Simon Peter.

The Four Chambers of the Human heart and the Four Pillars of the Spiritual heart are almost seamless. Just as in the human heart, the top two in-flow chambers receive life-giving blood from the lungs etc, the Spiritual heart's top two pillars (of a King and Warrior) receive their commission from the Giver of Life.

Just as the lower two ventricles of the Human Heart pump the blood received from the upper chambers out, the last two pillars of the Spiritual heart (of a mentor and friend) are meant to be used for Kingdom work. I take this to mean that the Power and Love we get from Christ and every part of the Holy Spirit is meant to be poured out of us into those around us in the world. To do anything else would make us bloated on our own self-righteousness and fat in our own favor.

FOUR PILLARS OF A WOMAN'S HEART

You are probably asking what book this is out of! None! The only mention I ever heard of the words "Four Pillars of a Woman's Heart" was a sermon by the great Christian apologetics genius Ravi Zacharias. Even he did not say what they are!

Being neither a counselor nor a full time preacher, it took some time to research and talk to people. My wife Vicki gave me what sounded like a combination of a Love Language and a Pillar in my search for the Pillars of a Woman's Heart.

(We all know the affable Dr. Gary Chapman's Five Love Languages and have done his studies in our churches. These are basically the Five Ways people speak and understand emotional love, according to Dr. Chapman....and he is correct! The Five Love Languages enable us to communicate better with our spouses, even our children; just by speaking a language they understand.

The Five Love Languages are Words of Affirmation; Quality Time; Receiving Gifts; Acts of Service and Physical Touch – such as a hug etc.) 6

Vicki Lutchman is not only a rock, she is solid on this. The Love Language portion comes from Words of Affirmation but only after the most solid Pillar of a Woman's Heart has been identified!

Therefore, I hereby, with no shotgun to my head, announce that the **First of Four Pillars of a Woman's Heart is TO BE LISTENED TO**!

Here is what Almighty God said in Psalm 46:10 (KJV) "Be still and know that I am God". The New American Standard Bible says "cease striving and know...." This is a more literal. My favorite Psalm commentator Dr. Walter Zorn of Lincoln Christian Seminary says if we want to know God, we have to come to see Him, since the Evidence is Observable. God is active in the affairs of all men so basically quit babbling and trying to outtalk Him!

Look at it this way. Through prayer and fasting; through months of courting (even years) and many years of marriage; God reveals to us plainly that it was HE who chose our wives! There is no doubt about this for the Christian. This book is written for Christians and those who aspire to be. I can not speak for the non-believer. To wit, God is my Father-in- law!

Do I want to make my Father-in-Law mad at me? Ask yourself the same question! I am not a marriage counselor or on Dennis Rainey's staff, but seems to me when thy wife speaketh, thou hast the obligation to pay attention or as in the King James Version – "speak, my Lady, thy servant heareth!!"

It takes a man out of his natural configuration to pay attention when his dear spouse speaks. This means he has to get out of his waffle square, look away from the computer or TV screen and look directly at this speaking wife or fiancée! Our wives are our ambassadors from Christ. We are to love them as He loves the church. We love like Christ when we listen attentively.

If we choose to listen selectively or just tune in our wives like an AM radio station, we will do the same when the Lord is shouting Basic Instructions Before Leaving Earth (B.I.B.L.E.) at us from on high! I have missed a number of important things in conversation this way and who knows how many blessings I missed from above because I was not in the Word as much as I am now or maybe watching that football game was more important than this study over here.

By extrapolation, we deduce that listening to your wife is listening to God, period!! The applicable Love Language is Language number one: Words of Affirmation. This affirmation is vital for her self-image; her peace of mind and joy in Christ! The paraphrased version of this is "if mama ain't happy, ain't nobody happy"!! Conversely, the male version is thus: "if daddy ain't happy, nobody cares"! (Not true, but it sounds good!)

The Second Pillar of a Woman's Heart is her Security. This security is first of all, Eternal Security. This knowledge of spending all eternity in the Presence of the Lord Jesus Christ must be secured first of all. No one seeketh after God, not one. It is God who calls us to Himself and through the Blood of Christ we are washed clean and justified through Faith.

The gift of Faith is ours in our depravity. The gift of faith is ours in our insecurity. The gift of faith is ours for our purity. The gift of faith comes through the Holy Spirit sealing us and our wives, once we have yielded all to Christ. He seals us until the Day of Redemption so no one can snatch us out of His Hands. God says so in Romans 8:30 NIV "*And those he predestined, he also called; those he called, he also justified; those he justified, he also glorified*"

This is the first Security she seeks. Secondly there is the Security of the home. I do not mean the burglar alarm or a Louisville Slugger to anoint any intruder.

It is the security from knowing her husband is watching out for her.

It is knowing her husband's four Pillars are made of steel and grounded in 10 feet of cement.

It is knowing he can be counted on and will always come through.

It knows that while the dude ain't perfect he is a stand up guy who would never badmouth her at work around the water cooler when all the other men (unfortunately including professing Christian men) say things about their spouses which should never be even thought of.

It is knowing he is for the children the Lord gave both of them.

It is knowing he has her back.

It is knowing if things at work are not successful by the world's standards, he is transparent and working for the Lord.

After all this, physical security is a matter for the Lord. When all cylinders are firing and the fuel injectors are clean, the engine runs smoothly. Each one of us has an assigned Guardian Angel and He has a hedge of protection around us, against which not even the

Gates of Hell will prevail. Oh, Satan will buffet but Jesus shall reign. He is King and His Love endureth forever. Men, if we are Jesus to our wives, this could be her strongest pillar!

The Third Pillar of a Woman's Heart is Love and Tenderness. Of course we can break off into all kinds of popular songs by Elvis (Love Me Tender) or Otis Redding (Try a Little Tenderness). Growing up with three brothers and now having two sons, we are a little rough around the edges. Sure my mother taught me right and I have two sisters. But even now after all these days, my wife has to remind me I am not her football buddy and maybe a little less testosterone!! Of course now my 8 year old daughter is telling me the same thing, when I get too enthusiastic around her!!

By now, the reader has begun to think I done gone and lost it… especially writing in common folks language such as this! But hey, I am listening to the Gaither's Homecoming old Time Southern Gospel hour from the mountains of North Carolina, on Sky Angel while writing this! The Bible says in 1 Peter 3:7 "*You husbands in the same way, live with your wives in an understanding way, as with someone weaker, since she is a woman; and show her honor as a fellow heir of the grace of life, so that your prayers will not be hindered*"

> "*We have come to know and have believed the love which God has for us God is love, and the one who abides in love abides in God, and God abides in him*" 1 John 4:16

> *"There is no fear in love; but perfect love casts out fear, because fear involves punishment, and the one who fears is not perfected in love"* 1 John 4:18.

> *"Let your fountain be blessed, and rejoice in the wife of your youth."* Proverbs 5:18.

Nothing can say it better than Scripture and on that solid rock, this Third Pillar of a Woman's heart stands. She is the queen of our life, treat her like royalty. In Jesus Name, Amen!

The Fourth Pillar of a Woman's Heart is a Work to Enjoy. What? Now I am really heading for a frying pan upside the head!

Hold on! Most of our wives, at least mine are multi-tasking and busier than a bee on a cherry blossom. My wife is a high octane dynamo who has worked in the medical field for almost two decades. She started up the Children's church ministry at the church over six years ago and except for a year when she had some help, has taught a new crop of kids every couple years. She works with the kids, and does most of the running around during the day. She likes to cut the grass in the summer and I like to cook and so on and so on.

We have always worked two separate shifts so one parent will always be home with our three children. This is difficult on a couple and means we get to go out on a date, in the past, at least once or twice per year. However the development of our children is of prime importance at this stage of their lives. With all this activity, how do we overcome overload? How can we find the time to allow her to even read her book or watch a chick-flick while walking on the treadmill?

Sometimes for her, it is just going to the hospital for her part-time night shift. But for the most part it is scrap booking. As a former Creative Memory Consultant her joy is creating albums as a pictorial legacy for our kids to take with them to their own families one day.

Her ministry is witnessing to people. In 18 years of marriage, Vicki has witnessed to and played a part in the conversion to the Lord of many of her contemporaries. She inspired me so much to do the same, I pray for opportunities for specific people by name. This is her life's work - "Anyplace evangelism". Her work to do is the Lord's work. Whether it is teaching, witnessing, singing special music (as we do in churches), and a woman has to have a Work to do.

LEADERSHIP IN THE COMMUNITY

The voluminous work of the past more than a chapter and a half gets us to the point where we take who we are as men and women of Christ, into the community at large. For Christians to have an impact on the people around us, we must have the following:

A product to sell (The Good News).
A plan to accomplish it.
A process to implement

A plan B if plan A fails
A people to lead.
A Perfect God to Praise when the plan succeeds!

Most leaders are not born, they are made. Moses was a fugitive from Egyptian justice. Gideon was a coward from a family who worshiped idols. King David was a shepherd boy with a gift from God and the gift of God. Peter was a hot headed fisherman. All these Biblical heroes had one thing in common – Passion! They threw every fiber of their being into the Service of the Holy One of Israel.

I do not know if you are like me and love old Bible movies. There is one about King David and one scene in particular which had such an impact on me, I want to live it. (This movie has Jeff Chandler in the role of King David and was made in the 1950's.) Read the following narrative from 2 Samuel 23: 13-17 NIV.

> *During harvest time, three of the thirty chief men came down to David at the cave of Adullam, while a band of Philistines was encamped in the Valley of Rephaim. At that time David was in the stronghold, and the Philistine garrison was at Bethlehem. David longed for water and said, "Oh, that someone would get me a drink of water from the well near the gate of Bethlehem!" So the three mighty men broke through the Philistine lines, drew water from the well near the gate of Bethlehem and carried it back to David.* ***But he refused to drink it; instead, he poured it out before the LORD.*** *"Far be it from me, O LORD, to do this!" he said. "Is it not the blood of men who went at the risk of their lives?"* ***And David would not drink it.***
>
> *Such were the exploits of the three mighty men. (Emphasis mine).*

Look again at the bold underline phrase "and David would not drink it"!! The movie reenactment of this was more powerful than reading it. Here was the man who wrote in the Psalms about a dry, thirsty land. Yet he poured out the only water he and his warriors had as a Drink Offering to a Holy God. This was even more powerful than the widow's mite in the New Testament.

The question we need to answer from the deepest part of our being is, are we ready to pour ourselves out in the Service of the Lord like King David? Sometimes leadership in community service calls for just this kind of sacrifice. I have seen it in men who run the Christian Homeless missions in Springfield. I have seen it in minister to the Homeless Scott Payne, who is a close brother and a member of our Men's Ministry – Business Men in Christ. It is not easy, yet it is a testimony to your mission and Mission, when you turn away 500 people in one year, because your Inner City Mission is full to capacity.

From leading and participating in regular Bible studies at the IC Mission over the years, I have noticed the spiritual progression of certain folks, whom the world had turned its back on. All of this happened because men like Scott Payne, his wife and family and a committed Christian staff 'poured out the water to the Lord'. Am I saying secular homeless missions, especially those who take money with governmental strings attached are not capable of life-altering Transformations like the ones we witness at Inner City Mission?

Yes! There is nothing; no psychotherapy; no Darwin/Freud psychobabble teaching comparable to the Liberating Truth of the Gospel of Christ. A good exercise would be to invite the enemies of Christ and His Evangelical church to name the great missionaries and mission homes around the world OTHER than those run by North American Evangelical Christians! Despite all the money Arab sheiks make off selling oil to the West, how do their people live? Southern Baptist Franklin Graham's Samaritan's Purse can be even be found in Muslim countries providing food and medicine. Name its counterpart?!!!

There is no need to expound on the points laid out earlier on Community Leadership. However as we follow these points to effect solid Christian service in our communities, we do need to be aware of the pitfalls and how to deal with conflict.

Of the abovementioned steps, the most complicated is not the plan but the people who are being led. Everyone comes to the table with different gifts, backgrounds, values and principles. We must never assume everyone in Christian ministry or work is a saved, sanctified son or daughter of the Living God. Wait until you see the fruit.

The Effective Leader must prepare for conflict before it even happens and know the way out of it. When it comes do not avoid it, slight it or gloss over it. Deal with it head on. As usual, the Bible shows the way for competent leaders to handle situations.

Matthew 16:15-17 NKJV says "*Moreover if your brother sins against you, go and tell him his fault between you and him alone. If he hears you, you have gained your brother. But if he will not hear, take with you one or two more, that 'by the mouth of two or three witnesses every word may be established.' And if he refuses to hear them, tell it to the church. But if he refuses even to hear the church, let him be to you like a heathen and a tax collector*".

This is the model from Christ for Church discipline as well as Para-church organizations. The key is to do it in love, even if it is tough love. Jesus' guidelines in this passage are full of love. He gives the sinner many chances before the latter is to be cut loose from the team.

LEADERSHIP IN THE CHURCH:

The same principle of conflict resolution works inside the Church as it does in the real Harvest field for the Church. The requirements for leadership for Christ's church however are very different and more defined. There is a big reason for this. Pastors/ teachers, elders and deacons are more accountable for their stewardship than anyone else. (Hebrews 13:17 "*Obey your leaders and submit to them, for they keep watch over your souls as those who will give an account. Let them do this with joy and not with grief, for this would be unprofitable for you".)*

The church is supposed to represent Christ on earth. If the church has no influence in moving its immediate sphere of influence its leaders are going to have to account for everything they did. I was a deacon for almost three years. When I thought I could be more effective elsewhere – i.e. in the leadership of Business Men in Christ – I resigned.

QUALIFICATIONS OF AN ELDER, BISHOP, DEACON

The reason for including the following long passage from 1 Timothy 3: 1-15 AMP is to show the qualifications for Church leadership. If anyone reading this book feels called to this aspect of ministry, fill up with the measure of your call against these Scriptures to see if you are found wanting or affirmed.

1 THE SAYING is true and irrefutable: If any man [eagerly] seeks the office of bishop (superintendent, overseer), he desires an excellent task (work).

2 Now a bishop (superintendent, overseer) must give no grounds for accusation but must be above reproach, the husband of one wife, circumspect and temperate and self-controlled; [he must be] sensible and well behaved and dignified and lead an orderly (disciplined) life; [he must be] hospitable [showing love for and being a friend to the believers, especially strangers or foreigners, and be] a capable and qualified teacher,

3 Not given to wine, not combative but gentle and considerate, not quarrelsome but forbearing and peaceable, and not a lover of money [insatiable for wealth and ready to obtain it by questionable means].

4 He must rule his own household well, keeping his children under control, with true dignity, commanding their respect in every way and keeping them respectful.

5 For if a man does not know how to rule his own household how is he to take care of the church of God?

6 He must not be a new convert, or he may [develop a beclouded and stupid state of mind] as the result of pride [be blinded by conceit, and] fall into the condemnation that the devil [once] did.

7 Furthermore, he must have a good reputation and be well thought of by those outside [the church], lest he become involved in slander and incur reproach and fall into the devil's trap.

8 In like manner the deacons [must be] worthy of respect, not shifty and double-talkers but sincere in what they say, not given too much wine, not greedy for base gain [craving wealth and resorting to ignoble and dishonest methods of getting it].

9 They must possess the mystic secret of the faith [Christian truth as hidden from ungodly men] with a clear conscience.

10 And let them also be tried and investigated and proved first; then, if they turn out to be above reproach, let them serve [as deacons].

11 [The] women likewise must be worthy of respect and serious, not gossipers, but temperate and self-controlled, [thoroughly] trustworthy in all things.

12 Let deacons be the husbands of but one wife, and let them manage [their] children and their own households well.

13 For those who perform well as deacons acquire a good standing for themselves and also gain much confidence and freedom and boldness in the faith which is [founded on and centers] in Christ Jesus.

14 Although I hope to come to you before long, I am writing these instructions to you so that,

15 If I am detained, you may know how people ought to conduct themselves in the household of God, which is the church of the living God, the pillar and stay (the prop and support) of the Truth.

My friends do not take this lightly. There is going to be many a pastor, elder or deacon not in Heaven when the roll is called up yonder. They were not His in the first place. Others will be held accountable for missed opportunities; financial mismanagement and not listening to the people sent by the Holy Spirit.

1 Peter 4:17 gives a dire warning and please take it seriously. Peter says ***"For the time has come for judgment to begin at the house of God; and if it begins with us first, what will be the end of those who do not obey the gospel of God?***

Judgment Day will begin with Christ's people first and it will be decided if all the works of the church will burn up like wood, hay or stubble. Do not believe the lie of soft modern American Christianity. This is leading countless thousands into the Lake of Fire with weak theology and lack of teaching of the repentance of sin. Do not be weighed in the scales and found wanting.

Finally, do not be a non-praying church. Almost every church in America is a non-praying church. I do not mean a pastoral prayer during the service or prayer requests during Sunday school. I am talking a continued consecration and calling out to Christ to come and concentrate His Spirit in the presence of His Bride to the Glory of His Name. This can only come about through repentance and renunciation of our sins as a corporate body. The Evangelical church in America is not a praying church. Why? Because we think we have nothing for which to repent!

LEADERSHIP IN THE HOME:

I can add nothing to what the Bible says about Biblical leadership in the home for parents. Various ministries have cornered the market on this from Dennis Rainey's Family Life to Ken Canfield's Fatherhood Ministry. But Christ is always teaching me something I can never read in any books or learn at a seminar about being a father and conversely Vicki, about being a mother.

The job of parents is to raise our children to be God-fearing adults who are their own person, yet remain completely dependent on Jesus. This is the biggest job we will ever have, not the one with the Tuesday deadline at the office. That job can pass as we are disposable employees. As Christ's own, however, no one can snatch us out of His Hands.

There are several more criteria which can be added but here are some of the responsibilities we have as parent leaders. I got them no particular place. The following list is a collection of my wife's and my experiences learnt the hard way over the preceding years. **On behalf of our children, we are:**

- To lead them to a saving knowledge of Jesus Christ as their Savior and the way to eternal life.
- To lead them to excellence in education based on Absolute Truth and Christian values.
- To lead them to critical thinking on their own.
- To lead them to empower and enhance their own lives through that kind of thinking.
- To lead them to the realization that because of their standing in Christ, they have unlimited opportunity.
- To lead them to realize this is America and the sky is the limit.
- To set their eyes on several goals and ways to accomplish them
- To set the minds on the possibility of failure and how to deal with it.
- To set their eyes upon Jesus and all will be well, in failure and success.
- To set their hearts on Prayer and to do nothing without it.
- To learn to respect authority, especially when authority or they are wrong.
- To learn those in authority are more responsible to God, both believer and non-believer.
- To learn while those in authority may be unfair and discriminate against you, they are still more answerable to a Holy God than you are.
- To learn life is not fair, so get on with it.
- To learn from their parents' principles so they can pass them on to their children.
- To learn the attributes of the Warrior from the previous chapter as well as those of God's General Joshua.
- To learn to apply these attributes to everyday life in all aspects of adolescence and then adulthood.
- To learn purity in thought, word and deed in a morally perverse and corrupt world where even those placed in authority are more concerned with their ideology than your eternal welfare.

- To learn from young, the value of a dollar and moderation in everything.
- To learn from lean times how to manage limited resources, since they would not live in comfort and ease starting out as an adult or newlywed down the road.
- To learn healthy habits as the wages of the physical sins of lust, fornication, alcohol, tobacco and even misuse of fire-arms are DEATH.
- To learn to accept the Godly guidance of their parents so they can avoid going to secular, no-nothing, Freudian-influ-enced therapists when they get older.
- To learn to look to the Bible which has the answer to every single problem known to mankind?
- To learn there are no excuses on Judgment day before God. He will judge according to Truth, Deeds and what the Gospel says.
- To learn God will judge both action and attitude, so be careful of their attitude to both the ministry and Christ's ministers, even if some are hypocrites.
- To perform random acts of kindness.
- To perform Godly sacrificial service to the less-privileged among us.
- To develop a heart for service.
- To develop a mind of steel, welded unto the Gospel of Christ.
- To develop the mind God gave to live in Truth – don't lie, your lie would find you out.
- To develop the propensity and pray to God for Courage to defend the Truth – as many will denigrate and try to deceive them as life goes on.
- To develop the strength, through Christ to stand for the Truth, so they will never fall for the Lie.

LEADERSHIP AT WORK:

The majority of people are not in management and this could be a good thing! Uneasy is the head that wears the crown and ultimately - very uneasy if the crowned head is without Christ. But did you know we can be leaders at work in our own little way.

We assume this mantle from Kingdom Authority. We who are called by His Name carry His Authority with us. We are not responsible for creating the organizational plan. However, we are responsible for executing it. He is responsible for its success. We who have His Spirit, are empowered by THAT Authority over what He has given us and therefore can claim it in certain situations.

So how can we use this opportunity as a worker, even those of us at the lowest rung in the ladder, to bring Glory to God?

Well, we build off the same attributes of Joshua, the Ultimate Warrior. Those Biblical principles never change. The Four Pillars of both men and women still apply. These are the foundational truths. Where we work is a positional truth, FOR A TIME.

Our salvation and standing with Christ is NOT positional. It is eternal. Who we are is NOT defined by what we do to help pay the bills. This is the domain of small minded non-believers in a wealthy, materialistic society on their way to eternal Judgment. Who we are is defined by our Faith and Trust in Jesus Christ and Him alone, as Lord of our lives.

The job we work in, at the present time, was provided by God. This is true whether we believe it, or not. Therefore do your job as you would, unto God. This truth is for the majority of us in the fields, as well as those in a supervisory capacity over us.

Read the following narrative from Genesis 2:15-17 NKJV "***Then the LORD God took the man (Adam) and put him in the Garden of Eden to tend and keep it.*** *And the LORD God commanded the man, saying, "Of every tree of the garden you may freely eat; but of the tree of the knowledge of good and evil you shall not eat, for in the day that you eat of it you shall surely die." Emphasis mine.*

The highlighted first sentence above was the first work assignment in human history. God prepared the way and gave Adam simple instructions. Adam chose to disobey and blame. Since the Resurrection of Christ and our standing as His Hands and Feet, by HIS choice, we have several duties to fulfill before He moves us, promotes us, or allows us to be dismissed. The following list comes out of years of walking with Christ among folks who profess a belief or none in Jesus. **In the workplace we are:**

- To conduct ourselves with open integrity and character without reproach.
- To care for the soul of even the most unpleasant nonbeliever in the office, shop or factory.
- To condemn blasphemy among our work colleagues and not fellowship with unrepentant sinners, who refuse to refrain from such conduct.
- To correct what is not right about God and Christ with your co-workers, in a loving way.
- To carry His Name and the Truth of the Gospel to these same people.
- To speak up when He directs you.
- To silence yourself when He is about to do the work Himself to either convert someone His way, or mark them for destruction on Judgment Day, by their own conduct.
- To use every opportunity to reflect the Work of Christ in our lives.
- To use every opportunity to pray for your colleagues and share the Gospel in a way relevant to the situation.
- To use every opportunity to minister in every imaginable way, as the Spirit directs, to make a small difference in someone else's family's life.
- To refrain from inappropriate jokes and using profanity at all times.
- To refrain from sexual and other inappropriate comment about women at all times in all situations.
- To refuse to go along with others to bars and other after-working hours establishments to "celebrate" birthdays or other events. Such events compromise your witness and mark you as a hypocrite.
- To refuse to go to lunch with any member of the opposite sex alone.

- To not become involved in the personal problems of any member of the opposite sex, unless they ask you for pray for them.
- To not become involved in any man-made fraternal or any organization which DOES NOT have Christ at the center of its entire being.
- To minister to brothers in Christ (if you are a man) or sisters in Christ (if you are a woman) and encourage them to soar to greater heights in the Lord, as a result of you being there for them at all times. This strengthens our Testimony and we are fulfilling one mission of Christ – to show how easy His yoke is and how light His burden is.

To do these things prayerfully, day after day, takes maturity and discipline. The key is to become mature in the Ways of God through constant daily study and immersion in the Word of God. It is spiritually profitable to listen to only uplifting Gospel and Christian music of all varieties.

Modern technology makes this so easy in these last days, one can find Christian radio stations or videos and CDs everywhere from Wal-mart to your secular video store. Sky Angel is a much better choice of Television for the family than anything HBO or MTV could ever devise from the pit of hell.

We should fellowship constantly with fellow believers when in hostile environments. Remember we are the shrinking remnant of His people on this earth. Those of us who are stronger and more fearless for the Cause of Christ are responsible for those who are under assault by the forces of this world, and can not react. We are to pray for, cheer them up, supply them with resources and encourage as much as possible.

Marketplace Evangelism is the most effective of all. Sunday church is mainly for the flock. Dr. Adrian Rogers once said "we gather for worship; we scatter for witness". Jesus hardly spoke to large crowds. The Gospels record few instances of the Lord speaking to outdoor mega-churches and then He was Pastor/Teacher. It was deemed as few as to warrant prominence in the Gospels. All the major lessons Jesus taught for our benefit, were presented to either one person face to face or the small group of hypocrites (or Pharisees).

His Word ALWAYS pierced their very souls! When He called Matthew, the latter was Levi the corrupt tax collector as was Zaccheus. We have more opportunity to be salt and light in a tasteless, dark, dying world than the average Preacher in the pulpit. Let's git 'er done!

CHAPTER 7

EFFECTIVE CHRISTIANITY

THE POWER OF FOURTH QUARTER CHRISTIANS

"For I am already being poured out as a drink offering, and the time of my departure is at hand. I have fought the good fight, I have finished the race, I have kept the faith. Finally, there is laid up for me the crown of righteousness, which the Lord, the righteous Judge, will give to me on that Day, and not to me only but also to all who have loved His appearing."
2 Timothy 4: 6-8 (NKJV)

The majority of working Americans, including some Christians, spend almost all of the entire second half of their working lives counting down to retirement. Why? A lot of them, including some with whom I work, just can not wait to stop working – so they can do nothing! Many new retirees who rest build their financial nest eggs and obsess about them in their forties and fifties basically place them all in a proverbial basket. This basket puts complete human faith in a concept of life without the Sovereignty of God. Even our own Evangelicals forget who is in charge and map their lives out according to human plans.

Here is what the Lord said in Luke 12:19-21 (NKJV) *"And I will say to my soul, "Soul, you have many goods laid up for many years; take your ease; eat, drink, and be merry."' But God said to him, 'Fool! This night your soul will be required of you; then whose will those things be which you have provided?' "So is he who lays up treasure for himself, and is not rich toward God"*

Believers are never meant to spend the Fourth quarter of life playing golf, driving around in RV's, restoring classic cars and making them minigods or living the life of Riley on stock dividends. Each day is a gift of God to be cherished. Each breath is a grant from the Father. Each moment of life is Grace from above. Never assume He owes us anything except eternal punishment for our rebellion.

Were it not for the Savior's death on the Cross, we would be receiving our just rewards of eternal damnation. The above verses are Truth and should not be taken lightly. There is no allegory here, but literal fact! The poet Robert Burns said in his Poem (To a Mouse) – "the best laid plans of mice and men often go awry".

Christians are not supposed to look forward to another season of life as the world does. We know better. Our God placed us on this planet for His Service, His Pleasure, and His own purposes. It does not matter if you are a Calvinist or an Arminian or an in-between (belief in some free will, but accepting most of the TULIP of Calvinism). One thing is sure - He who made the Heavens knew us before the Foundation of the World.

(TULIP is the acronym for "the Total Depravity of man, Unconditional election, Limited Atonement, Irresistible Grace and Perseverance of the Saints. The TULIP is the backbone of Calvinism)

This is not an endorsement of Calvinism. Like a lot of other Literal Bible students, I have trouble with the Calvinist belief of Limited Atonement – meaning Christ only died for the elect. The Cross was for all, for all time. What this means is He set a path for us. Whether we choose to obey Him and stay on that path is totally up to us. We will all stand before the Judgment Seat of Christ one day, where He will test our works by fire for rewards. What we did with our time will determine our reward in Heaven.

Dr. Jerry Falwell was the head of Liberty University, Lynchburg, Virginia which is one of the finest of any educational colleges in America. Many years ago, he came up with some points about Fourth Quarter Christians (1) in ministry and life. We do not have to go back to Abraham, Joshua and Caleb and the Patriarchs of the Faith to see examples of men or women who 'died with their' boots on or changed the world in their latter years!

Think of Ronald Reagan who became president of the United States at age 70! His story is well known, except for the fact he was very private about being a born-again Christian (is there any other kind?). Think of the late Sir Winston Churchill who was called back to save Great Britain during World War II at age 65. Reagan won the Cold War against the evil Soviet communist empire and Churchill set the standard for generations of world leaders in the free world. (Churchill was not a believer as we see in his dying hopeless words. However the man had tremendous wisdom.)

So how should one approach the game in the Fourth Quarter? The main points **(in bold)** are from Dr. Falwell, *to which I added my own commentary*. They give us some guidelines whether we are in ministry in a church or a volunteer at a nursing home.

1. **You live life looking forward, but you understand life looking backward.**

   In other words, you can not know where you are going until you know where you came from. When Christ saved you and me, He brought us out of the Egypt of our own sin.

   He had already passed over our own door posts by dying on the Cross. He parted the Red Sea to get us onto dry, safe land. But He took us through the desert. He took us through thirst. He took us through rebellion as at the waters of Meribah. He took us through bickering and disappointment. Because of the Cross, we get to Cross the Jordan with Him into the Promised Land!

   We can not comprehend the Promised Land until we understand the Wilderness of Zin. We can not appreciate Heaven and Paradise, until we remember Egypt. We can not appreciate Grace until we look at the Law and see the vile nature of our forgiven, repented sin!

2. **Your success in the Fourth Quarter begins long before the game begins.**

This makes absolute sense. Whatever we plant, we sow. How many times have we watched a football game and seen the team leading with the score at halftime, sit down and try to run out the clock. Unfortunately, this describes a lot of Christians, even some of our more solidly mature ones! We all know the stories of 5% of folks in the churches, doing 100% of the work, while the other 95% wait to be served.

Do not sit on the lead! Do not run out the clock! How many times we have seen a team running out the clock, make a mistake, turn the ball over on downs and end up losing. If we lose the game in the Fourth Quarter, the Coach will not be too happy.

Coach Jesus called and gave us the correct play. He provided the strategic blocking for OFF TACKLE RIGHT which works every time He calls it. Why on earth would His people begin killing the clock right after half time? The audible calls we make on the line, changing the play on the fly after thinking we read the changing defense, will have impact more than we can ever know! Disobedience is a heck of a misread!

3. **The greatest thing about the fourth quarter is still being in the game.**

Following on point number 2, even if we are disobedient and change the play on the line from the one Coach Jesus sent in, He gives us 2nd and 3rd down to move the ball. There has never been and will never be another Coach like ours. He is the Alpha and the Omega and there is none like Him. He can yank us from the field. Many have been benched for rank disobedience because He will not allow His children to sully His Name. The fact is He allows us to be hit in the backfield, get up and run straight up the middle again right behind the center. Jesus is not into long bombs and Hail Mary's!! He is definitely not into Hailing Mary! He is methodical and sticks to the playbook. He was born of a virgin, but existed before she ever did.

4. **The longer you stay in the game, the more comfortable you get playing the game.**

Those of us who became believers and Warriors late in our lives wished we had done this, years ago, when we were in our teens! The problem is we were not mature enough back then to even notice we were in need of a Suffering Savior. We needed to go through the Valley of the Shadow of Death, die to our sins and be redeemed by the Blood of the Lamb.

Psalm 23 says in Verse 4 (KJV) says "*yea though I walk through the Valley of the Shadow of Death, I shall fear no evil…*" We fear no evil because a Shadow can not hurt us! Jesus defeated death on the Cross! King David was living in victory (Psalm 110: 1, KJV…"*the LORD said to my Lord, Sit Thou at My Right Hand, while I make Thine enemies a footstool*!).

Yet he got so comfortable in the Lord, he broke all the Commandments in the Bathsheba incident, repented in Psalm 51 and was restored. Then he fumbled the ball again when he pride fully took a Census, against the specific instructions of God and his people were punished by the LORD in a severe famine. Again David was restored! The lesson to learn here is thus – do not get so comfortable in what we think we are doing FOR God that we fail to protect the ball with both arms wrapped around it, and try to carry it with one arm. The enemy's linebackers are cunning and evil enough to go for the knees and knock the ball loose! Hold on to Jesus! Do not fumble; we are in the Red Zone!

5. **Even though the game gets more comfortable in the fourth quarter, it never gets any easier.**

Many things in ministry seem easier to deal with as time goes by due to the fact of Christ's power dwelling or abiding in us. Abiding is a sweet word. The original Greek word is MENO and among its meaning is "to continue to be present". It is a present tense. Roget's Thesaurus gives a number of words we can use to expand on the true meaning of "abiding". They are: establish oneself, hole up, hang out, live at, lodge, occupy, reside, room, stay and tarry! I like the first phrase "establish oneself".

Once we are established in Christ Jesus and live in His Word, it does get easier to fellowship with Him. It is more comfortable being in the heat of battle on the field. No matter what the opposing side throws at us, we can rest in the Knowledge of the Holy. Psalm 119:32 (NIV) puts it succinctly: "*I run in the path of your commands, for you have set my heart free.*"

Now this is good news BUT NEVER sit on a lead, as we discussed earlier! Our enemy, the Devil, roams the earth like a roaring lion seeking to devour whomever he can. He takes extreme pleasure in bringing down God's people who allow the power of sin to cloud their new nature in Christ. The deeper we get into the Red Zone with First and Goal; it is hard enough to score. We also lose yardage by willfully sinning and giving up yardage to the devil.

6. **I'm a better team player in the fourth quarter.**

This is very true! Age does not equal maturity. I have seen younger men who live more in Sabbath rest, in Him, than men who are older by 20 or 30 years.

First of all, we acquit ourselves by the very manner and attitude by which we perform these necessary duties. I speak from experience from one who still cleans church bathrooms with my family for the past 12 years. When one is faithful in little things, one is then entrusted with weightier matters. Furthermore the Body of Christ has already been designed thus, as in Ephesians 4: 11, 12 (AMP*): "And His gifts were [varied; He Himself appointed and gave men to us] some to be apostles (special messengers), some prophets (inspired preachers and expounders), some evangelists (preachers of the Gospel, traveling missionaries), some pastors (shepherds of His flock) and teachers. His intention was the perfecting* *and the full equipping of the saints (His consecrated people), [that they should do] the work of ministering toward building up Christ's body (the church)."*

7. **The longer you stay in the game, the better perspective you have of the big picture.**

In the game of Life, one does not expect a rookie to start the first game of the season. The more experienced quarterback always gets the call because he knows the plays, can read the defense and can audible to change the play on a dime.

One does not expect Broadway Joe Namath of the New York Jets to fall for a stunt by a Baltimore Colts linebacker in Super Bowl III when he was reading almost every counterattack as if it were written in large print. So it is with the Christian. Once I came off the bleachers and was sent in with a play called by Coach Jesus, I was on a horizontal playing field. This meant both my peripheral and distance vision were equally horizontal. But the Plan He has laid out involves Vertical line of sight! We must look upward to get the only accurate big picture there is. Likewise, our vision is perfect like Namath.

Too many Christians think and play horizontally. The Cross is made up of two pieces of wood: one horizontal and the other vertical. Christ's arms are open wide in the horizontal position. His Head and Heart are pointed north into Heaven. Never lost sight of the Heart of Christ as we move ahead on the ground. Both directions together give us the correct perspective on why we are even in the game!

8. **In the fourth quarter, you're not as distraught about your past failures.**

H. Duane Black (who ever he is!!ha) once said "if at first you don't succeed, think of how many people you made happy!!" We believers chuckle at this but have a different point of view on our past failures. What the world calls a failure, Christ uses as a training tool! I like the verse from

Job 13:15a "though He slays me, I will hope in Him!" This is the ticket.

This is the way to look at the Lord's molding us into a people called out for His work. Hebrews 12: 6 says "those whom the Lord loves, He scourges". Look however at verse 11 which *says "All discipline for the moment seems not to be joyful, but sorrowful; yet to those who have been training, afterwards it yields the peaceful fruit of righteousness".* The many failures in my own life were my own fault. They came about because I was not walking with the Lord or was disobedient. But the merciful Lord He is, He brought me through it! The Breakthrough He provided was more that I ever deserved! It is worth repeating; when He tests are with fire, DO NOT ignore!

Playing in the best part of the game – the Fourth Quarter – allows us the wisdom to recognize when the Lord is in something we consider fierce or unfair. A lot of times He is not. This is when Satan's demons work in the lives of the mostly non-believing people we work with or for in our secular jobs. How we respond to these satanic attacks, even if they bring failure, exhibits the level of our spiritual maturity.

9. **In the fourth quarter, you return to your tried and proven methods**

In the section on Leadership, we looked at some proven methods from the best of the best. I am talking about men like Bobby Welch who applied several proven military leadership to Evangelism methods. The Christian world is full of all kinds of "new" and "exciting" other ways to reach the lost.

I was at the Southern Baptist Convention in Greensboro, North Carolina in June 2006 at a breakout session to show off the up and coming new pastors and some of them were excellent! Kerry Shook is a solid man and Erwin McManus who pastors Mosaic Church in downtown Los Angeles, is in a class by himself. Some of the other things I saw were motocross jumping on church platforms and an over-reliance on contemporary music.

It is amazing the sizable percentage of the mainly "mega churches" (relative to city size) who have shucked their old members, gone millions into debt and gone totally into the post-modern marketing model of church philosophy. In the process, some of them lost some of their older members who are opposed to these massive seeker-sensitive structures.

It is also amazing the lengths certain ministry leaders think they have to go to appeal to their favorite demographic – the young and restless! In all this, I fail to see the relevance to the Reverence towards the Holy One of the Universe. I am sorry, but I am not a fan of the modern ways emerging out of the darkness.

The fear of many of us forward looking evangelists, who are grounded in the solid hymns of the faith and traditional faith, is these seeker-sensitive based churches are creating a number of converts who were not regenerated by conviction of their sins! Our fear is they are swayed by nice sounding music, drama, dance and tickling of the ears by non-offensive preaching from the paraphrase versions of the Bible! The Tried and Proven methods are still the only way, whether it is the Fourth Quarter or the opening kickoff. There is a reason Ray Comfort (www.livingwaters.com) and Kirk Cameron are exploding all over Christian TV with ***the Way of the Master*** weekly program. The only way to bring the Good News of the Gospel is the way Christ did and Charles Spurgeon preached – use the Law to show the need for a sinner. There is no sugar coating this!!

10 **The greatest thing about the fourth quarter is the confidence you develop.**

Some of the great college football teams from my favorite Alabama Crimson Tide to the black and blue Big Ten Division teams like Michigan and the Illinois Fighting Illini always stress the fundamentals. The great Bear Bryant of the Tide was a stickler for the book but also bucked the system. It is well known among football fans what Bear did to bring black football players into the Tide back in 1971. He was strong enough as the Bama coach to integrate the Tide when then Democratic Governor George Wallace was in full reign against the Civil Rights movement. Bear's confidence came from a non-nonsense modus operandi his entire life.

It is not an accident his attitude led to his preaching fundamentals on the field – discipline and the fundamentals. Roll Tide! With the proper foundation, any one in the game will be confident of his or her place in Christ.

We have seen it in organizations, sports teams and the like, the more the fundamentals are executed with precision, the more confident they become. I would actually use Dr. Falwell who came up with the eleven header points I selected as an example. He may not be everyone's favorite Christian or preacher, but if you look at him or Franklin Graham or Dr. John Macarthur, these men are unflappable. The secularists in the media in their elitists interrogations of their positions always see men of God who are smiling and SPEAKING TRUTH! They do not flinch or waver. Their confidence in the Christ we serve is awe-inspiring!

11. **In the Fourth Quarter you learn how to play with pain!**

We serve a Suffering Savior. The entire chapter of Isaiah 53 is about the Suffering Servant of Almighty God the Father. He, who had no place to lay His Head, was beaten so much He was beyond recognition. One of the many objections to Mel Gibson's Passion of the Christ was its bloodiness. But in a major sense, that was one of the most accurate things about the movie. The world, including some weak-kneed Christians, did not want to face up the bloodguilt it has by what was done to Jesus Christ.

The whips laced with metallic scraps which tore into His flesh were graphic and historically accurate. The Lord's face was unrecognizable. By the way, this makes the famed Shroud of Turin a major hoax. So how do we play with pain?

Most avid football fans remember the Miami Dolphins – San Diego Chargers Monday Night Football game in Miami back in 1981. It is a game which makes highlight reels for the great Tight End of the Chargers, Kellen Winslow. Winslow was dehydrated and suffering numerous injuries. That game has stuck in my memory for the past 25 years for its sheer magnificence of a man who gave it all on the field.

Not only did he block a field goal, in his pain, but had 13 receptions for 166 yards and 1 touchdown – an NFL record at the time. He had a pinched nerve, severe cramps that rendered him almost immobile as he walked in slow motion, a cut lip with 3 stitches and dehydration. The memory of two teammates almost dragging him off the field at the end of the game which the Chargers won 41-38 is an NFL classic replayed over and over again.

We are not Kellen Winslow. However when the devil knocks us down; blindsides us; hit us below the belt; chop blocks our knees; clotheslines our necks or gives us an illegal contact upside our Helmet of Salvation, we get up; praise the Lord; take a swig of Living Water and get right back in the game!

This game of Life which Christ calls us to is not for the weak. When He saves us He not only puts us on the field but expects us to put on the uniform He provides for us. Ephesians 6 gives us a full description of the Armor of God. This will be described in detail in the next chapter because too many of our fellow travelers go out in the marketplace of ideas without their Armor. They subsequently get beat up, defeated and then turn away from the fight or in some cases, from the faith completely. The latter were never saved in the first place.

Just as a football team has specialized positions for each man, so Jesus has provided gifts and talents to His men and women who are called by His Name.

Dr. Robert Lewis has a phrase in his public church ministry Men's Fraternity 3 (The Great Adventure) where he teaches "function follows form". In other words, you can not take a duck and try to train it to fly like an eagle. A duck is a duck. A church pianist should strive to be the best she or he can be. The friendly usher/greeter has a special function in the church and so on.

Not everyone is called to be a pastor, and believe me, not everyone who is a pastor was called either! The regular church member in the pew can be more of an evangelist than the entire church staff put together. She or he has the opportunity to reach more worldly doubters at the office or the marketplace and witness by their words and deeds.

I am in awe sometimes at my wife Vicki who is bolder than I in sharing face to face in the simplest way I wish I was able to (as previously mentioned)! Over the past decade and a half, I have known of countless people she has evangelized. Sometimes one can try to reason too much and appeal to the intellect with people who are steeped in Darwinism and their own self-righteousness.

This is the case with me at times in my encounter with the secular world weekly. So how the Lord has gotten around this, is to have me fellowship with a very small select group of fired up believers known only to ourselves at work! He has His Own way of training you for His Work here on earth.

MID LIFE CRISIS

One can not speak of Fourth Quarter Christians without addressing what is a classic North American phenomenon – the Mid Life Crisis! Countless men, wiser and more educated than I, have addressed this in seminars, books and other teaching tools. I do not seek to be like them! I come from a conservative Christian Caribbean background. This thing about men in their forties or fifties suddenly ditching their beautiful wives of their youth to buff up in the gym then go driving a red corvette accompanied by a 20 year old blonde bimbo, is totally anathema to me….and to Christ!

Where did that come from? Sure I have doubts about life. Who does not? I work in what many consider the bottom of the barrel type of job in the State of Illinois and drive a 1989 Beige Crown Victoria we purchased from my wife's grandfather estate after he died. I tell you what; the car only had 29,000 on it at the time and glides like a Sherman tank on a cloud! Both my wife and I have to work. We have bills like everyone else and braces to pay for etc. *So why is this man smiling?!!* Nehemiah 8:10 "....the Joy of the Lord is my strength!"

No man or woman of God should to succumb to this secular pattern of misbehavior. Do not buy all this garbage you see advertised in these lurid magazines and tabloids at the check out line in the supermarket. These things such as Cosmopolitan and Redbook give such much filthy advice to women; it can only come from the pit of hell! These so-called self-help magazines and their book counterparts sell the lie of a "guilt-free" fantasy life "as long as you do no act it out". This is another lie from the master of lies, Satan.

Why buy counsel from some columnist in New York City who sits behind a word processor transferring his or her own twisted thoughts to print while stopping in a bar on the way home to drown whatever their demons are? Beware this so-called Fantasy life. Jesus warns in Matthew 5:28 (AMP) *"But I say to you that everyone who so much as looks at a woman with evil desire for her has already committed adultery with her in his heart."*

This applies to both men and women.

One's thought life is the first thing which should be guarded from the evil one. The great Zig Ziglar, appearing on the Focus on the Family radio broadcast many years ago gave the best application to guard your heart from straying. He prays every morning for the Lord to build a Wall of Fire (2) around his heart, so NOTHING can penetrate it – no harlot, no temptation, and no compromising situation. I have since taken his advice.

The minute one allows a thought to take hold; it leads to situations I have seen numerous times in my past 35 years of work, to the destruction of families.

Here is what pop psychology tells you about a Mid Life Crisis. Jean Coleman, MSC, a consultant clinical psychologist says *"mid life crisis is characterized by low mood, dissatisfaction with life, a feeling of pointlessness in life. It is not always distinguishable from clinical depression."* 3

She also says those in crisis may show their distress by reacting in several different ways: *"by denial (by escape or overcompensation), by decompensation (with anxiety, depression or rage), or by regression. An individual may become discontented at work, resort to alcohol or risk taking behavior.*

*The range of feelings experienced have been variously described as hollowness and lack of genuine enjoyment, emptiness and uncertainty, a mixture of strain and boredom, floating unfocussed melancholy and depression. This is the time when people are believed to be vulnerable to hypochondria, accidents, illness, alcoholism and suicide. **

Midlife crisis is described as an existential crisis, that is to say, it is centered about issues of meaning and purpose in life. *(Emphasis mine).This is why it arises at the time it does, because by the mid thirties, young people have often achieved their initial goals in life (or realized they are not attainable"*

AHA!! There it is! **EXISTENTIALIST CRISIS**! To understand the modern North American version of Midlife Crisis, one has to delve into what Existentialism really means and how American society has become so totally wrapped up in this humanistic philosophy.

The best description I can find is from Dr. Bob Corbett, Professor Emeritus of Webster University of St. Louis, Missouri. Dr. Corbett is a very nice man and has since retired to his garden, gourmet meals and watching European Soccer!! From all he said, life is good even with a six month stint on a Federal Grand Jury in Missouri! He gave me permission to us this very classic and textbook explanation of the characteristics an Existentialist, to wit: 4

- They are obsessed with how to live one's life and believe that philosophical and psychological inquiry can help.
- They believe there are certain questions that everyone must deal with (if they are to take human life seriously), and that these are special — existential — questions. Questions such as death, the meaning of human existence, the place of God in human existence, the meaning of value, interpersonal relationship, the place of self-reflective conscious knowledge of one's self in existing.

Note that the existentialists on this characterization don't pay much attention to "social" questions such as the politics of life and what "social" responsibility the society or state has. They focus almost exclusively on the individual.

- By and large Existentialists believe that life is very difficult and that it doesn't have an "objective" or universally known value, but that the individual must create value by affirming it and living it, not by talking about it.
- Existential choices and values are primarily demonstrated in ACT not in words.
- Given that one is focusing on individual existence and the "existential" struggles (that is, in making decisions that are meaningful in everyday life), they often find that literary characterizations rather than more abstract philosophical thinking are the best ways to elucidate existential struggles.
- They tend to take freedom of the will, the human power to do or not do, as absolutely obvious. Now and again there are arguments for free will in Existentialist literature, but even in these arguments, one gets the distinct sense that the arguments are not for themselves, but for "outsiders." Inside the movement, free will is axiomatic, it is intuitively obvious, it is the backdrop of all else that goes on.

There are certainly exceptions to each of these things, but this is sort of a placing of the existentialist-like positions.

In high school, one of my literature books was "The Stranger" by Albert Camus. This book messed up my mind for years because I was not a regenerated, Holy Ghost- saved, sanctified believer. I was a 16 year old pup who had written the US Navy the year before so I could join and go fight in Vietnam! I thought there was some kind of glory in getting anonymously shot down on the battlefield!

However it said a lot about my philosophy – namely, I had none!! I went to church, youth group, missions, etc...but I was Camus' Stranger on the beach. Camus is one of the leading Existentialists of the 20th Century. I did not know until now he was an atheist! So were all the others like Franz Kafka or Jean-Paul Sartre.

So the Midlife Crisis' roots ARE existential and totally wrapped up in self, devoid of God. The Christian who is living by the Life of

Another (a favorite phrase of my friend, the great Bob Warren, Bible teacher and former San Antonio Spur) is NOT an existentialist.

The Christian exists to please Christ and walk in His Light. How many times do we hear in the latest fad book, talk show, song, TV show....basically the secular American culture, the following, in no particular order nor author, just from observations over 30 years :

- You are free! So love yourself. Be yourself. Do what you wish. You are not hurting anyone!
- Think big! Think outside the box! You better think!
- You deserve that car! Charge that coat! Take that cruise, pay later! Just charge!
- Live like there is no tomorrow! Grab all you can now! Tomorrow never comes!
- The choice is yours! "Go on try it, you'll like it!"
- "She won't know, you are only looking!"
- "Oh I love him....and I don't care if he is married with four kids...."

You get the picture! Sorry for all the exclamation punctuation marks but these and variations of them are heard daily screaming at us from all directions. They are meant to get us off our game; out of comfort zone. It is the vilest, most subtle attack from the enemy you can imagine. If anyone thinks something bad can not happen to us, because "we have it all together and we are all fine", THINK AGAIN!

By now, you are saying, "well these are just people speaking or writing who have no influence or nothing to do with me!" Well... how about Rick Warren, pastor of Saddleback Church in California? Pastor Rick is the best selling author of over 26 million copies of the Purpose Driven Life and the leader of the seeker-sensitive church movement.

Rick Warren is now a regular columnist for Ladies Home Journal. In March 2005, he wrote an article which included his famous Five Points on how to "Learn to Love yourself". These were : **"Accept yourself.....Love yourself.....Be true to yourself.....Forgive yourself.....Believe in yourself"**...5.On the surface, this sounds like good psychological advice. The problem is none of this is based on Scripture and ALL OF IT IS BASED ON SELF! As believers, or even, if someone reading this has not come to Faith in Christ yet, everything about our lives, has to be filtered through Jesus and the Word of God. There is no other way.

Rather than follow Warren's advice in Ladies Home Journal, we should choose to use his five points to say …..**"Accept what Christ did on the Cross"….Love the Lord your God with all your heart, soul and might and love your neighbor as yourself…..Be true to the Word of God because you are the only Bible 99% of the world is going to read…..Forgive others as the Father in Heaven has forgiven us….. and Believe in the Lord Jesus Christ and ye shall be saved!!"**

This love of self is what is placing a cancer in American evangelicalism and causing some otherwise rational Christian men to fall. Needless to say, even the strongest among us must take heed, lest we fall. For goodness sake though, why participate is this New Age sacrament? A person, male or female, whose life is so full of prayer and is totally sold out to Christ, would seek to do NOTHING which would hurt the Heart of God. When we were saved by Him, we took on His Nature. Our old Adamic Nature was disposed with. Let us act like the saints we have become.

The following verses from Romans 6: 1-13 (AMP) are so rich and relevant to any Christian's life that they must be quoted fully and in context. (Emphasis mine). Like it did Martin Luther over 500 years ago, these verses in Romans opened my eyes permanently with a peace which passeth all understanding! These verses are the only way to glorious living, living by the Life of Another, and living in Victory:

> *1 WHAT SHALL we say [to all this]? Are we to remain in sin in order that God's grace (favor and mercy) may multiply and overflow?*
>
> *2 Certainly not! How can we who died to sin live in it any longer?*
>
> *3 Are you ignorant of the fact that* ***all of us who have been baptized into Christ Jesus were baptized into His death?***

4 We were buried therefore with Him by the baptism into death, so that just as Christ was raised from the dead by the glorious [power] of the Father, so we too might [habitually] live and behave in newness of life.

5 For if we have become one with Him by sharing a death like His, we shall also be [one with Him in sharing] His resurrection [by a new life lived for God].

6 We know that our old (unrenewed) self was nailed to the cross with Him in order that [our] body [which is the instrument] of sin might be made ineffective and inactive for evil, that we might no longer be the slaves of sin.

7 For when a man dies, he is freed (loosed, delivered) from [the power of] sin [among men].

8 Now if we have died with Christ, we believe that we shall also live with Him,

9 Because we know that Christ (the Anointed One), being once raised from the dead, will never die again; death no longer has power over Him.

10 For by the death He died, He died to sin [ending His relation to it] once for all; and the life that He lives, He is living to God [in unbroken fellowship with Him].

11 Even so consider yourselves also dead to sin and your relation to it broken, but alive to God [living in unbroken fellowship with Him] in Christ Jesus.

12 Let not sin therefore rule as king in your mortal (short-lived, perishable) bodies, to make you yield to its cravings and be subject to its lusts and evil passions.

13 Do not continue offering or yielding your bodily members [and [a]faculties] to sin as instruments (tools) of wickedness. But offer and yield yourselves to God as though you have been raised from the dead to [perpetual] life, and your bodily members [and [b]faculties] to God, presenting them as implements of righteousness.

My brother in Christ Bryan McKenzie, Pastor of Grace Bible Church in Lake Jackson, Texas, uses verse 11 in teaching application to turning from the sins of the flesh or "become dead to that sin".

These sins can be anything from coveting a friend's new Mercedes to looking more than once at temptation as she passes by. Let us consider ourselves "dead to those sins", live in peace, joy and contentment in Christ and watch any so called Mid-life Crisis become just another man-made theory. In other words picture yourself like Paul in Philippians 4:11 *"Not that I speak from want, for I have learned to be content in whatever circumstances I am."*

HOW THEN SHALL WE LIVE IN THE FOURTH QUARTER?

If there was one man in the Bible who lived a permanent Midlife Crisis it was King Solomon! His prayer at the dedication of the Temple when he chose Wisdom over riches one of the most beautiful, heartfelt prayers in the entire Scripture is still the standard for believers. I used this prayer to pray the Lord for wisdom, His Wisdom, more than anything else in my own life.

However from then on for old King Solomon, it went downhill. The wonderful love of his life in the Song of Solomon has become the benchmark for couples Bible studies nationwide. From the Song of Solomon, he went to Proverbs 21:9 ("*It is better to live in a corner of a roof than in a house shared with a contentious woman").* He went from the Love of his life to his 700 wives and 300 concubines (1 Kings 11: 1-3)! He came full circle in the final quarter of his life when he repented and wrote the book of Ecclesiastes.

Chapter 11 of this book gives us wonderful direction on life. The entire chapter is a joy but the key verses in my opinion are verse 1-2 (NIV): *"Cast your bread upon the waters, for after many days you will find it again. Give portions to seven, yes to eight, for you do not know what disaster may come upon the land."*

The original Hebrew translation of these verses is *"Send your substance [out] over the face of the water [i.e., the sea] that you may find it [again] many days hence. Give a share to seven, or even to eight, for you cannot know what [sort of] disaster may come upon the land."* This is even richer than the English translation!

Ecclesiastes 11 (NIV)

1 Cast your bread on the surface of the waters, for you will find it after many days.

2 Divide your portion to seven, or even to eight, for you do not know what misfortune may occur on the earth.

3 If the clouds are full, they pour out rain upon the earth; and whether a tree falls toward the south or toward the north, wherever the tree falls, there it lies.

4 He who watches the wind will not sow and he who looks at the clouds will not reap.

5 Just as you do not know the path of the wind and how bones are formed in the womb of the pregnant woman, so you do not know the activity of God who makes all things.

6 Sow your seed in the morning and do not be idle in the evening, for you do not know whether morning or evening sowing will succeed, or whether both of them alike will be good.

7 The light is pleasant, and it is good for the eyes to see the sun.

8 Indeed, if a man should live many years, let him rejoice in them all, and let him remember the days of darkness, for they will be many. Everything that is to come will be futility.

9 Rejoice, young man, during your childhood, and let your heart be pleasant during the days of young manhood. And follow the impulses of your heart and the desires of your eyes yet know that God will bring you to judgment for all these things.

10 So, remove grief and anger from your heart and put away pain from your body, because childhood and the prime of life are fleeting.

Solomon was the wealthiest man in the world and had diversified into all kinds of products which made him the envy of the known world! But his uncontrollable lust led him to worship the pagan gods of his many pagan wives. He set the table for the utter devastation, decline into depravity and death of the nation Israel!

His legacy was a split Kingdom with his sons and their descendants becoming some of the vilest enemies of the Living God. So when he repented and wrote Ecclesiastes, we need to listen to him, who was once a man after God's own heart.

So what "Cast your bread" mean?" First of all, we must be bold. Boldness runs throughout the rest of the chapter. By being bold and not afraid to take risks, we are encouraged to invest wisely. One invests wisely in seven or eight different ways to avoid putting all one's eggs in one basket. He is using metaphors not just for financial prosperity but in any aspect of life.

Some Bible teachers also point out the larger meaning of verses 1 and 2 to the mature Christian. I can not remember where I heard the following but it reveals a lot of truth. For instance, Middle Eastern bread is light and can float on water for a while. By this random act, one is almost doing what some say: "do good, throw your bread out in the water, if the fish does not know it, God does!" I take this to mean when one constantly thinks of others in the context of investing time, resources and the Love of Christ in them without expecting a return, one is less likely to obsess in the worldly standard of "SELF" above all else. Hence verses 1 and 2 of Chapter 11 carry a double meaning which is so rich and poignant.

The rest of the verses are full of life changing truths to support the poor and be generous. He encourages us not to wait for the weather to change but to do today whatever we can do. A person whose life is hidden in Christ, Colossians 3:4 (Christ is my life), will be joyful (verse 7) and enjoy life by thanking Him for each new day.

Solomon warns in verse 9 not be become dazzled by the things of the world, supposedly as he did. Finally in verse 10 he admonishes the reader to make the most of our years, as youth and life is so fleeting.

Chuck Swindoll summarizes the entire chapter rather well in one of his many sermons on the radio: "Start activating your life today and never quit...Refuse to let your life collect dust. Start today. If you don't start today, chances are good you never will. Don't wait for the weather to change. Don't wait for the kids to grow up. Don't wait for your husband to come back or your wife to return. Don't wait until you have spare time or more money or stronger health or a better job or a bigger house. Don't wait for conditions to be perfect. Be bullish about this, starting today. And never quit". [6]

One can almost see Swindoll flashing the big smile of his as he expounds this truth!

The mature Christian who has been in the game for all four quarters and lived Ecclesiastes 11 can look forward to walking off the field when the whistle blows and the Roll is called up Yonder to a crown of glory for a life well –lived.

As Solomon says, there is 100% unemployment in the grave, so let's get to work now and seize the day!

CHAPTER 8

EFFECTIVE CHRISTIANITY

THE POWER OF A LEGACY

"What you leave behind is not what is engraved in stone monuments, but what is woven into the lives of others"
Pericles, General of Athens, ruler of Tyre (495-429BC) [0]

JACOB AND THE TWELVE TRIBES

In Genesis 49, verse 1-28, we read a stunning blessing pronounced by a dying Jacob upon his twelve sons. Many years after reuniting with his son Joseph in the Land of the Pharaohs, Jacob (Israel) brings down a hammer on the heads of most of his sons as he prepares to die. Ten of his twelve sons had caused him pain.

Most of them had violated many of the statutes of the Holy God of Abraham, Isaac and Jacob, even if the Law of Moses would not be given for almost 500 years! The following account of the sons and the blessings from their dying father is significant for its course change in human history.

There is application to Gentiles across the spectrum of the past 4500 years. Many people today think God is asleep because He may not punish us for our sins right away, "therefore He must be looking the other way, and it is alright to continue in this sin!" Not so, my friend. What the world and its followers are actually doing is storing up Wrath for themselves, on the Day of Judgment, unless they are washed CLEAN by the Blood of the Lamb!!

With this in mind, here are the blessings on each of the sons of Jacob and what became of them, over time. When they became the Nation promised by God.

REUBEN **(Genesis 49: 3-4a) NKJV:**

Reuben, you are my firstborn, my might and the beginning of my strength, the excellency of dignity and the excellency of power. Unstable as water, you shall not excel, because you went up to your father's bed; then you defiled ... (with Jacob's wife Bilhah) (Reference: Genesis 35:22)

The issue with Rueben applies to a lot of Christians (and non-Christians sometimes). We may not do vile things. We may be impetuous and full of vigor and virtue, but if there is an unconfessed sin in our lives, all of that means absolutely nothing to a Holy God. Reuben had tried to save Joseph from being murdered by his other brothers. The sin of Adultery against God, and the curse upon him from Jacob ("you shall not excel"), eventually led to this tribe being wiped out in Israel when the Syrian King Tiglath-Pileser captured them and the half tribe of Manasseh (1 Chronicles 5:26).

Not surprisingly the Reubenites TOTALLY abandoned the faith of the God of Abraham, Isaac and Jacob. Not one prophet, judge or hero came from this first son of Jacob...NOT ONE!

SIMEON AND LEVI **(Genesis 49: 5-7) NKJV:**

Simeon and Levi are brothers; instruments of cruelty are in their dwelling place. Let not my soul enter their council; let not my honor be united to their assembly; for in their anger they slew a man (Reference Genesis 34:24-26), and in their self-will they hamstrung an ox. Cursed be their anger, for it is fierce; and their wrath, for it is cruel! I will divide them in Jacob and scatter them in Israel.

Most of us will never let our discontent, even anger, rise to such a point that double-cross and premeditated murder (the entire chapter of Genesis 34) result. But thinking such thoughts are just as evil. Jesus preached many times against the sin of the mind (*anyone who looks at a woman with lust for her has already committed adultery with her in his heart...* Matt.5:28). Simeon and Levi dishonored their father by this vile murderous act. They brought the Wrath of God upon their own heads, even though the Levite tribe produced some notable Biblical stalwarts.

The Simeonites faded away and blended into the pagan Northern Kingdom of Israel, fulfilling the prediction of God through Jacob, in verse 26. 1 Chronicles 4: 41-43 reveals what a useless, Godless people they had become, just like Simeon, the father of that tribe. There was nothing more abominable in the sight of God that the Northern Kingdom.

Levi's descendants (the Levites) were of no major account until the time of Moses and his brother Aaron. God Himself chose the Levites out of the Twelve to be His priests and minister in the Tabernacle and later Temple. He consecrated them unto Himself and gave specific instructions for their conduct.

Aaron, the first priest of Israel, almost set the tone for the Levites later on in their awful rebellious history. He did so right from the beginning. In Exodus 32, while Moses was up on the Mountain of God getting the Law from the Hand of the LORD, Aaron was making a golden pagan calf to pacify the ungrateful mob. In verse 32, he blamed the people, even though the calf was HIS idea! Then he said *"I threw the gold into the fire and OUT CAME THIS CALF*!" (Verse 24). But Moses, writing in Verse 35 said *"God smote them..... because of the calf Aaron had mad*e". I suspect Aaron will be held responsible for that on the Day of Wrath! When will God's people ever learn!

The Levites engaged in vile abominations at times, just like their Tribal Father Aaron. From the sons of Eli (1 Samuel 2:11-13) to the Pharisees and Scribes of the New Testament, they are shining examples of disobedience and total violation of the Word of God.

The Chosen Prophet Jeremiah was the son of the Levite Priest Hilkiah who was part of the corrupt priestly system during the reigns of Kings Jehoiakim and Zedekiah. Both these kings had pagan gods in their palaces and bowed down to them, all the while claiming they worshipped the one true God of Israel! The priests went along with their rulers in this corruption.

In Ezekiel, the house of Israel was so vile, the priests were committing abominations right in the temple!

Jesus Himself scolded Nicodemus in John 3: 10 (*Jesus answered and said to him, "Are you the teacher of Israel and do not understand these things*?) The Levites themselves were condemned to Hell by Jesus. I would urge the reading of the entire Chapter of Matthew 23 for context!

The Pharisees and high priests of the Temple were so caught up in their man-made traditions and "rule on rule, rule on rule....a little here and a little there" (from Isaiah 28:13) they could not discern the prophesies of their own prophets. By the way, these are the same Prophets they murdered or exiled!

So the heritage of these Simeon and Levi is significant, to the larger context of the God's Original plan. The application the LORD wants us to take from this, as mothers and fathers, is "actions have consequences". It is so easy to fall from Grace if one is not careful. But more important than this is the Lord has a warning in Luke 12: 48 *"But he who did not know, yet committed things deserving of stripes, and shall be beaten with few. For everyone to* ***whom much is given****, from him* ***much*** *will be required; and to* ***whom much*** *has been committed, of him they will ask the more."*

Jesus had this warning for the descendants – the Scribes and Pharisees - of the Levite priests in Matthew 23 NIV who were about to kill Him for speaking God's Truth :

> *"You snakes! You brood of vipers! How will you escape being condemned to hell? Therefore I am sending you prophets and wise men and teachers. Some of them you will kill and crucify; others you will flog in your synagogues and pursue from town to town. And so upon you will come all the righteous blood that has been shed on earth, from the blood of righteous Abel to the blood of Zechariah son of Berekiah,*

whom you murdered between the temple and the altar. I tell you the truth; all this will come upon this generation"

These men, placed in a high position by God, through the Levitical priesthood even as it was coming to a close due to the New Covenant of Christ, bore the blood of Isaiah, Zechariah, John the Baptist and other Old Testament prophets on their hands. They did not actually commit these acts, but came from a murderous generation which did. The Key word here is Legacy. Blood guilt and damnation was their legacy.

Even as Aaron's rod, which budded, lay in the Ark of the Covenant, his priesthood and God's covenant with his tribe is now history. We have a new High Priest forever and ever, and His Name is Jesus. His is the True Legacy from the Father. The Twelve Tribes of Jacob have their symbolic place in the Kingdom of Heaven, as do the Patriarchs Abraham, Isaac and Jacob, but those actual members of the body of Israel are another story.

JUDAH:

The blessing to Judah was stunning in its Messianic prophesy. Our Savior, Jesus Christ came from this line and is known as the Lion of Judah. Jacobs blessing, from the Amplified Bible, Genesis 49: 8-11 reads thus (emphasis mine)

Judah, you are the one whom your brothers shall praise; your hand shall be on the neck of your enemies; your father's sons shall bow down to you. ***Judah, a lion's cub!*** *With the prey, my son, you have gone high up [the mountain]. He stooped down, he crouched like a lion, and like a lioness—which dares provoke and rouse him? The scepter or leadership shall not depart from Judah, nor the ruler's staff from between his feet,* ***until Shiloh [the Messiah, the Peaceful One]*** *comes* ***to whom it belongs, and to Him shall be the obedience of the people.*** *Binding* ***His foal*** *to the vine and His donkey's colt to the choice vine,* ***He washes His garments in wine and His clothes in the blood of grape***

It is fitting God took the Priesthood away from the corrupt, murderous Levites, and gave it permanently to His Son, from one Tribe to another! This legacy from Judah's line came about only because Jesus was the God-man! He is/was God who became man, identified with His Flock (us), died a real death on the Cross, and rose to the Father as our Intercessor. He could only be our Intermediary before the Father because of the Cross!!

You wonder why liberal theologians and the world, doing the bidding of Satan, deny the Cross. They do because Jesus walked into Heaven after the Ascension, forty days post-Crucifixion, victoriously as permanent High Priest on our behalf! That is something NOBODY can take away for us!

> Hebrews 4:14-16 (AMP) reveals as much here: *Inasmuch then as we have a great High Priest Who has [already] ascended and passed through the heavens, Jesus the Son of God, let us hold fast our confession [of faith in Him]. For we do not have a High Priest Who is unable to understand and sympathize and have a shared feeling with our weaknesses and infirmities and liability to the assaults of temptation, but One Who has been tempted in every respect as we are, yet without sinning. Let us then fearlessly and confidently and boldly draw near to the throne of grace (the throne of God's unmerited favor to us sinners), that we may receive mercy [for our failures] and find grace to help in good time for every need [appropriate help and well-timed help, coming just when we need it].*

There is no underestimating how significant this fact is to the Believer in Jesus Christ. Even the other part of the Blessing to Judah in Verse 11 (*He washes His garments in wine and His clothes in the blood of grapes)* talks of the Lord when He returns in Glory to take down the secular kings of the earth in Revelation 19:13 with the Armies of Heaven dressed in white linen on white horses.

This prophecy from the dying Jacob wraps up in this verse from Revelation 19:13 "*He was clothed with a robe dipped in blood, and His name is called The Word of God*". Jesus as our Savior/High

Priest means not only His confession of our name on Judgment Day but as Intercessor to our prayers on this side of Heaven!

There are many other things to be written on this topic but for now, suffice it to say, this blessing to Judah, is the most important of the Twelve by Jacob to his sons. Here are the other blessings, briefly and how the Tribes fared in the annals of history.

ZEBULON; ISSACHAR; DAN:

> Genesis 49:13, AMP: *Zebulun shall live toward the seashore, and he shall be a haven and a landing place for ships; and his border shall be toward Sidon.*

Zebulon was an obscure son. He almost faded into the shades of history except for one big mention in the Book of Judges. His tribe fought valiantly alongside Naphtali's tribe and was mentioned by the Judge Deborah in Judges 5:18.

> Genesis 49:14,15, AMP: *Issachar is a strong-boned donkey crouching down between the sheepfolds and he saw that rest was good and that the land was pleasant; and he bowed his shoulder to bear [his burdens] and became a servant to tribute [subjected to forced labor].*

Issachar's tribe settled in some of the richest land in the land of Palestine, at the time, just as Jacob predicted! They were not noted for much else, except being hardworking farmers!

> Genesis 49: 16, 17, AMP: *Dan shall judge his people as one of the tribes of Israel. Dan shall be a serpent by the way, a horned snake in the path that bites at the horse's heels, so that his rider falls backward.*

Samson and the Judges of Israel came from the Tribe of Dan (see the entire Book of Judges). One of God's greatest Generals was the great Gideon, a Danite. In 1 Chronicles 2:12, Dan is omitted and in Revelation 7. The Angel of Heaven left Dan out of the 144,000 saved out of the Tribulation by Jesus, at the End times!

GAD; ASHER; NAPHTALI:

> Genesis 49*: Gad—a raiding troop shall raid him, but he shall raid at their heels and assault them [victoriously].*

The name Gad means "a troop". His tribe was vicious and warlike. They moved to East of the Jordan and occupied part of the mountainous area, intermingling with the Ammonites. However 12,000 of them were sealed by the Angel of God in Revelation 7, of the 144,000…as were 12,000 of each tribe EXCEPT Dan!

Genesis 49: 20, AMP: *Asher's food [supply] shall be rich and fat, and he shall yield and deliver royal delights.*

Asher also settled into rich farm land in Palestine. They lived very close to the Mediterranean coast.

Genesis 49: 21, AMP: *Naphtali is a hind let loose which yields lovely fawns.*

The tribe of Naphtali was recorded fighting valiantly alongside Zebulon in the book of Judges

JOSEPH AND BENJAMIN:

> *Genesis 49: 22-26, AMP: Joseph is a fruitful bough, a fruitful bough by a well (spring or fountain), who do branches run over the wall. Skilled archers have bitterly attacked and sorely worried him; they have shot at him and persecuted him. But his bow remained strong and steady and rested in the Strength that does not fail him, for the arms of his hands were made strong and active by the hands of the Mighty God of Jacob, by the name of the Shepherd, the Rock of Israel, by the God of your father, Who will help you, and by the Almighty, Who will bless you with blessings of the heavens above, blessings lying in the deep beneath, blessings of the breasts and of the womb.*

The blessings of your father [on you] are greater than the blessings of my forefathers [Abraham and Isaac on me] and are as lasting as the bounties of the eternal hills; they shall be on the head of Joseph, and on the crown of the head of him who was the consecrated one and the one separated from his brethren and [the one who] is prince among them.

The tribe of the great Joseph, Prime Minister of Egypt, was split into Ephraim and Manasseh. Ancient Jewish Tradition says Joseph wanted to have reconciliation with his brothers after Jacob's death, something Jacob did not bless him with. Like the first time, tradition says, his brothers double-crossed him again. While Joseph himself was a blessed man and his bones were buried right next to Jacob's well, until it was desecrated in 2005 AD by Palestinian guerrillas, his tribes later split.

However these tribes are also sealed by the Angel of God in Revelation 7, while Ephraim and Dan are left out! Both Joseph and his sub-tribe are mentioned as saved by the Spirit. Dan was accountable for introducing worship of worthless pagan gods and idols.

Genesis 49: 27, AMP: *Benjamin is a] ravenous wolf, in the morning devouring the prey and at night dividing the spoil.*

The Benjamites were a ferocious fighting lot. King Saul, the first king of Israel, came out of this tribe. They were eventually swallowed up by the Tribe of Judah and not heard from again in the rest of the Bible. Famous Benjamites were the Apostle Paul and Jonathan, friend of the great King David.

The reason for examining the Blessings of Jacob on his twelve sons to a certain depth was to provide the background for a Biblical understanding of Legacy. These are not just stories which occurred 3700 years ago in a vacuum, but events led by people who have impacted several millennia, cultures and everything up to this point in time.

An important thing to note here, is how much Jesus Christ is in the picture from Genesis to Revelation and what an outstanding presence He has even from the Blessing to Judah until the Sealing of the Tribes and the 144,000 evangelists who are the Remnant of the Tribes in the End times.

LEGACY

Webster's Dictionary defines "legacy" as *"something transmitted by or received from an ancestor or predecessor or from the past"*. What some of these men, Jacob's sons, transmitted was more than bad news. It was the worse news ever in terms of Eternity. Their lot was smeared with the foul mud of their pre-Egypt conduct and their uniting with Joseph again. But their deeds found them out right after both Jacob's and Joseph's deaths, as successive Pharaohs forgot the deeds of Joseph with the passage of time.

What are we transmitting to our children and future descendants? On our dying beds, what type of blessings would we confer on our surviving children? Are blessings like Jacob's even done today; in terms of its meaning of "formal approval"?

Proverbs 14:26: *"He who fears the LORD has a secure fortress, and for his children it will be a refuge (NIV)."* This is our battle cry and prerequisite as parents who can carry on the Biblical traditions of the great Patriarchs of Genesis!

But we do have a more modern example of a Jacob-like giant of the Faith, who has given us the example to be the kind of all-pro parents we should be, as we pass on to eternity. Read on!

THE LEGACY OF EDWARD WIGHTMAN, MARTYRED BY KING JAMES OF ENGLAND! [2]

In the course of researching and seeking permission to use published materials concerning their family, I had the privilege of speaking to Ron Wightman. This fine gentleman currently lives in Salt Lake City, Utah and is a font of every knowledge concerning an American hero named Obadiah Holmes! I learnt something really important from him in the Legacy Line from Obadiah to Abraham Lincoln! Did I just say Abraham Lincoln, 16th President of these United States? Yes!

Ron told me about an important member of his family - Edward Wightman who was burnt at the stake in on April 11, 1612 by King James in England. This is the same King James after whom the KJV Bible is named! James was the keeper of the Church of England as the ruling monarch of Scotland and England. Edward was called a heretic because he was of the same Christian mindset as the Pilgrims who came over on the Mayflower!!

This simply meant he wanted the Freedom to worship God the way the Bible prescribed. One man, who did not come over to the U.S. but was persecuted by the English Church authorities around the same generation as Edward Wightman, was John Bunyan. We know him as the hero of the Faith who wrote Pilgrims Progress while in prison for preaching the Gospel Truth!

Edward was the last person ever burnt at the stake in England and is listed in Fox Book of Martyrs. His execution took place in Litchfield, England. History has it that as he was set ablaze by the king's henchmen, Edward screamed and said some seemingly unintelligible words.

The people nearby thought he was recanting his beliefs and put on the fire quickly! Then Edward began preaching the Gospel again and did what all good martyrs do – he stood firm on the Rock of Christ. They burnt him again.

The Wightman family still has his King James Bible in their prized possessions!

This historic family has bloodlines going all the way back to the founding of the Modern Christian church of America and its Baptist roots. For instance, one of the Martyred Edward's descendants is the Rev. Valentine Wightman whose line churched at Quidnessett Baptist Church.

His brother Daniel was co pastor of Second Baptist Church of Newport, Rhode Island. Any visitor to the super affluent Newport would not recognize its Christian heritage. It has fallen a long way from its innocent yet powerful God-inspired roots.

Now here is the reason Legacy is so important. Daniel's first wife was Susannah Holmes, granddaughter of the great Obadiah Holmes (see the rest of this chapter). Holmes was the pastor of First Baptist in Newport. Susannah's mother was Mary Sayles, the great-granddaughter of Roger Williams. Wightman family history calls Roger Williams (also see later on in this chapter) "that dauntless apostle of freedom of conscience".

Obadiah Holmes was one of the first Christian martyrs in the United States. A hero of the Baptist Faith, he was sentenced on May 31, 1651 for guess what – preaching and baptizing (by immersion) on the Lord's Day!! Holmes was born in Lancashire, England in 1607. He came to America like a lot of Baptists, escaping persecution from those in the Church of England (whose current branch is the Episcopalian church of America).

Married to Katherine Hyde in 1646, Holmes was granted two acres in Salem, Massachusetts. A little known fact of history is he is the first man in America to manufacture glass!!

Most of the Baptists moved to the New York (then New Amsterdam) area to live around the Dutch, but Holmes settled in Massachusetts. The Pilgrims who lived in New England were Congregationalists who believed in Infant Baptism. This immediately caused a problem. By definition, Baptists believe in the Biblical form of Baptism.

(Infant Baptism comes out of theory from an early church father named Hippolytus in the 3rd Century who was the Bishop of Rome around 220. He was not a pope. The Apostle Peter was not the first pope of the Catholic Church either. This has been mythology passed down over centuries going back to Constantine in the 4th Century. Hippolytus inferred and basically created infant baptism out of whole cloth from earlier writings from the great martyr Polycarp, a friend of the Apostle John. There was wide disagreement over it and the controversy continues today.) 1

Obadiah Holmes found the same stringent old world practices from the protestant, yet Monarch-run Church of England, in the new American colonies. He rebelled. 1

His relative by marriage, Roger Williams, the founder of the Baptists in America, took a stand for the new Free Church in America against the Establishment (who had only a couple decades before come over on the Mayflower!). On November 13th 1644, an act was passed stating that any person who did not have their children 'sprinkled" (infant baptism), among other things, would face banishment. 1

Holmes was a teaching brother at the time. He was fined for acting like a real Baptist in the face of the same kind of persecution Martin Luther and others faced against the powerful Catholic Church, at the time of the reformation. A number of other brothers were arrested and fined for that "transgression". All the other men's fines were paid, but Holmes refused to have his paid, even though it was one of the heavier fines of thirty pounds, a huge amount in the 17th Century! So the Pilgrims, who fled England for religious freedom, had Obadiah flogged! 1

He was whipped in public so badly; he was unable to do anything except rest on his elbows and knees in jail...by the authorities! On behalf of religion! Holmes soon left Salem for Rhode Island where he became co-pastor of First Baptist Church of Newport. 1

By the way, the Congregationalist church which persecuted Holmes was started by the Pilgrims. It is now one of the most liberal churches in American and part of the extreme leftist denomination, the United Church of Christ. Salem is well known throughout American history for its famous 'witch trials'.

On a parallel basis, Roger Williams was once the pastor in Salem He moved to Plymouth and then back to Salem in 1635. He too ran into trouble with the church authorities in the colony for his 'radical behavior'! His now mainstream evangelical views were heresy to the governing authorities. They banished him from Salem. When he continued speaking out, the authorities came after him to send him to trial in England where he would have no doubt met the same fate as Martyr Edward Wightman.

Williams set out in a canoe with five other men and landed at a new settlement on the Moshassuck River. Because he said he got there by the "providence of God", he named the settlement Providence - now the capitol of Rhode Island.

(During our three year stay in Hartford, Ct., my wife Vicki and I were members of the Immanuel Congregational Church (right across the street from Mark Twain's house where he wrote Huck Finn, Tom Sawyer and others! We spent most of our time in that church teaching the Bible to kids in the basement, while the service was going on upstairs. It was one of the biggest blessings of our lives. Most or all of them did not know what was in the Bible. The Lord brought several children to an initial knowledge of Him and we were able to see fruit in less than three years with the same kids. This was our mission in Hartford.)

Apart from his persecution, a requisite for a true man of Christ, Obadiah Holmes is better known for what he did just before he died. His letter to his nine children is a masterpiece, still quoted in devotionals by many family ministries. It stands as a loving testimony of a father on his way to be with Jesus. Here are parts of his famous letter to his nine children, a treatise which will inspire you!

My Dear Children:

A word or two unto you all who are near and dear unto me, and much on my heart as I draw near to my end and am not likely to see you nor speak to you at my departure. Wherefore I am moved to leave these lines for your consideration when I am gone and you shall see me no more.

Above all things in this world let it be your care to seek the Kingdom of Heaven and His righteousness first. Be you thoroughly convinced of that and, by actual transgressions, that you are sinners. Yet, know that such great love as cannot be expressed by man or angels has the Lord sent and held forth: even his Son, his only Son, to save and deliver you from wrath....

My soul has been in great trouble for you, to see Christ formed in you by a thorough work of the Holy Spirit of the Lord that it may appear you are born again and engrafted in the true vine; so you, being true branches, may bring forth fruit unto God and serve Him in your generation. Wherefore, wait on Him with care and diligence; carefully read the Scriptures and mind well what is therein contained, for they testify of Him.

Obadiah Holmes started his letter with the most important issue in life: repentance from sin and faith in Jesus Christ. He knew that if his descendants missed Christ then they would miss life. And now my son, Joseph: Remember that Joseph of Arimathea was a good man and a disciple of Jesus; he was bold and went in boldly and asked for the body of Jesus, and buried it.

My son, John: Remember what a loving and beloved disciple he was.

My daughter, Hope: Consider what a grace of God hope is, and covet after that hopes that will never be ashamed but has hope of eternal life and salvation of Jesus Christ.

My son, Obadiah: Consider that Obadiah was a servant of the Lord and tender in spirit, and in a troublesome time hid the prophets by fifty in a cave.

My son, Samuel: Remember Samuel was a chief prophet of the Lord, ready to hear his voice saying, "Speak, Lord, for thy servant heareth."

My daughter, Martha: Remember Martha, although she was encumbered with many things, yet she loved the Lord and was beloved of Him, for He loved Mary and Martha.

My daughter, Mary: Remember Mary who chose the better part that shall not be taken away and did hearken to the Lord's instructions.

My son, Jonathan: Remember how faithful and loving he was to David, that servant of the Lord.

My daughter, Lydia: Remember how Lydia's heart was opened, her care borne, her spirit made to be willing to receive and obey the apostle in what the Lord required, and was baptized, and entertained and refreshed the servants of the Lord.

"Be you content with your present condition and portion God has given you. Make a good use of what you have by making use of it for your comfort (solace). For meat, drink or apparel, it is the gift of God. Take care to live honestly, justly, quietly with love and peace among yourselves, your neighbors and, if possible, be at peace with all men.

"In what you can, do good to all men, especially to such as fear the Lord. Forget not to entertain strangers, according to your ability; if it be done in sincerity, it will be accepted, especially if to a disciple in the name of a disciple. Do to all men as you would have them do to you.

"If you would be Christ's disciples, you must know and consider that you must take up your cross and follow Him, through evil

report and losses. But yet know, he that will lose his life for Him shall save it.

"Thus, my dear children, have I according to my measure, as is my duty, counseled you. May the good Lord give you understanding in all things and by His Holy Spirit convince, reprove and instruct and lead you into all truth as it is in Jesus. So that when you have done your work here, He may receive you to glory. Now the God of truth and peace be with you, unto Whom I commit this and you, even to Him be glory forever and ever, Amen."

ABRAHAM LINCOLN!

One of the reasons for including Obadiah Holmes in this book was to exhibit how a man, with a lineage of pastors, judges and college presidents from the great Jonathan Edwards, can leave a legacy with his blessing, much like Jacob left his with Judah. One of Obadiah Holmes descendants was none other than **Abraham Lincoln**!!

Old Honest Abe, claimed by the states of Kentucky, Indiana and of course, Illinois (the Land of Lincoln) was a direct descendant of Holmes's daughter Lydia! She moved to New Jersey and had a daughter named Sarah, who married Richard Salter. Salter's daughter Hannah married a man named Mordecai Lincoln.

Mordecai Lincoln's son was John Lincoln; called "Virginia John" His son was Captain Abraham Lincoln! He was killed by Indians in Kentucky in 1780. Captain Lincoln's son was Thomas Lincoln, the father of ABRAHAM LINCOLN – now called the greatest president of the United States of America.

Both Springfield's own Honest Abe and his grandfather were named Abraham. They came out of the legacy of Obadiah Holmes. Let's reread this part of Reverend Obadiah Holmes' last letter to his children, as he prepared to go home to Jesus. Here again is the part to Lydia Holmes. Lydia was the great, great, great, great grandmother of President Abraham Lincoln.

My daughter, Lydia: Remember how Lydia's heart was opened, her care borne, her spirit made to be willing to

receive and obey the apostle in what the Lord required, and was baptized, and entertained and refreshed the servants of the Lord.

Look at the love and Godly counsel passed on by this man of Christ – Obadiah – to his daughter Lydia. He recognized the commitment her daughter made to Christ, was baptized in the power of the Holy Spirit into the Kingdom of God. Lydia's descendants, through their pioneer spirit, led to the rail-splitter of Illinois.

From Obadiah to Abe Lincoln, the Legacy of Christ remained the thread. This does not mean everyone in this line were saved, justified, sanctified, glorified sons and daughters of Christ and are in heaven with him now. It does mean they had the opportunity to do so, along with coming from solid God-fearing American stock.

Other descendants of Obadiah Holmes include Baptist pastors and ministers down to this day! Some of his descendants on the Wightman side came down from Obadiah's granddaughter Susannah. She has been previously mentioned as the first wife of Rev. Valentine Wightman. The family grew and some settled across state lines in the great state of Connecticut, a state dear to me heart.

The Wightman Family moved from Montville, Connecticut to Herkimer County, New York. Later on, a descendant Benjamin fought in the American Revolutionary war for the Tryon Country Rangers of New York. The family grew in Herkimer County. Some of the Wightman line was also born in Kirtland, Lake County, Ohio. In 1835, one of Obadiah's descendants Charles Billings Wightman joined the Church of the Latter Day Saints – the Mormons.

He moved with his family in 1865. Traveling 2000 miles from New York by wagon into the Rocky Mountains, Charles settled in Payson. This was only 65 miles south of Salt Lake City, Utah. This is the line from which my new friend Ron Wightman descends. I am extremely grateful to Ron for supplying all this super family history from Edward the Martyr to Ron himself! There is so much rich American, Church and Family history in his story. This is Legacy; the legacy of three persecuted men of God – Edward Wightman, Obadiah Holmes and Roger Williams. To Him be the Glory and Honor and Praise, Amen.

All Wightmans are cousins of the Abraham Lincoln line! You can even say Ron Wightman is one of the last known 'kinfolk' of Honest Abe himself, even if Lincoln has no direct descendants!

"The conclusion, when all has been heard, is: fear God and keep His commandments, because this applies to every person. For God will bring every act to judgment, everything which is hidden, whether it is good or evil". (Ecclesiastes 12:13-14)

CHAPTER 9

EFFECTIVE CHRISTIANITY

THE POWER OF HOLINESS:

"When God seems far away, guess who moved!"
The Navigators.

Picture the scene: it is around 739 BC and the long, prosperous and some say, even too prosperous, reign of King Uzziah was coming to an end. It was a time not unlike prosperous America! It was like today: the church and God's people awash in massive new structures, fancy electronics and corporate-type marketing plans. The Sacred Scriptures are treated lightly as charlatan TV preachers sell prayer clothes and prosperity gospel. Multiple versions of the original word are watered down to the lowest common denominator....you get the picture.

Now rewind to 739 BC. Isaiah (which means "the Lord is Salvation) is married to a prophetess (Isaiah 8:3) and has two sons whose names are given to him directly by the LORD. Their names are prophetic: Shear-Jashub (7:3) meaning "the remnant shall return" and Maher-Shalal-Hash-Baz (8:3) meaning "the seed spoileth and the prey hasteth". This man was the prophets of all prophets! The Book of Isaiah is even called the "little Bible".

In these booming economic times in Judah, the Southern Kingdom, it seems obvious Isaiah was living a comfortable life as well! We pick up the account from Isaiah 6:1- 5 (KJV):

> *1 In the year that king Uzziah died I saw also the LORD sitting upon a throne, high and lifted up, and His train filled the temple.*
>
> *2 Above it stood the seraphims: each one had six wings; with twain he covered his face, and with twain he covered his feet, and with twain he did fly.*
>
> *3 And one cried unto another, and said, Holy, holy, holy, is the LORD of hosts: the whole earth is full of His glory.*
>
> *4 And the posts of the door moved at the voice of him that cried, and the house was filled with smoke.*
>
> *5 Then said I, Woe is me! for I am undone; because I am a man of unclean lips, and I dwell in the midst of a people of unclean lips: for mine eyes have seen the King, the LORD of hosts.*

Two things of major importance to the Christian here: Isaiah comes apart at his own personal situation and secondly, he was in the Presence of the Most Holy God!

Can you imagine how he felt??!! Imagine how we would feel as believers (or not) in the Lord Jesus Christ. We are so well-fed, over-indulged and spoilt that the Christians of the First Century would look at us as the biggest cry-babies ever! We think we have it so hard. In fact, I once heard a story on Moody Radio WLUJ about an American Missionary who was visiting a Chinese martyr not too long ago in the pagan Chinese mainland. The U.S. missionary asked the martyr "what I can I pray for you for?" To which the Chinese persecuted man said "pray we do not become like you!" OUCH!!

We watch Television and movies which has so desensitized us by its sexual and secular imagery; we have subconsciously accepted it as normal! We listen to contemporary Christian music by artists most of whom do not even mention the Name of Jesus in their songs. When they are asked, most of them say "He is inferred!" Look at Revelation 3: 15-16 (NKJV) to see what Jesus says about "inference": *"I know your works, that you are neither cold nor hot. I could wish you were cold or hot. So then, because you are lukewarm, and neither cold nor hot, I will vomit you out of My mouth!"*

Have we ever asked ourselves if we would rent this or that movie or watch the new culturally-popular sitcom if Jesus were sitting right next to us??!! NO!! But we do now!

Well Isaiah found out first hand he was not fit to have the Lord sitting next to, in front or above Him!! This first hand account of the Scene at the Throne, which goes on now as you read this. Isaiah found out face to face just how Holy Almighty God is!

He not only found out how Holy God is, but he saw how Glorious He is and worthy of Worship!! In fact this scene in Heaven is our Living Example of worship...not the soft, toothless sermons of modern American Christianity or the mindless pap of 711 songs. (The 711 song syndrome means the same 7 words sung 11 consecutive times!)

Look at Chapter 6:1 again where we have the LORD *"high and lifted up"*. This shows His Stature in the annals of Time and Space. Basically He towers above all else and we are basically nowhere near in stature as the prophet acknowledges. Then, "His Train fills the Temple". The words "of His robe" were added by the translators to explain this Train. This long, flowing garment is indicative of His Majesty as King of all which exists!! Only a king would wear such a robe!

So the prophet sees a towering, Holy and Majestic Sovereign. No wonder he falls flat on his face in total shame....AS SHOULD WE!!

Dropping down to Verse 5, he (whose name means Lord of Salvation) says "*woe is me; I am a man of unclean lips!*" No matter how Holy or righteous a man appears on earth to his peers, in the Presence of Holy God, we are still impure! We are all people of unclean lips and we do not have to cuss like a sailor to be this way!

Jesus says in Matthew 15:11 (paraphrase) what comes out of a person's mouth is what defiles him/her, not what goes in! No one is exempt. No pastor, elder, deacon, preacher, president, teacher, student or laborer. We are ALL unclean, even as a saved people.

Here was a man from Prophet Central, with a prophetess wife feeling the intense heat of Judgment in front of the Throne. But while the Laodecian church did not yet exist in Judah, its equivalent did and Isaiah lived in this environment. Just as we do today with all these Christian book fads and movements going on!

My guess is Isaiah lived like a southern Californian mega pastor, ate the best food, wore the finest linen and had a well-appointed terrace upon his house. He had a prosperous life just as we did. He admits he lives amongst a godless people as the Southern Kingdom had become and did not appear too much different than they were with their speech etc! This was so, even though he was God's prophet!

One theological note here, Isaiah mentioned in Vs 5 his eyes saw *"the King, the LORD of Hosts."* This phrase is mentioned over 200 times in the Old Testament and each time it means the same thing! LORD is the Holy One of Israel – Yahweh, Adonai. The word LORD also implies ruler, sovereign, master, self-existent (all attributes of God).

The word "Hosts" could means both armies and multitudes! Revelation 19:14 describes "*the armies of Heaven*" clothed in clean, white linen as they follow King Jesus down from Heaven as He returns on His white horse to destroy the enemies of God! This prophetic scene should inspire us to daily search ourselves and beg Jesus cleanse us! It is the inspiration for the rest of this chapter on being an Effective Christian and living a Holy Life.

It is a life which we see God calling Moses too at the Burning Bush. The ground was so Holy when the LORD was there; Moses had to remove his sandals. The next two sections will attempt to lay out the case for Holiness and how we can apply it. It comes out of my own study on the subject and do not represent a theological dissertation for a Masters degree. Rather it is a work of an ordinary layman who seeks wisdom from the Scriptures. My goal is to share this wisdom in the simplest possible form.

Two amazing things happened to the prophet in Isaiah 6: 6-8 (KJV)

6 Then flew one of the seraphims unto me, having a live coal in his hand, which he had taken with the tongs from off the altar:

7 and he laid it upon my mouth, and said, Lo, this hath touched thy lips; and thine iniquity is taken away, and thy sin purged.

8 also I heard the voice of the Lord, saying, Whom shall I send, and who will go for us? Then said I, Here am I; send me.

The Angel over the Throne of God flew over to the eternally burning flame in Heaven, took a burning coal and touched Isaiah's "*unclean lips*"! This occasioned his sin to be not just immediately taken away from him but purged or cleansed thoroughly. Fire is used many times throughout the Bible as we see in the chapter on Repentance and Revival.

The second amazing event is Jesus speaking and the prophet taking up the Commission from the Lord, (i.e. "*here I am, send me*"). Look at how He says "*whom shall I send? Who shall go for us?*"

If you or I were in Isaiah's place, in front of a Holy God and His Son, how would we respond to these questions?

Note here the error of all rabbis, priests, Pharisees and Sanhedrin. They have been wrong for 2000 years now! How wrong? Dead wrong! Here is an Old Testament prophet proving God is more than One Person! Jesus predicted (Matthew 24:2) the destruction of the Temple which happened in 70 AD.

This buried Old Testament Biblical Judaism. It had already died on the Cross when the Lord as God/Man died. The Veil of the Temple was torn in half and it was over for the Mosaic Covenant. **Anyone who still follows this Covenant to this day will be judged against the requirements of the Law.**

When Roman Governor Titus destroyed Jerusalem, he destroyed the Temple and the blood sacrifice system was also ended for good in practice. Jesus was the Ultimate Holy Blood Sacrifice. He already put a permanent stop to it in terms of God's requirements! This is the true meaning of Propitiation! His Blood was the fulfillment of the requirements of all law Moses wrote, concerning sacrifice.

WHY HOLINESS?

The writer of Hebrews writes in Chapter 12:14 said: "*pursue peace with all people....AND HOLINESS, WITHOUT WHICH NO ONE WILL SEE THE LORD* (N.K.J.V.) The quote from the Navigators above brings it even closer to home. The word Holiness implies "separateness" unto God. God is above all else Holy and has never moved from His Throne.

Those who are called His people are summoned to the same characteristic. When a person saved he/she is made right by God, through the finished work of Christ on the Cross. This is called Justification.

The Process of Sanctification then begins. The verb "to sanctify" means to set apart. We are/were set apart for God's service and to be holy unto Him. This is a process which can take a lifetime.

We need to avoid a lot of the new Christian fads and new movements out there so our minds are not complicated with things which will distract from Him. There is something inherently wrong with the way the modern gospel preached by even the best of our Evangelicals. Congregations are told about the free gift of the GRACE of God, without the Holiness of the God who demands purity! Enough of this "Jesus loves you, man....just say this prayer....walk this aisle.... listen to this song on Contemporary Christian radio!!"

Here is the Command from the Word of God: "*Therefore, prepare your minds for action, keep sober in spirit, and fix your hope completely on the grace to be brought to you at the revelation of Jesus Christ. As obedient children, do not be conformed to the former lusts which were yours in your ignorance, but like the Holy One who called you, be holy yourselves also in all your behavior; because it is written, "YOU SHALL BE HOLY, FOR I AM HOLY."* I Peter 1:13-16.

The Apostle Peter got the last phrase "***YOU SHALL BE HOLY, FOR I AM HOLY***" from Leviticitus 11:44a: *For I am the LORD your God. You shall therefore consecrate yourselves, and you shall be holy; for I am holy.* (NKJV)

The things to note from the original command from God in Leviticus are Consecration and Holiness. **CONSECRATION or**

to be consecrated, is the act of CONTINUALLY separating ourselves from everything EXCEPT what God has called and selected us to do! This means from the moment we are saved, we are to begin putting our sinful life styles behind us.

Peter is the Rock and the man selected by Jesus Himself to build the church. He explains Consecration best in the above passage, which is not surprising since the Word of God is richer and purer than anything else!!

PREPARATION:

Peter in 1 Peter 1: 13-16 (from above) reveals the following to us:

a. **PREPARE YOUR MINDS FOR ACTION**. How do we do that? Read the previous column titled "...to dwell in the House of the Lord..." and read any commentary on Psalm 1: 1-3. Prepare your minds with prayer and power-reading the Word of God. Power read with the Spirit of God as your guide... "meditate on His Word, day and night!" Prayer and Scripture are the key components. However, in my opinion, there is a subtext.

   The Battle of ideas and reason are won in the mind. If the mind is not buffeted by complete submission to the Supreme Will of God; if the mind is not completely broken along with the will; if the mind is not fixed and focused on Him, we are susceptible to the wiles of the power of sin.

b. **KEEP SOBER IN THE SPIRIT**: The Christian life walked in step with the Lord is not a sprint or something which needs contrived emotional highs to sustain it. Certain worship styles or televangelists are great about leading their congregations to jump, prance and dance in the aisles while "getting slain in the Spirit". The latter is not Biblical. Nowhere is "slain in the Spirit" mentioned or commanded. There is a huge problem with emotions not grounded in Biblical Truth, because our enemy, the Devil, is the king of manipulating basic human feelings.

BE LEVEL-HEADED! Think clearly. Worship with every fiber of your being. I have been moved to tears by preaching in Conventions, worship songs with my hands held high and prayer which moved me when I felt the Spirit of the Lord so powerfully present in the place. There is absolutely NOTHING wrong with True love and devotion in such worship.

c. **FIX YOUR HOPE COMPLETELY ON THE GRACE TO BE BROUGHT TO YOU AT THE REVELATION OF JESUS CHRIST**: If most people were to be asked about where they would spend eternity, they would say "Heaven". HOWEVER we believers in the Lord Jesus Christ are the only ones who can rest in the Blessed Assurance that not only Jesus is mine and thine, but because a Holy God has revealed Himself through His Son Jesus and His Life, death and Resurrection 2000 years ago, we can live in His Grace and Mercy, after having repented of our sins.

Now friends, here comes the caveat, because these are the things a Holy God can not abide with. Peter says:

AS OBEDIENT CHILDREN, DO NOT BE CONFORMED TO THE FORMER LUSTS WHICH WERE YOURS IN YOUR IGNORANCE: God demands total obedience from His elect. I know first hand, as do most true believers, the Mighty Hand of the Lord on those who have slipped up in even the smallest way! We all know the Lord disciplines those whom He loves but there is more. From the moment of Salvation, when we died, were buried and rose with Christ (the act of Regeneration) and became Saints by Calling, we lost our Adamic Nature with which we were born.

HOWEVER, because we are still human, the power of sin still exists in the mortal man, this side of Heaven. We will be tempted, tossed and tried in the truest way. Satan will buffet us to test our Transformation into Christ. Show him we are not conforming to his temptations for lust of the flesh because we do not belong to him!! We, who are called by

Him, are not ignorant of our status in Christ. THEREFORE, LET US ACT LIKE HIS CHILDREN!!

BUT LIKE THE HOLY ONE WHO CALLED YOU, BE HOLY ALSO, IN ALL YOUR BEHAVIOR: No matter who we are or were. No matter what we have done, when God calls a person to Him, it is in our eternal interest to respond!! Look at the kind of people He called – Matthew a corrupt tax collector, Zaccheus another corrupt Tax collector, Saul/Paul a murderer and persecutor of Christians these people immediately changed their behavior upon being called by the Lord Jesus! Zaccheus repaid all the money and more, which he had defrauded people. Saul became Paul and immediately began preaching the Gospel of Christ. What are we to do? How are we to live? It is in the Book! ***"Therefore, beloved, since you look for these things, be diligent to be found by Him in peace, spotless and blameless,"*** **2 Peter 3:14**

How do we live that last Bible verse? Can we even begin to compare with the standard a Holy God has set before us? Before we can even begin to compare, we have to know what the standard is! We have all seen, read and heard the discussion, for instance, on Gay "marriage", for instance.

Some people, even some "clergy" go to the Bible and misquote Scripture to support their contention that Jesus never said anything against their perversion! Yes He did! He stated clearly, both in **Genesis 2:24, Matthew 19:5 and Mark 10:7-8 that** ***"a man shall leave his father and mother and be joined to his WIFE and the two shall be called one flesh!"***

What these apostates are attempting to do is alter God's Moral Law and Government. Before we examine this briefly, look at how Moses had to approach the Burning Bush in **Exodus 3:2**. God Almighty told him to remove his sandals because the ground on which he was standing was **"holy ground" (verse 5**). Wherever God is, that place is Holy! Simple as that! By the way, the vegetation on the same part of the mountain at Hereby, in the middle of the desert, is green and alive!!

THE MORAL LAW:

The Moral Law of God is well known as the Ten Commandments **(Exodus 20:1-17).** Why the Commandments are called the Moral Law? Moral Law is based on the premise of Absolutes.

There is such a thing as Absolute Truth. Things are either right or they are wrong. There is black and white. Western Society, whether modern day politicians admit it or not, was built on the Moral Law and Absolute Truth.

Where there was/is Moral Law, there had to be a moral lawgiver! That Lawgiver is God Almighty Himself! Adonai and His Son Yeshua. The atheist and the agnostic have said in their hearts "there is no God!" They have denied Absolute Truth. However, they have just contradicted themselves!

They have made an absolute statement under the terms of Logic. They are also dead wrong eternally in their sins, as God Himself has written the Moral Law on the hearts of every man and woman. Romans 2:15 says: *"in that they show the work of the Law written in their hearts, their conscience bearing witness and their thoughts alternately accusing or else defending them"*... this literally means that anyone , ANYONE, who dies without Christ will face the Fearsome Hand of Judgment which leads to eternal death in Hell! This is ABSOLUTELY TRUE!!

We know what the Moral Law is. Where it was given was on Holy Ground on Mt Horeb in the Sinai desert. Why the Moral Law was given was for the following reasons:

1. To show mankind the Absolute Holiness of God.
2. To show the complete need for a Holy Life
3. To show us the need for Mercy from that Holy God!

God shows His Holiness right there in the first three commandments. Look at His commands from Exodus 20:1-7

1 Then God spoke all these words, saying:

2 "I am the LORD your God,ʾ who brought you out of the land of Egypt, out of the house of slavery.

3 You shall have no other gods before Me
4 You shall not make for yourself[1] an idol, or any likeness
of what is in heaven above or on the earth beneath or in the
water under the earth.
5 You shall not worship them or serve them; for I, the
LORD your God, am a jealous God, visiting the iniquity of
the fathers on the children, on the third and the fourth gener-
ations of those who hate Me,
6 but showing loving-kindness to thousands, to those
who love Me and keep My commandments.
7 You shall not take the name of the LORD your God in
vain, for the LORD will not leave him unpunished who takes
His name in vain."

Several things are evident! God is God alone! As a Holy God and Righteous God, He must uphold His own Law and only He can define what it means.

He is a jealous God because He is holy. Nothing made by the hands of man, at Satan's prompting, will stand on the Day of Wrath. Nothing preached from the false gospel of certain modern day "Christian" leaders, will stand before His Throne. Nothing spoken in blasphemy will be tolerated from He who knows our every thought.

We see in these commandments given to Moses what God demands up front – total awe and respect of WHO He is and What He stands for. The Name of God was so holy to the Israelites, even the ones going around in a circle in the desert for 40 years (just 12 miles from the Promised Land!!) that they would not even speak it!

Contrast this to our modern culture where the Names of both God and Jesus Christ are blasphemed in almost every aspect of life! God was called יהוה or YWHW (read the Hebrew from right to left and pronounce it YAHWEH).

By the way, if anyone has been fortunate to see a copy of the Torah Scroll in any Messianic Synagogue (Jewish believers in Christ), you will be amazed at how meticulous the Scroll was written….and think Moses…by free hand writing!!

The rest of the Commandments are obvious guideposts for life. The other 600 plus laws in Torah are the Ceremonial Laws, which do not apply to the Christians! Christ ended all of that on the Cross.

Because God has told us who He is in the Old Testament, we are expected to live holy lives!! One problem – we can't...or we won't! Why? Because man is a fallen creature! The new agers, the non Christians and others say man is good...no, he isn't!

Taking a look at the Ten Commandments or the Moral Law, there has been only One Man who could ever keep every letter of every law written in stone there!! Anyone who says he has kept them is a liar and God hates liars!

Therefore, since Jesus is the only Perfect Man, a Holy God has to be angry at sin. He hates sin! When Jesus was dying on the Cross, His Own Father could not stand to look at the Cross because it carried the burden of sin and death.

It was only when Jesus cried out "*Eloi, Eloi, lama sabacthani.... My God, My God, why has Thou forsaken Me*?" (Mark 15:34) did He expire and was glorified in Heaven!

God is so angry at sin, He has to punish it. Don't believe the garbage on Oprah and others like her these days, who preach that all people go to Heaven and only the Adolph Hitler's and Saddam Hussein's of the world go to Hell!

These false prophets have their own coming to them one day. If you want to know the truth about Judgment and Hell, read the greatest sermon ever preached in America.

It was on July 8, 1741 by Jonathon Edwards called "Sinners in the Hands of an Angry God". On that day, over 500 people were saved! I recommend obtaining the Max McLean reading of the Greatest Sermon in America ever to get the full effect of what it means! The terror modern man faces on that Day will be unequalled and there will be many surprised "Christian" people who will hear, from Jesus: "*And then I will declare to them, I never knew you; DEPART FROM ME, YOU WHO PRACTICE LAWLESSNESS*", Matthew 7:22-24.

God knew we could not keep His Moral Law, so He sent us the best way out of Hell – His Son Jesus Christ! God knew we could not keep the Ceremonial Law and its many blood Sacrifices, so He made one Blood Sacrifice for all time; past, present and future.

God knew He wanted us to be a distinct people. He called us away from the darkness of the world, to the Light of His Glory, so He redeemed us by the Blood of the Lamb. God knew His Anger at man had to be satisfied by blood, so He gave up Jesus on the Cross for all time.

The word "satisfied" comes from two Latin words: "satis" meaning "enough" and facere "to do". Jesus did enough on the Cross to satisfied God's anger at man's filth and sin.

PROPITIATION:

An important word used in the Bible is PROPITIATION, which simply means "an averting or satisfying of the Wrath of God. Christ died on the Cross, as a propitiation or satisfaction of our sins. He made us righteous (when we trusted Him completely) or justified us. The Holiness of God could only be found, therefore, through the Person of Jesus Christ!

There are only two choices really: either Trust and Live or go your own way and face Judgment! The modern church seeks to bring happiness to its pew dwellers, instead of the righteousness of Christ. It seeks to show Christ as the means to an end or the way to fill a need, rather than teach the Christ who is the fulfillment of the Moral Law. It seeks to teach an easy gospel of free Grace without linking it to the Sin which brought out the absolute need for Grace!!

Apart from the Holiness of God, Grace is empty talk dressed up in a nice suit.

Apart from the Holiness of God, sinners take it upon themselves to save themselves OUTSIDE of the Word of God!

Apart from the Holiness of God, there is no difference between new age pop psychology and the feel good message of the "best life now".

Apart from the Holiness of God, our churches have become mega-theatres full of skits, loud bands etc.; where entertainment trumps true worship.

Dr. David Wells of Gordon Conwell Seminary said in his book "No Place for truth…whatever happened to Evangelical Theology" (1993) "Sin is defiance of God's holiness, the Cross is the outworking and victory of God's holiness and faith is the recognition of God's holiness. Knowing that God is holy is therefore the key to knowing life as it truly is, knowing Christ as He truly is, knowing why He came and knowing how life will end."[2] Precisely!

WHAT IS THE MATTER WITH US?!

If you have gotten this far into this chapter, you are now wondering "why is he doing this? I get it! I have to be holy"." Does this mean I have to dress in a long robe, grow a beard and walk with a shepherd's staff? What will my friends AT CHURCH think about me?! I don't know how to do this!"

Therein, the final statement lays the crux. The majority of ordinary churchgoers have no idea what Holiness or Sanctification is or why it matters. The seminaries out of which their pastors graduate are riddled with professors of psychology and weak theology.

When was the last time you heard a message on hell in church? When was the last time you were called to repentance of current sin before a Holy God? When was the last time you had a church board embark the local body on Forty Days of Prayer and Repentance instead of some man-made five points of light?

"Hardly ever" is the answer to every one of those questions! The scariest part of it all is God is not amused by what He sees in His churches today. Modern American Christianity has reduced Him to an uninterested party whose major focus is more and new massive buildings and fancy multimedia messages.

We sing Holy, Holy, Holy but live Oh- me, oh-me, oh-me!! Lord have mercy on us, folks! All the programs, Starbucks, small group management and websites have taken the place of True Discipleship which leads to us being consecrated true saints of the Living God!

If you were to ask a Jewish Rabbi, at any point in history, what he thought about our God in Heaven, without a doubt, the Rabbi would be in awe and say confidently "God is Holy!" The God of

Israel, the same God whom we serve and whose Son is our Savior, is so Holy to practicing Jews they do not call His Name.

Even now, the Messianic Jewish movement reveres the name of God so much; they call him G-d (leaving the vowel out). Lord is spelt L-rd. (By the way the word Messianic describes Jews who believe Jesus is the Messiah....therefore, all the Disciples and the first Christians were Messianic!)

If you were to ask any person in America or even western culture in Canada or Europe (where you may find a few Christians still), what their opinion of God is, they would reply "God is Love". Well, this is true. God IS love....but first God is Holy!

Somehow cheap western Christianity has brought the Attributes of the Almighty to a 5 second TV sound bite to satisfy our compartmentalized busy life of doing much and accomplishing little! You hear God referred to as "the Man upstairs", a kindly old grandpa or a loving parent who will continue to look the other way. Is this correct? NO!!

God's Purity is His major attribute. This Purity is indicative of His Perfection. It is His Nature, the very essence of His Being. In Psalm 89:35 God says: "*Once I have sworn by <u>My Holiness</u>; I will not lie to David*". The Psalms carry the poetry of this perfection, even while other mentions can be found in Hebrews 6:13 and Amos 6:8 or Leviticus 11:44, 45.

Psalm 96:9 says "*Worship the Lord in the Beauty of Holiness*" (NKJV). My favorite Bible verse Psalm 27:4 talks about the "*beauty of the Lord*". This beauty can only be found in His Perfect Glory and Light..."*Who will not fear, O Lord, and glorify your name? For You alone are holy; for ALL THE NATIONS WILL COME AND WORSHIP BEFORE YOU, FOR YOUR RIGHTEOUS ACTS HAVE BEEN REVEALED.*" Revelation 15:4. This has not changed in 2000 years!!

From Moses to Revelation, this describes the awesome fearsomeness and Holiness of Our God. So what do the Ancient Oracles of God say about Jesus, the Holy One of God (Psalm 16:10)?

As an aside, the Pharisees and Teachers of the Law Jews denied the Son-ship of the Lord to their detriment, but they had to ignore the very Scriptures they profess to teach which said "*Who has ascended into heaven, or descended? Who has gathered the wind in His fists? Who has bound the waters in a garment? Who has established all the ends of the earth? What is His name, and what is His Son's name, if you know?"* Proverbs 30:4 (NKJV)

These lost ones, who are now in Hell, are not too different from the modern world, which has also denied the reality of the Son of God, who became the Son of Man and now sits on the Throne alongside the Father! Hebrews 1:9 gives a clear view of Jesus and His relationship to the Father, vis a vis Holiness. : *"You have loved righteousness and hated lawlessness; Therefore God, your God, has anointed you with the oil of gladness more than your companions."*

Revelation 3:7 carries the words of the Apostle John who was ushered into the Presence of Jesus and was told by the Angel to write these words in part because *"these things saith He that is Holy"* (KJV). There are countless other examples in God's Word but point is well taken. This is what we are summoned to.

When Christ saved us, He "justified" us – imputed or transferred unto us – His Own Righteousness. In other words, He made us "right" with Him. Were we Holy? NO!! No matter how moral of full of integrity we thought we were, our behavior, in relation to Him, was zero!!

However, if the person was truly saved, born again (first), baptized and bought through the Blood of the Person of Jesus Christ, he has been regenerated and now F.A.T. (not fat!!haha) F- FAITHFUL, A- AVAILABLE AND T- TEACHABLE. Thus the new believer has given the gift of Faith which makes him/her available to Christ for instruction by the Holy Spirit of God, or teachable.

Jesus is the Prophet, Priest and King of the Most High God. Read the entire chapter of John 17 in the Gospel. As Prophet, He is the Word of God. As Priest, He is separate and Holy. As King, all His Words are pure and Judgments true. He will come to judge the world in righteousness. He said: *"Heaven and earth will pass away, but my Words will never pass away."* (NIV) These Words are True doctrine. These Words cut to the core, the core of even the unbelieving sinner.

If you read His teachings and admonitions, especially in the last five chapters of the Gospel of Matthew, they should scare the living daylights out of anyone who is not a true follower of Christ! Matthew 23 was not written only to the SAD-duccees, the Pharisees and their "seminary" law teachers...one of whom was Gamaliel, the mentor of a certain Saul of Tarsus (the Apostle Paul), it was written to us.

Chapter 23 was written to anyone in this day and age who is just like them!! In reality, the modern day poltroons (abject cowards condemned to Hell because they can not see the Truth before their faces) are the Apostates who write books like the Da Vinci Code.

They are the ones who compare God to rocks and trees and brooks.

They side with terrorists against the Holy Land of Israel, which while a secular country at the current time, is set for the Return of the King who will reside there.

They question the Resurrection.

They say "Christ was just a good moral teacher" from their Ivory Towers in their universities.

They deny the Divine Inspiration of the Bible. Woe to them!

They are worse than the Pharisees because they have 2000 plus years of history and truth. But their eyes have been blinded.

They have confirmed the Teaching where Jesus talks of the perverse generation who is ever seeing, ever hearing but never learning.

Beware of anyone who calls themselves a Christian or a "Biblical scholar". Even the devil knows Scripture and perversely uses it out of context to his own purposes. These modern day Caiaphas's and their like were never born again or saved because they do not have the Spirit of the Lord living in them.

It is the Spirit of the Lord who reveals Christ. The Spirit of the Lord, who convicts, cuts to core, teaches Truth and brings us to a place where we long for, seek and pray for a more meaningful relationship with the Living God through Christ Jesus. The Spirit of the Lord who is Holy.

The Holy Spirit! He is the Third Person of the Trinity and not to be trifled with. The Greek word for the Holy Spirit is PARAKLETOS... meaning "one who consoles or intercedes on our Behalf".

Here is what Jesus says in John 14:26 – *"But the Helper, the Holy Spirit, whom the Father will send in My name, He will teach you all things, and bring to your remembrance all that I said to you."*

Then, the Apostle John writes in 1 John 2:1 – *"My little children, these things I write to you, so that you may not sin. And if anyone sins, we have an Advocate with the Father, Jesus Christ the righteous."* (KJV) The word "ADVOCATE" here is the same word in Greek for the Holy Spirit (PARACLETE) meaning Christ and the Holy Spirit in 1 John 2:1 and John 14:26 are ONE!!

Now I don't know of any better news than this! Because Christ saved, justified and brought us into His Kingdom, we actually have Him....ALL of Him...living within us! No one can show me or any true believer any better news than this! Therefore, my brothers and sisters, because Christ has made us right we are to move to the next level as sure as the sun rises in the east. He did not save us to leave us where we are but to sanctify us, or make us Holy like Him!!

The believer has no ties with Jesus if he or she refuses that Sanctification, which can only come by the conviction and teaching of the Holy Spirit. 2 Thessalonians 2:13 NKJV says *"But we are bound to give thanks to God always for you, brethren beloved by the Lord, because God from the beginning chose you for salvation through sanctification by the Spirit and belief in the truth.."* (Emphasis mine).

> 2 Peter 1:2-4 NKJV says: *"Grace and peace be multiplied to you in the knowledge of God and of Jesus our Lord as His divine power has given to us all things that pertain to life and godliness, through the knowledge of Him who called us by glory and virtue, by which have been given to us exceedingly great and precious promises, that through these you may be partakers of the divine nature, having escaped the corruption that is in the world through lust"* (Emphasis mine)

We note here the underlined Key Words: Sanctification, Belief, Truth, Knowledge, Divine, Power, ALL THINGS, Great, Promises, Divine and Nature.

The Holy Spirit or Christ who inspired Peter to write these words put them there for a reason. Every word of every phrase of every verse was put there by the Triune God for a specific purpose. That purpose is to make us like Christ.

Peter notes in the last part of Verse 4 *"...having escaped the corruption that is in the world through lust".*

Because the Holy Spirit has convicted us of our sins and directed us towards His Holy calling.

Because we are now purified in our hearts by Grace through faith.

Because we have been washed in the Precious Blood of the Lamb and made sons of God, we are now set apart from the evils of the world. We are set apart...i.e. made Holy. Now have to change our behavior from zero, when we got saved to gradually move up the scale towards as close to 100% as we can.

Do we achieve that is this lifetime? NO!! But we can try!

This is not a doctrine of Good Works, which many so called religions and even ones claiming Christianity, used to justify themselves as belonging to Jesus. This is a conscious, proactive, firm decision to turn away from the sinful nature we were born with, and let the Holy Spirit do the work He was sent to do in us.

Ephesians 4:30 says *"do not grieve the Spirit of God, by whom you were sealed until the Day of Redemption."* Because we have all of the Holy Spirit, we have all of Christ. Jesus says His Yoke is easy and His Burden light. It just takes self-discipline.

So if the believer lives in misery or defeated all his/her life, it is a choice. The believer is saved, due to the promise in this verse, but has not grown into the Holiness of Christ, who *"committed no sin, nor was any deceit found in His Mouth"* Hebrews 7:26 KJV.

OLD NATURE, SAME HEART PROBLEM:

Folks, we have a heart problem. The human heart is corrupt and sinful since the Fall in the Garden. When Christ saved us and placed

His Holy Spirit within us, the Battle was joined. He took away our Adamic Nature, but the power of sin still remains while we are here on this earth.

That power goes up against the Power of the Holy Spirit all the time!! This battle of epic proportions rages in the heart of every believer. The heart can be deceived, even in the strongest believer.

The true servant of Christ does not walking around trying to sin lustfully, actively or passively. How many of us can relate to Romans 7:15-20!! We looked at them in a previous chapter and some people call them the "Do-do" passage! Basically Paul is saying that the very thing he is trying to avoid (sin) he ends up doing because of the sin which lives in his mortal body!!

He is NOT saying "the devil made me do it!" The devil has no sway over us unless we let him. When we got saved, Christ became our Master and Lord of our lives. But while we are alive on earth in this dying body, even the most saintly believer is susceptible to sin.

There are some life lessons Paul wants us to learn from this passage in Romans 7. Along with all the solid meat from the Scriptures already quoted, he set out in these few verses a simple outline we can grasp on to and live.

- Knowledge of the Law is not the answer (Romans 7:9).
- Depending on your OWN moral code to do right, does not work either (vs. 15).
- Becoming a Christian does not do away with all sin and temptation (vs. 22).

When we got saved, it took the flash of a moment. However it takes a lifetime to grow more like Christ.

Understanding the "heart" is important in striving to attain to the Holiness of our Lord. The great Webster's Dictionary has ten definitions of the word heart with the number one description as "the locus (or dwelling place) of feelings and intuitions."

It is the latter which gets us in trouble as humans. Intuitions, unless it is from God, who has revealed Himself only through His Word, are a dangerous thing.

The devil uses deceit and feelings can land a person in heap big pile. Still, as believers, we do not even know our own hearts! 1 Corinthians 4:3-5 says: "*For I am conscious of nothing against myself, yet I am not by this acquitted; but the one who examines me is the Lord. Therefore do not go on passing judgment before the time, but wait until the Lord comes who both will bring to light the things hidden in the darkness and disclose the motives of men's hearts; and then each man's praise will come to him from God*".

Deceit is in the heart, but another "D" word which lands us in trouble is "desire". The devil uses the desires of our heart to cause us to sin. From Adam and Eve, he has appealed to the baser, lustful instincts of human nature, to cause us to stumble.

BEWARE OF THE DECEIT OF THE HEART!

Beware of people who say "LISTEN TO YOUR HEART"...that would be the sinful, deceitful heart of humankind! This can lead to all kinds of temptation and unless one is strengthened by a daily, vital walk with the Savior and fully involved in His Word, deceitful desire will win over Godly reason. Paul says in Ephesians 4:22 NIV "*You were taught, with regard to your former way of life, to put off your old self, which is being corrupted by its deceitful desires*".

It is our own desires, evil and those which are but do not seem that way, which lead us into Temptation. This is the ground zero of our battle for Holiness. One more thing about sin. These verses stand out as a trumpet blasting against backsliding: Romans 6:1 says "*What shall we say then? Shall we continue in sin that grace may abound?*" In Jude 4, Jude, the half brother of our Lord Jesus Christ condemns those who "*turn the grace of our God into lewdness*".

When we do that, we depend on the Mercy of God to forgive us, instead of focusing fully on how much He actually hates what we did and how Holy He is. This has been a personal battle for years for every person alive, to varying degrees. It takes many years to fully fathom the depth of human depravity. So the only way to attain the victory necessary to not hurt the heart of God is OBEDIENCE!

There is so much more which can be said or written about understanding the nature of our hearts and souls, but I wish to end here by offering practical steps to Holy Living in Christ and the Holy Spirit.

The Book of Romans has changed the face of Christianity beginning with Martin Luther almost 500 years ago. Luther actually read the Bible, studied it. He got convicted by the Book of Romans, saved, justified and sanctified then left the Catholic priesthood to serve the Lord.

KEYS TO HOLINESS:

A friend of mine got saved after listening to a tape on the Study of Romans Chapters 1-8 by Bob Warren (www.lifeonthehill.org). Why? Why do the devil and his apostate preachers fight against the preaching of Romans, especially Romans 1? Because it has the keys to Victory and victorious Holy living in Christ!!

> Romans 6: 6-11 reminds us "*knowing this, that our old man was crucified with Him, that the body of sin might be done away with, that we should no longer be slaves of sin for he who has died has been freed from sin. Now if we died with Christ, we believe that we shall also live with Him, knowing that Christ, having been raised from the dead, dies no more. Death no longer has dominion over Him. For the death that He died, He died to sin once for all; but the life that He lives, He lives to God. Likewise you also, reckon yourselves to be dead indeed to sin, but alive to God in Christ Jesus our Lord.*" (NKJV…emphasis mine).

Here is the key to Holiness (see underlined phrases in above passage): when we got saved, we died with him (crucified). Christ died for all sin for all time. Therefore death (we died with Christ) has been defeated.

Because we died this death, sin have no pull over us (or it should not)!! We ROSE with Him (Christ having being raised from the dead) and in light of that, or therefore….RECKON OURSELVES DEAD TO SIN AND ALIVE TO GOD IN CHRIST JESUS!!

We have victorious living here! How you ask? Because we are ALIVE TO GOD IN CHRIST JESUS...we have all the Power HE has given us...how ...through the Holy Spirit! We have 100% of the Spirit, if we do not live Spirit-filled lives; sins of omission (and even commission) are to blame!

"Our goal is to help young and even older stagnant believers grow in their sanctification as Jesus intended", 1 Thessalonians 5:23.

So get into the habit of reminding yourself YOU ARE ALIVE, in the Power of the Holy Spirit, to God IN CHRIST JESUS!! Drill that into your consciousness until it is second nature!

Use the Faith God gave us to summon His Holy Spirit from the back of your being where you have hidden Him.

Pray the Spirit of God to give you the strength daily to combat the devil and his deceit!

Rely on the Holy Spirit (Romans 8:11 "*And if the Spirit of him who raised Jesus from the dead is living in you, he who raised Christ from the dead will also give life to your mortal bodies through his Spirit, who lives in you).*

The Spirit shows us God's high standard for Holiness. Read Jeremiah 17:9.

The Spirit was sent to minister to us. Jesus said so. Read 2 Corinthians &:10.

The Spirit therefore shows us our sinfulness. Read Philippians 2:13; Romans 7:13.

The Spirit uses Scripture (which He breathed into its human authors) to teach us. This means we HAVE to be in the Word daily. THIS IS MANDATORY! .

This last one is primary. In Isaiah 66:2b God says *"But to this one I will look, to him who is humble and contrite of spirit, and who trembles at my word"*

Read the Word and PRAY!! PRAY DAILY WITHOUT CEASING. Pray for Holy Living or Holiness. Read Ephesians 3:16

where Paul exhorts his fellow believers *"to pray that out of his glorious riches he may strengthen you with power through his Spirit in your inner being"* (NIV).

Remember you are totally dependent on the Holy Spirit for growth in Holiness. 100% DEPENDENT, for the Spirit did not come to just read us the riot act of righteous living but to testify to the Character of God. He is a God so Holy that He demands completes Obedience.

So Conform to the Character of God.

Conform to the Image of Christ (James 1:2-7).

Conform to the Mind of the Spirit (Read the following verses: 1 Thess 2:12; Eph. 4:1; Col. 1:10; and then 1 Cor 9:24 and Philippians 3:13)

Here are Ten points of practical Holiness as laid out in part by **Dr.Joel R. Beeke** in his book "HOLINESS" 3

1. God called us to Holiness (1 Thessalonians 4:17).
2. He has made Holiness as evidence of our justification and election (1 Cor. 6:11)
3. Without Holiness, all things are defiled (Titus 1:15).
4. Holiness augments our spiritual health because without it, no one will see God. (Hebrews 12: 11-12)
5. Holiness fosters assurance (2 Peter 1:10).
6. Holiness is essential for effective service to God (2 Timothy 2:21)
7. Holiness makes you resemble God
8. The God you love, loves Holiness
9. Holiness preserves your integrity.
10. Holiness fits you for Heaven (Hebrews 12:14).

The next ten points are proactive habits to adopt RIGHT NOW. 3

1. Know and relish Scripture (John 17:17)
2. Strive for constant Faith in Christ....FLEE TO HIM...RUN TO HIM!
3. WWJD (my paraphrase) (1 Corinthians 11:1)
4. Seek the Holy Spirit's counsel (my interpretation).

5. Associate with older or wiser mentors in the Faith or Church etc (Proverbs 13:20)
6. Pray for Holiness. Read Job 14:4 and Psalm 51:10
7. Recognize (as we discussed) we are dead to sin and alive with God (Romans 6:11)
8. Nurture and persevere in Personal Discipline in all things... from the job to the home to the stores to the church. Read Proverbs 24:16
9. Develop a Biblical formula for action. Ask yourself constantly "does this glorify God?" Read 1 Corinthians 10:31; 7:23; 11:1; 6:9-12; 8:13 and 10:33.
10. Totally commit to not sinning at all. Don't willfully disobey now on the grounds you will ask forgiveness tomorrow. Read 1 John 2:1; 2 Corinthians 10:5 and most definitely PROVERBS 23:7!!

Dr.Beeke's blog recently taught on why we should read the holy writings of the Puritans. Who? The Puritans! "Why, Bernie man, you are a freak! Those guys have been dead for 300 plus years, man...this is the 21st Century!" Yes, it is and hence the reason we need to seek their wisdom on we should apply the Bible to daily living!

Here are Dr. Beeke's quotes from a book I intend to find soon. They are from Richard Baxter's "The Saint's Everlasting Life". If you want to live the life of the Five Solas of the Protestant Reformation – read the Puritans.

The Five Solas are Sola Fide (Faith Alone); Sola Scriptura (Scripture Alone); Sola Christus (Christ Alone); Sola Gratia (Grace Alone) and Sola Gloria (Glory to God Alone). You have heard the saying "Grace Alone, through Faith Alone in Christ Alone"....This is Reformation Theology. Live it, love it, and pass it along! If you study these five attributes of Biblical Christianity and do a real good study on the Book of Romans, you too would desire instant holiness. The only thing is nothing is instant, it requires commitment and determination.

Here are nine reasons to read the Puritans, and I suggest we start with Stephen Charnock (quoted elsewhere in this book):

Puritan writings help shape life by Scripture.
Puritan writings show how to integrate biblical doctrine into daily life. (Think Jonathan Edwards.)
Puritan writings show how to exalt Christ and see His beauty.
Puritan writings reveal the Trinitarian character of theology.
Puritan writings show you how to handle trials.
Puritan writings explain true spirituality.
Puritan writings show how to live by wholistic faith.
Puritan writings teach the importance and primacy of preaching.
Puritan writings show how to live in two worlds.

Do these things. Effective Christianity demands it. Therefore you will understand why the entire point of Holiness is "He must increase and I MUST DECREASE!" (John 3:30) This is what He set us apart for! This is what He meant us to live the True Life of Peace, Joy and Contentment.

CHAPTER 10

EFFECTIVE CHRISTIANITY

THE POWER OF CONTENTED LIVING.

"Contentment is a pearl of great price, and whoever procures it at the expense of ten thousand desires makes a wise and a happy purchase."

- John Balguy

What do the Keys to a Contented Life look like and where do they cut them? 1 Timothy 6:5-7 NKJV says intense participation with a contentious life leads to "*useless wranglings of men of corrupt minds and destitute of the truth, who suppose that godliness is a means of gain. From such withdraw yourself. Now godliness with contentment is great gain. For we brought nothing into this world, and it is certain we can carry nothing out*".

In light of this absolute truth it would appear that Godliness and Contentment are two sides of the same coin. Why should they not be?

The one who gave us life and created this world had these words for us in Matthew 6: 28-34 NIV:

> *"And why do you worry about clothes? See how the lilies of the field grow. They do not labor or spin. Yet I tell you that not even Solomon in all his splendor was dressed like one of these. If that is how God clothes the grass of the field,*

which is here today and tomorrow is thrown into the fire, will He not much more clothe you, O you of little faith? So do not worry, saying, 'What shall we eat?' or 'What shall we drink?' or 'what shall we wear?' For the pagans run after all these things, and your Heavenly Father knows that you need them. But seek first His kingdom and His righteousness, and all these things will be given to you as well. Therefore do not worry about tomorrow, for tomorrow will worry about itself. Each day has enough trouble of its own.

This narrative from Jesus holds the keys to this life. We could stop right here and we can pack it up for the evening. The salient point is life has become more complicated than this. There is no doubt the True Christian and even the professing ones wish to live by the Words above from the Savior. What causes us pause is the Rat Race.

CONCERNING THE RAT RACE:

What is the rat race anyway and who came up with this term about a race of 56 different types of omnivorous disgusting vermin rodents? [1] The rat race is described *as "a term used for an endless, self-defeating pursuit. It conjures up the image of the futile efforts of a laboratory rat trying to escape whilst running around a maze or in a wheel."* This is an accurate description of the lifestyle we lead daily at Mach 3 (or high supersonic) speed.

Look at the adjectives in this definition. First, we have "endless". The daily routine of work feels never-ending. This is compounded by most working people claiming dissatisfaction with their jobs. It is endless because the cycle of life demands we work to pay bills, eat, clothe ourselves, provide for and entertain our families.

What modern affluent North American society has done is perfected this past the basics of life (food, shelter, transport etc) into the realm of large homes, cars, boats, and bank accounts and so on.

Most have now engaged in the non-stop pursuit of temporal wealth without an eternal perspective. The definition of the rat race is accurate because this pursuit is self-defeating. The word pursuit has the imagery of say, Sheriff Buford T. Justice and Junyah in a multi-state car chase of a speeding Bandit (from the 1970's era Burt Reynolds movie "Smokey and the Bandit").

If you remember the movie, old Bandit had a good old time (as a good 'ole' boy) going pedaled to the metal across Louisiana, Alabama and Georgia on the lam from an enraged Sheriff Justice. A resulting series of mishaps to the ***pursuing*** law enforcement caused the one ***in pursuit*** to get the worse of the exchange.

Who can forget the Jackie Gleason character, smoking mad, getting out of his car with no hood, doors or roof....and he still had not caught the Bandit (Reynolds) and his TransAm!

Sheriff Justice is modern man (and woman). He/she keeps chasing the elusive worldly dream halfway across Creation. In the meantime, the vehicle (or body) we are charged with maintaining and the soul we are responsible for nourishing are taking huge hits in the back draft of the speeding TransAm of life way ahead of us. It is so beat up at the end of the chase as to be unrecognizable.

In life, the damage is most often unseen, so we think nothing is wrong. Sheriff Justice's son, Junior (or Junyah!) is a metaphor for our children who pay the price for our madcap chase for the 'good life'.

We have all been a part of this race at one time or another. Even those of us who have eschewed material pursuits for the Heavenly realms are still caught up in the maze. We still have families and have to run them to violin lessons or symphony practice, ballet class and so on. We have seen the SUV-driving soccer parents who is so high-strung and obnoxious on the sidelines of little Emily's soccer game, you would think it was a World cup match!

There are reasons these people in our towns act like complete buffoons at harmless kid sports games which we will not get into. That is another book by itself. Maybe Dr. Dobson wrote one, I don't know!

All I know such misconduct is a major reason my family ceased participating in local team sports after about 5-6 years of this unchristian, unsportsmanlike conduct from the prosperous looking laboratory rats in the rat race of life. The root of all this hostility and anger (not to mention lack of any sense of what awful things they are passing on to their children) can be found in overwhelming overreach, overwork and overloading.

In order to deal with this kind of life, I aim to present in the rest of this penultimate chapter God-given keys and remedies. Several topics will be examined with its authenticity tested through the Full Counsel.

CONCERNING AFFLUENZA:

Dr. Steve Farrar in his excellent book "Overcoming Overload" had a wonder description of AFFLUENZA (paraphrase: an epidemic or plague which comes from the rat race). Here is the modern prayer of those afflicted by this virus affecting most of Suburban minded America: 2

Now I lay me down to sleep
I pray my Cuisanart to keep
I pray my stocks are on the rise
And that my analyst is wise
That all the wine I sip is white
And that my hot tub's watertight
That racquetball won't get too tough
That all my sushi's fresh enough
I pray my cell-phone battery works
That my career won't lose its perks
My microwave won't radiate
My condo won't depreciate
I pray my health club doesn't close
And that my money market grows
If I go broke before I wake
I pray my Volvo they won't take!
Amen

If this is your prayer, we have to talk! Unfortunately I have seen people like this up in the very affluent suburbs of Chicago land. My wife's parents are probably the only modest folk living up in this part of Creation. You see the affluenza-afflicted everywhere. You can then instinctively know what they have to do to maintain the lifestyle described in the previous section.

They can be someone who has ninety minute commute each way by BMW or Dodge Durango to the stockbrokerage firm in downtown Chicago or some similar career in medical sales; kids with the finest money can buy yet left alone until late in the evening when mom and day returns....and on and on. Then on Sunday, the Lord's Day, they have no time for Him who made everything on earth.

While His remnant leaves on their way to church, the affluenza-afflicted lay in their rat race induced daze recovering or doing work on their laptops for the never-ending cycle starting again in less than 24 hours. Of course it is a Starbucks latte-induced daze. This also makes for false self-diagnosis.

They claim there is no God, because they have no time for themselves. They claim there is no God because they have to work so hard for what they have. They claim there is no God because "look at all the bills we have" or "look at this $11000 Cook County property tax bill"!

It seems as if the stereotypical overworked American can not get off the treadmill of work, work and more work for a variety of reasons. A survey of a number of Americans in the private sector found 44% of Americans say they were overworked in 2004 and while they multi-task now more than ever, they can not seem to get things done.

Chronic overwork is even more pervasive as the employee usually takes the office back home to their families daily. This causes their family life no end of friction. The results of overwork, found by the Families and Work Survey [3] are not surprising:

- More mistakes are being made at work, as lack of rest and recreation takes a toll.
- The employee is more inclined to become antagonistic to their bosses, thereby creating the potential for all kinds of conflict.
- The potential for intense competition between coworkers for promotions raises etc increases to a dangerous level.

- The potential for intergenerational conflict worsens as the young Turks go after the more entrenched forty and fifty-something types and the latter hits back.

Every one of these items results in stress and even worse- major health problems. Here are some of the symptoms the Mayo Clinic [4] describe as stress-related: headaches; chest pain; high blood pressure; back aches; constipation; stomach ailments; sleep problems; sex problems; weight gain or loss and fatigue. This is only a partial list!

Psychological problems are anxiety; worry; depression; anger; mood swings; job dissatisfaction; insecurity; forgetfulness; guilt; bad attitudes; resentment and burnout. This is another partial list.

Unless the "participant" gets a grip on the physical and psychological, behavior patterns careen out of control and can lead to overeating; alcohol and drug abuse; angry outburst; conflict at home and social situations and ultimately divorce.

In this demographic, divorce is higher than the national average. Sadly the marriages of evangelical Christians can be caught up in this downward spiral, if they are not grounded in Biblical Truth. Now in all this, did you see the name of God mentioned? And Jesus Christ? Fuggedaboudit! These folks have no time for the Lord. Even their kids complain they hardly have time for them!

Coming back to Dr. Farrar. He directed me to his book on Overload which he later described perfectly on a Focus on the Family broadcast in 2007 during a two part series on Affluenza. The type of parent I described here who is so caught up in their careerism, their cash-driven success develops children who are:

- given too much freedom and too little attention
- given too many things and too little time.
- given too much information too early (which takes away their child like innocence).
- given a sense of values whereby image is more important than character.

- given a mandate to succeed at all costs immediately, while neglecting the natural development which comes with God-given talents and Grace. 2

HOW DID WE GET HERE?

Modern America has created a Frankenstein we now see in their reality Television shows. Some of them are so seductive they attract a type of twenty something or older teenage girl or boy who become so unscrupulous they would do anything to get to the next level. They do all this in the fleshly search for fame and fortune.

We see the results of no Godly foundation in these young people with the popularity of YouTube.com and MySpace.com. These two hugely popular websites contribute absolutely nothing to the Kingdom of God, except maybe a free website from some of the more modern Contemporary Christian artists. The MTV generation has thrown away everything their secular feminists predecessors marched for in the 1970's to achieve respect for women.

All we have now is the gangster – rap induced degradation and extreme disregard for the mystique of female virtue. We now have beautiful young female teachers in an epidemic of sexual molestation of teenage boys in their classrooms. We now have drunken orgies on college campuses all over America to the point politicians want to mandate our God-fearing parents give our daughters anti-HPV vaccine.

We now have values of the Affluenza- afflicted causing young women posting nude photos of themselves all over creation and then weeping on Fox News channel about their indiscretions when it all comes back to haunt them.

This kind of thing leads to young men, who are not taught respect for women at school, home or even the church, impregnating young women and some even disowning the institution of marriage. Then again why should they own this God instituted tradition (Genesis 2:24) when they see their boomer and Generation X parents bowing down at the pagan altar of the new American Dream – wealth, success and expensive toys?

However the book is not about what is wrong with the family. What role did the "greatest Generation" play in the present American condition? (This is the great World War II generation who gave it all to change the world during the 1940's and grew up during the harsh Depression – era 1930's).

The greatest generation created the Great Post – War economic boom which built American into the Economic and Military Giant and Superpower it has become and still is, no matter what the world may think. This is the greatest country in the world.

While all this great expansion was taking place, the seeds of trouble began to be sown as success gave way to folks letting down their guard against the dangers of Spiritual warfare. The greatest generation's parents knew about Spiritual warfare and depending on the Lord. But when wealth and interstate highways blossomed across America, the first strains of Affluenza started showing up.

Little by little the churches went soft on Biblical teachings. Preachers and evangelists warned about the watering down of the Gospel back in the early 1950's. No one listened. The U.S. Supreme Court led by Hugo Black slowly and steadily began chipping away at Christianity and God in America. Two major Supreme Court decisions: Everson versus Board of Education in Trenton, New Jersey (1947) and Engel versus Vitale (1962) [5] set the stage for what is occurring not only in the schools of America today, but with EVERY social and family ill.

Both these decisions were read in the majority by Hugo Black who is looked at as the single symbol of the removal of God from American public education.

The upheaval of the 1960's had its roots in 1940's and 1950's Affluenza and its rejection of Biblical Christianity. The now aging 1960's rebels and retiring baby-boomers got caught in a dichotomy of the good life and self indulgence. Together they are a falsely related. They passed their values to the You Tube generation of today who now also demand their first job as the one which should buy them a new Ford Mustang, a Blackberry and a condo by the lake!

There is no good life without God. The Supreme Court can not mandate you a good life, neither can any self-righteous politician. We have already examined how a leader is supposed to act at work.

To expand briefly, we need to look and see what the Lord says about work since Adam's sin brought us work as we now know it.

CONCERNING WORK

Concerning Work, there are several guidelines in the Bible which we need to read for ourselves and study. Here are a few:

- We must be careful not to exploit people for financial gain, especially for the employer. In 1 Kings 12: 4, the people came to the late King Solomon's son Rehoboam and begged him saying "*Your father made our yoke hard; now therefore lighten the hard service of your father and his heavy yoke which he put on us, and we will serve you.*" Rehoboam foolishly refused to stop the exploitation of his people and the Kingdom of Israel promptly split in two.

- We must be careful to work for the benefit and provision of others and not just for our own selfish pursuits. There is nothing wrong with wanting to live in a nice, warm comfortable home etc…within reason. However Scripture commands us to *"He who has been stealing must steal no longer, but must work, doing something useful with his own hands, that he may have something to share with those in need."* Ephesians 4:28 NIV.

- We must be careful to never make work a false god and worship at the altar of the office. Who we are is not what we do. Who we are is who Christ says we are, IF we are in Him!!

  Read Ecclesiastes 2: 17-26, but here are a few encouraging verses to remember: "*A man can do nothing better than to eat and drink and find satisfaction in his work. This too, I see, is from the hand of God, for without Him, who can eat or find enjoyment? To the man who pleases Him, God gives wisdom, knowledge and happiness, but to the sinner He gives the task of gathering and storing up wealth to hand it over to the one who pleases God. This too is meaningless, a chasing after the wind.* Ecclesiastes 2: 24-26 NIV.

- We must be careful to acknowledge work is a gift from God and we need to have the proper perspective. It is He who puts us in the jobs we have now and we are there to not only make a living for our families, but to glorify Him. Ecclesiastes 5: 18-20 NIV says "*Then I realized that it is good and proper for a man to eat and drink, and to find satisfaction in his toil-some labor under the sun during the few days of life God has given him—for this is his lot. Moreover, when God gives any man wealth and possessions, and enables him to enjoy them, to accept his lot and be happy in his work—this is a gift of God. He seldom reflects on the days of his life, because God keeps him occupied with gladness of heart*".\

- We must be careful to realize our toil on this earth will continue until that day, when Christ reestablishes His physical rule over the earth. Romans 8:18-21 NIV says "*I consider that our present sufferings are not worth comparing with the glory that will be revealed in us. The creation waits in eager expectation for the sons of God to be revealed. For the creation was subjected to frustration, not by its own choice, but by the will of the one who subjected it, in hope that the creation itself will be liberated from its bondage to decay and brought into the glorious freedom of the children of God*".

- We must be careful and watchful for the day when all His children come into the Kingdom of heaven and we will work, without the burden of sin. People are under the impression Heaven is boring, floating on a cloud and playing a harp. In fact the world tells you they would rather be in hell where all their friends and Marilyn Monroe is (I have actually heard this) are!

They have no clue what hell is and even if you tell them, their hearts are so hardened they are ever hearing and never understanding. Here is what the great Prophet Isaiah wrote and prophesied about the Coming New Heaven and Earth. Remember Isaiah is the man who was allowed into Heaven and was face to face with a Holy God (Isaiah 6). In Chapter 65, he writes in verses 17 and then 21-23 NKJV: "*For behold, I create new heavens and a new earth; and the former shall not be remembered or come to mind......*
21 They shall build houses and inhabit them;
they shall plant vineyards and eat their fruit.
22 They shall not build and another inhabit;
They shall not plant and another eat;
For as the days of a tree, so shall be the days of My people,
And My elect shall long enjoy the work of their hands.
23 They shall not labor in vain,
nor bring forth children for trouble;
for they shall be the descendants of the blessed of the LORD,
and their offspring with them.

I spent a long time here on work as it is the activity which provides for the family and what God has ordained for man to do with the best part of his waking hours. The amazing thing to behold from this dissertation is the work awaiting us in the new heavens!! My reaction from the above passage in Isaiah is "WOW"!! Most people have no idea about this as prophesy is not really taught in churches much anymore. There are several very good prophesy teachers on Television who stick closely by the Word. These men are John Hagee and Dr. Ed Hindson.

So you wish to know what Heaven is like? Read this partial account from Revelation 22: 1-5 NKJV: *1 And he showed me a pure river of water of life, clear as crystal, proceeding from the throne of God and of the Lamb.*

2 In the middle of its street, and on either side of the river, was the tree of life, which bore twelve fruits, each tree yielding its fruit every month. The leaves of the tree were for the healing of the nations.

3 And there shall be no more curses, but the throne of God and of the Lamb shall be in it, and His servants shall serve Him.

4 They shall see His face, and His name shall be on their foreheads.

5 There shall be no night there: They need no lamp nor light of the sun, for the Lord God gives them light. And they shall reign forever and ever.

IT IS RIGHT TO SUFFER

"...So they went on their way from the presence of the Council, rejoicing that they had been considered worthy to suffer shame for His name"...Acts 5:41

"...and if children, heirs also, heirs of God and fellow heirs with Christ, if indeed we suffer with Him so that we may also be glorified with Him"...Romans 8:17

"...Suffer hardship with me, as a good soldier of Christ Jesus"...2 Timothy 2:3

"...And who is he who will harm you if you become followers of what is good? But even if you should suffer for righteousness' sake, you are blessed. "And do not be afraid of their threats, nor be troubled. But sanctify the Lord God in your hearts, and always be ready to give a defense to everyone who asks you a reason for the hope that is in you, with meekness and fear; having a good conscience, that when they defame you as evildoers, those who revile your good conduct in Christ may be ashamed. For it is better, if it is the will of God, to suffer for doing good than for doing evil"...1 Peter 3:13-17

We see a trend here from three different authors of the New Testament. Dr. Luke, the gentile crusader for Christ wrote the book of Acts. The Apostle Paul wrote Romans and 2 Timothy and Simon Peter wrote 1 Peter. However, the message was the same!! This message was "when it comes to Christ, no pain – no gain"!

For instance, what would cause two men of Christ – Peter and John, to go away from the Jewish religious authorities proclaiming Peace and Contentment? This occurred right after the Pharisees and hypocrites had imprisoned and flogged them severely!

What would cause the Apostle Paul to say "if indeed we suffer with Him...we may be glorified with Him"?

What would cause him to exhort others like the young Timothy to be like him as he lay chained in the filthy sewer prisons saying "come suffer hardship with me, as a foot soldier of Jesus Christ"?

What would cause Peter to say "if you should suffer for righteousness' sake, you are blessed"?

What would indeed? It is the Suffering Savior of Isaiah 53: 1-3. Here are the verses from the New King James Version of the Bible:

1 Who has believed our report?
And to whom has the arm of the LORD been revealed?
2 for He shall grow up before Him as a tender plant,
And as a root out of dry ground.
He has no form or comeliness;
and when we see Him,
There is no beauty that we should desire Him.
3 He is despised and rejected by men,
A Man of sorrows and acquainted with grief.
And we hid, as it were, our faces from Him;
He was despised, and we did not esteem Him.
(Emphasis mine)

The Contented Life does not come to us unmarked and unscathed. Politicians, sociologists, activists, mainstream media and assorted atheists tell us we should have no troubles in life. They tell us we can have life and life abundantly if we trust in ourselves and believe in the power of positive thinking and action.

We have million selling books from name it and claim it preachers showing us how to invest mammon seed money and claim earthly riches. They never tell you about a Holy God. They never tell you about what He demands from His people. They never tell you about the Wrath which is to come.

> Listen to what 1 Thessalonians 5: 2-6 NKJV says "*For you yourselves know perfectly that the day of the Lord so comes as a thief in the night. For when they say,* ***"Peace and safety!"*** *then sudden destruction comes upon them, as labor pains upon a pregnant woman. And they shall not escape. But you, brethren, are not in darkness, so that this Day should overtake you as a thief. You are all sons of light and sons of the day. We are neither of the night nor of darkness. Therefore let us not sleep, as others do, but let us watch and be sober". (Emphasis mine)*

Everyone, including professing Christians, who trust in man-made organizations like the United Nations, the vile anti-Christian European Union and politics, will suffer sudden destruction on that Day. The book of Revelation warns they will run into the hills and beg the mountains to fall on them. They shall not escape.

Anyone who thinks armies and governments can protect them from the Wrath of God is delusional. Anyone who thinks peace treaties and contemplative chanting and mumbo-jumbo eastern mystic prayer will deliver them, in that Day, is trusting in the god of this world.

But we who are called by His Name are expected to persevere. The perseverance of the saints come from the realization this world is not our home. Every one of those verses in this section calls on the saints to suffer. Why? Jesus told us we have to, for the sake of His Name. From the minute He won the Victory on the Cross, Satan's days were numbered.

The world's systems set out to wipe out anyone and any institution which bears the Name of Christ. Even the destruction of the ancient city of Jerusalem in 70 AD (and it is Anno Domini – the Year of the Lord, NOT C.E. as the atheists now try to claim) did not stop the agents of evil. The destruction of the old Jewish Temple and its sacrificial system was in partial judgment for what was done to Christ.

The book of Hebrews begins with a warning to Jewish Christians to not lose their nerve and go back under the law of the Pharisees. Anyone who remained faithful to Christ and left the city escaped destruction from Titus' Roman army and the massacre at Masada. God used pagan armies many times to punish His own people. When Israel and Judah worshipped vile pagan idols and snakes, He sent Jeremiah to warn them. They tried to kill him. Then Almighty God sent the armies of Babylon to destroy the city. Nebuchadnezzar later became a believer in the one True God.

The persecution of believers has never been more intense as it is now and will become even worse. Liberal congressmen in Washington D.C. are now trying to pass laws to prevent pastors from preaching against Homosexuality. In Canada and other places, you can not preach out of Romans 1. The love affair with Evolution in seemingly conservative states like Kansas is a sign of a people turning to the gods of the earth.

The scare tactics used to promote theories of global warming and the draconian steps proposed to "stop" it shows the evil arrogance of man and how he is now elevating himself above the Creator.

Anyone who challenges these theories or anyone who trusts in the Lord who created the climate is made fun or and silenced. Judges have taken the place of parents and school districts try to decide what is best for your own kids. It used to be against the law to corrupt the morals of a minor, now it is intolerant NOT to expose even first graders to every perversion under the sun.

So the saints will be persecuted as corporate body. The modern Christian church actually helps the world persecute us by its conduct, moral relativism and weak or NO Truth Doctrine at all! Sometimes you can not tell the difference between a professing Christian and those of the world. This is the worst testimony of all.

THE SUFFERING SAINT(DEPRESSION)

But suffering also comes to the individual. While we shall suffer under the hands of those in our non-believing neighbors, co-workers and even our families, we also suffer in our bodies and even our hearts, minds and souls. How we handle these situations determine if we live in victory or not.

We can choose the path of depression and use excuses; even blame God for our troubles. OR we can choose to accept the path He has chosen and see Him in everything. Throughout Biblical history we have had even God's prophets suffering from depression. Elijah went hiding in a cave in 1 Kings 19: 4-16. This is a great study to do for the Christian who feels like giving up.

In fact a lot more believers suffer from depression than we acknowledge. The problem is they turn to the world for answers. They turn to secular therapists and even sometimes professional Christian counselors who are not usually Biblically sound. If we are able to defeat the tendency towards depression, then anything else will be put in perspective.

If we can our physical pain from cancer to canker sore as an opportunity to grow closer to Him and fellowship through the Holy Spirit, we are living in Victory. Here is the story of a depressed Elijah, using only verses from 1 Kings 19: 4-10 NKJV:

> *4 But he himself went a day's journey into the wilderness, and came and sat down under a broom tree. And he prayed that he might die, and said, "It is enough! Now, LORD, take my life, for I am no better than my fathers!"*
>
> *5 Then as he lay and slept under a broom tree, suddenly an angel touched him, and said to him, "Arise and eat."*
>
> *6 Then he looked, and there by his head was a cake baked on coals, and a jar of water. So he ate and drank, and lay down again.*
>
> *7 And the angel of the LORD came back the second time, and touched him, and said, "Arise and eat, because the journey is too great for you."*
>
> *8 So he arose, and ate and drank; and he went in the strength of that food forty days and forty nights as far as Horeb, the mountain of God.*

9 And there he went into a cave, and spent the night in that place; and behold, the word of the LORD came to him, and He said to him, ***"What are you doing here, Elijah?"***

10 So he said, "I have been very zealous for the LORD God of hosts; for the children of Israel have forsaken Your covenant, torn down Your altars, and killed Your prophets with the sword. ***I alone am left; and they seek to take my life."*** **(Emphasis mine)**

In our pain of a troublesome disease

In our pain of the loss of a loved one

In our pain in the trials of raising Godly teenagers in a corrupt world

In our pain of facing financial ruin as the cost of living explodes

In our pain of troubles at home in marriage or family

In our pain of isolation from a friendly face

In our pain of loneliness in a cold city or church where everyone is totally wrapped up in their own worlds…in that kind of pain, comes the Loud and clear voice of God to us in our 'caves' "What are you doing here, Elijah…or Sam….or Joyce or Lori?"

Indeed, what in the world are we doing down on our face? We have the best news, the only God and the smiling Savior of true love. What more do we need? He poured it on the Cross and we have His entire love letter to mankind in 66 Books of the Bible. It is the handbook for us to be strong, fearless and fully surrendered.

If we get ourselves in the habit of going to His Word in prayer; if we get ourselves in praying the Scriptures to Him and truly opening up our hearts in prayer, it is impossible to stay depressed. We can get down at times. This is a human attribute. But when we feel ourselves slipping in a downward spiral, it is only the Blood of Jesus which can stop us. I encourage us to pray for the covering of the Blood all over ourselves.

Find some real prayer warriors to surround you with and make yourself available to pray and intercede for others with them. I notice when I pray for others, the Lord uses others to pray for me and it becomes a circle of life-giving power with Him right in the middle of it. I have seen time and time again, the Lord use others to bring the prophetic word to me.

He has used certain people to bind the strongholds of darkness which are attempting to bring me into the defeat of depression. He has used these same people to lift my spirits. At each occasion, He used a Scripture to speak victory to me. This kind of depression-defeating combat can only come from first accepting the Literal Word of God as Truth and secondly praying through each verse as it is written.

This is important in defeating the demons of depression. If the Christian is led to the extreme of suicide, then we have failed to reach this person with the Truth.

I recommend praying through EACH SINGLE VERSE of 1 Peter. Nothing is more beneficial for the Soul and its peace than to pray back the Scriptures to Him and to cry out for deliverance - THROUGH these verses.

First Peter is important because it is a handbook full of guidance on suffering for the Cause of Christ. I can write a five point purpose plan on suffering here, but it could actually short-circuit what the Lord wants you to get out of praying through each one of these verses. When do you this, you will want to do your own 10 point plan...and then tell somebody else!

It is not a surprise to be persecuted for Christ nor is it a stigma. So use the time of trial to focus on what God calls us to do. Use it to focus on the essentials of our Faith. Use it to find the True Source of all power.

Suffering for Christ:

- enhances our testimony.
- exhibits our Faith.
- eradicates our emphasis on earthly comforts.
- eliminates phony believers.
- strengthens us for the long race ahead.
- strengthens our Faith.

- strengthens our Witness.
- strengthens our Integrity.

How do we defeat the depression which can sometimes result from some really intense trial and suffering. Job's long speeches showed a tendency towards depression when he kept wishing he was not born. However we can get out of hiding in our own caves like Elijah when we eat the hot cake and drink the water of life, found in the Sacred Scriptures. If we obey and trust God, He will take over our case. He is then in charge of everything in our lives and we just go along with Him.

Notice in the passage about Elijah, he (Elijah) was the one who went into the cave. God did not send him there. In fact God asked him what he was doing hiding in there even though He knew the answer completely. These are the days of Elijah and the days when absolute surrender and obedience to the Will of God will bring us true peace, joy and contentment.

Defeat depression, self-pity and self-worthlessness and defeat the tendency to self-defeat when troubles and trials hit us very hard. Defeat the tendency to raise Holy hands in church while hanging your head down inside. Go to the Feet of Him who brings Good News NOW! **This** is your best life NOW!

The following poem is one we can all relate to, in order to live in victory. It urges us to get off our face. It urges us to get out of the cave. It urges to stay the course. It urges us to never, never surrender to the darkness of depression.

Don't Quit

When things get wrong, as they sometimes will,
When the road you are trudging seems all up hill;
When the funds are low and the debts are high
And you want to smile, but you have to sigh;
When care is pressing you down a bit,
Rest if you must, but don't you quit.
Success is failure turned inside out;
The silver tint of the clouds of doubt.

And you can never tell how close you are
It may be near when it seems afar;
So stick to the fight when you're hardest hit –
It's when things seem worst that you mustn't quit.
(*Don't* Quit from The Complete Speaker's Sourcebook
by Eleanor Doan pg. 207 © 1996, Zondervan Treasures;
Zondervan Publishing House) 6

SABBATH REST

The natural progression in this chapter from overwhelming overload and suffering is to Sabbath Rest. The thing to notice about Sabbath rest is – it is not for the Sabbath, but for a lifetime! Hebrews 4: 1-11 AMP has a tremendous passage on Sabbath rest which I encourage you to stick with, even though it is long:

1 THEREFORE, WHILE the promise of entering His rest still holds and is offered [today], let us be afraid [to distrust it], lest any of you should think he has come too late and has come short of [reaching] it.

2 For indeed we have had the glad tidings [Gospel of God] proclaimed to us just as truly as they [the Israelites of old did when the good news of deliverance from bondage came to them]; but the message they heard did not benefit them, because it was not mixed with faith (with the leaning of the entire personality on God in absolute trust and confidence in His power, wisdom, and goodness) by those who heard it; neither were they united in faith with the ones [Joshua and Caleb] who heard (did believe).

3 For we who have believed (adhered to and trusted in and relied on God) do enter that rest, in accordance with His declaration that those [who did not believe] should not enter when He said, As I swore in My wrath, They shall not enter My rest; and this He said although [His] works had been completed and prepared [and waiting for all who would believe] from the foundation of the world.

4 For in a certain place He has said this about the seventh day: And God rested on the seventh day from all His works.

5 And [they forfeited their part in it, for] in this [passage] He said, they shall not enter My rest.

6 Seeing then that the promise remains over [from past times] for some to enter that rest, and that those who formerly were given the good news about it and the opportunity, failed to appropriate it and did not enter because of disobedience,

7 Again He sets a definite day, [a new] Today, [and gives another opportunity of securing that rest] saying through David after so long a time in the words already quoted, Today, if you would hear His voice and when you hear it, do not harden your hearts.

8 [This mention of a rest was not a reference to their entering into Canaan.] For if Joshua had given them rest, He [God] would not speak afterward about another day.

9 So then, there is still awaiting a full and complete Sabbath-rest reserved for the [true] people of God;

10 For he who has once entered [God's] rest also has ceased from [the weariness and pain] of human labors, just as God rested from those labors peculiarly His own.

11 Let us therefore be zealous and exert ourselves and strive diligently to enter that rest [of God, to know and experience it for ourselves], that no one may fall or perish by the same kind of unbelief and disobedience [into which those in the wilderness fell].

Sabbath rest is when we live in a perpetual state of eternal empowerment, equipping and endeavor to see others come to knowledge of the same.

In the beginning, God rested on the seventh day. He did not rest because He was tired but as a guideline for man to follow. Therefore we are to look upon the Sabbath as a time of rest, receptivity to the Truth of His Word as well as time to refocus on Him as the new week begins.

For most of western civilization, in the Church Age, the Sabbath (Sunday for Christians) was set aside for rest and relaxation. Those of us over 50 years old can remember the blue laws – when not even a grocery store would open on Sundays out of respect for the Lord's Day. The Orthodox Jews in Israel and parts of the United States have taken this to an extreme. They would not drive or even press an elevator button on their Sabbath (Saturday).

Somewhere along the line, as western humankind lost its first love and reverence for God, they dismantled all the blue laws. One by one, everything was opened up for business. Now one can buy hard liquor early on Sunday morning. We are not under the Law, since the Cross. However, some of our activities must have the Lord shaking His Head.

We have seen Americans are the most overworked people in the world. The Western Europeans have taken this in the other direction in their socialist utopian world. However we have the edge on them in this: we have Christ, they do not. As an entire continent the Europeans have denied not just Christ the Savior, but the God of this world. They can have all the government socialist welfare programs and six weeks paid vacations they enjoy now. This is their reward.

The following passage from Hebrews 4: 3-5 NKJV describes both us believers as well as those in America, Europe and the rest of mankind who will spend eternity in restless agony, separated from God*:* ***Now we who have believed enter that rest****, just as God has said, "So I declared on oath in my anger, 'They shall never enter my rest.' "And yet his work has been finished since the creation of the world. For somewhere he has spoken about the seventh day in these words: "****And on the seventh day God rested from all his work." And again in the passage above he says, "They shall never enter my rest."*** (Emphasis mine).

To be sure, we are not commanded to keep the Jewish Sabbath. Paul warns the Galatians in Chapter 4: 10-11 about having to legally observe certain days. These include their Sabbath. John Calvin explains it best this way:

> *"...As the truth therefore was given to the Jews under a figure, so to us on the contrary, truth is shown without shadows in order, first of all, that we meditate all our life on a perpetual Sabbath from our works so that the Lord may operate in us*

by His Spirit. Secondly, in order that we observe the legitimate order of the Church for listening to the Word of God, for administering the sacraments, and for public prayers. Thirdly, in order that we do not oppress inhumanly with work those who are subject to us...." 7

Calvin explains the beautiful requirements for the Lord's Day.

But Sabbath Rest is more than just a day to rest on Sunday. It is more than just a day of relaxation or reading a book. It is more than just even a time of rejuvenation of mind, body and soul. It is more than a day of refocusing our energies, time and resources. It is more than just a time acquiring ability to let certain things go and receive the blessings of the Lord in return. It is our call to live through Him, in Him and have His Mind – the Mind of Peace, Joy and Victory as we cry "Abba, Father"!

PRESENT REST, SABBATH REST

No, my friends, Sabbath Rest is a lifestyle. Hebrews 4:9 is the only time in the entire Bible the Greek word "sabbatismos" appears. The word means "Sabbath Rest" in the PRESENT time. All other times, the word "rest" is translated from the Biblical canon "katapausis" or Spiritual rest.

We children of God are currently in Sabbatismos if we live by His Principles and walk in His Ways. This Present Rest comes from being disciplined and obedient. I encourage the reader to read again Hebrews 4:3-11 to get the full picture of present rest and the rest to come.

The rest to come can be capsulated in the wonderful Gospel song.

What a fellowship, what a joy divine,
Leaning on the everlasting arms;
what blessedness, what a peace is mine,
Leaning on the everlasting arms.
Leaning, leaning, safe and secure from all alarms;
Leaning, leaning, leaning on the everlasting arms. 8

This "sabbatismos" or present Sabbath Rest is found only in this New Testament passage. Therefore it is meant ONLY for those who believe in Christ as Savior. No other religion can make such a promise! A lost people will never have true peace in this life without Christ. This is a cold, hard fact and reality, whether it sounds harsh or not.

Spiritual rest is promised and spoken of throughout the entire Bible, from Deuteronomy 3:20 to Revelation.20:6. Along the way, we have many mentions of rest. Psalm 94:12-13 promises rest from adversity. Psalm 95 is the Sabbath psalm. Isaiah prophesied about freedom from bondage in Chapters 11: 10 and 14:3 and 7. Rest is going on right now, alongside Present Rest (sabbatismos), in this mortal life.

The believer goes from this life, after death, into eternity with our Lord. In the Old Testament, those who lived by Faith (or the Great Cloud of Witnesses in the famous Faith Chapter of Hebrews 11) went directly into the "Bosom of Abraham". After Christ died on the Cross and paid for all sins for all time, it was only then the Old Testament saints were ushered into the Kingdom. Victory had been won at the Cross.

1 Peter 3:18-20 NKJV describes Christ as going into the other world of the damned during His physical death on earth, to proclaim the Good news*: For Christ also suffered once for sins, the just for the unjust, that He might bring us to God, being put to death in the flesh but made alive by the Spirit, by whom also He went and preached to the spirits in prison, who formerly were disobedient, when once the Divine longsuffering waited in the days of Noah, while the ark was being prepared, in which a few, that is, eight souls, were saved through water.*

However the ultimate Spiritual Rest is our entry into the eternal gates of Heaven! This begins with those of us who return with Christ to reign with Him in the Millennial Kingdom. This has been prophesied by the great Old Testament prophets as well as in Revelation 20: 1-6.

Here is the final Spiritual rest. It is found in Revelation 21: 3-4 NIV "*And I heard a loud voice from the throne saying, "Now the dwelling of God is with men, and He will live with them. They will be His people, and God Himself will be with them and be their God. He will wipe every tear from their eyes. There will be no more death or mourning or crying or pain, for the old order of things has passed away."*

This is not just leaning on the Everlasting Arms, this is complete Victory!! This is the complete fruit of living in Sabbath Rest!

TRUE WORSHIP

How do we respond to this Indescribable Promised Gift of Heaven, which we can not even fathom? Look at what Jesus says in John 4:23-24 NIV: "*Yet a time is coming and has now come when the true worshipers will worship the Father in spirit and truth, for they are the kind of worshipers the Father seeks. God is Spirit and His worshipers must worship in spirit and in truth."*

When Jesus said this to the Samaritan woman it was a completely new paradigm. Up to this point the Jews in Jerusalem, having ALL the Old Testament Scriptures followed the Mosaic commandments to the letter. They did not follow it in the Spirit of God as we see in all the Gospels, as they had no Truth in them, but these teachers of the Law and Pharisees – the Hypocrites – knew the Law inside out.

The Samaritans only had the Torah – the first five Books of the Word and had a reputation for making up some other worship practices. This was not of God either. However both peoples knew of the coming Savior!

When the Savior Himself made this statement about "true worshippers" it heralded in a new way of worship. An important thing to note here is whenever Jesus made a life changing doctrinal or other command, He never called a press conference or His Public Relations firm!

He spoke them Himself to people like this unnamed Samaritan woman, the many handicapped people He saved and the woman with the blood issue. Even the rich young ruler evoked a Truth – "it is easier for a camel to go through the eye of a needle, than for a rich man to enter the Kingdom of lHeaven".

But what about Worship? In the Old Covenant, Tabernacle worship was given to Moses. When The Book of John was written around 85 AD, the destruction in 70 AD of the Temple which Jesus predicted back in 33 AD had already occurred. The old worship system was destroyed as one brick was not left upon another from the Temple.

The new True Worshippers did not now need to go to the Temple in Jerusalem to worship God the Father, but can now worship Him "in Spirit and in Truth". In the Old Testament, the word Worship is translated "shachah" which means to bow down or prostrate yourself in obedience. Indeed this kind of reverence to God is missing today not only in the world, but in His Christian churches!

Worship in the New Testament has another meaning in the original Greek language. It is acknowledged that the great English Martyr William Tyndale was the first to translate the New Testament Greek into English. He immediately translated "proskuneo" 9 as "worship". His old English meaning is 'worth-ship' or 'to assign the attribute of worth or value to'.

The Dictionary description of the word "worship" gives us only a small glimpse of what we need to know as children of the Living God. Webster describes its meaning as "profound love and admiration" as well as (in the verb) "love unquestionably and uncritically". Indeed!!

Worship is giving back to God the gifts He has given us.

Worship is acknowledging His Majesty, Sovereignty and dominion over all.

Worship is listening to Him, as He said in Psalm 46: 10 "Be still and know that I am God".

Worship is preparing our hearts to receive His Word.

Worship is prostrating ourselves at the Foot of the Cross, for that is where we belong.

Worship is praying His Word back to Him in awe and reverence.

Worship is praising Him for Who He is and What He has done.

Worship is practicing His Statutes for they are true and worthy.

Worship is providing all of us to all of Him.

Worship is precisely why He called us to Himself.

In Heaven, we will spend an eternity worshipping the Lord. In this earthly body, we do it in Spirit and in Truth. Those of us who are called by Christ to be His have the Holy Spirit. Our spirit is joined with His until the Day of Redemption. That is a fact.

Because of this relationship we are to continually seek the Lord who gave us His Spirit through the Truth of His Word, found ONLY in the Bible and NOTHING else! No, we do not need to go to the Temple anymore in Jerusalem. Our bodies are now the Temple of the Holy Spirit of God and we can assign Him His worthiness at any time and in any place.

RETURN OF FAMILY WORSHIP

Until World War II and its post-war boom, America with its frontier spirit spent a lot of time on its collective knees. However, this was never true of ALL of America. The country was founded on Christian principles from Jamestown to Plymouth. You would never know it in Jamestown, Virginia today as we celebrate the 400th Anniversary of the Settlement. The politically correct have removed all mentions of Christ and the Christian foundation of Jamestown.

It was in the World War II after-glow when the late Supreme Court Justices Hugo Black and Earl Warren accelerated the War against Christianity by two decisions as previously mentioned (Everson v Board of Education, 1947 and Engel v Vitale, 1962).

These two court decisions took The Bible and Prayer out of Public Education, under dubious reasoning. Justice Black, a former member of the Ku Klux Klan (Google it yourself), went beyond comment in his majority speeches and virtually attacked religion. When the courts took God out of the school, Satan moved in. Today we see the fruit of those decisions. The seeds were sown long before these judges, who have since met the Real Judge – to their dismay!

Leaders in our evangelical churches are the remaining standard-bearers in this escalating war which will end on the plains of Armageddon. Unfortunately, apart from the conservative Southern Baptist Seminaries, Moody Bible Institute, John MacArthur's Masters and a few other seminaries, the quality of our upcoming church leaders is very worrisome.

Even with some of our current popular and local churches, the teaching may be good, but there is no movement of prayer or family worship anywhere. In Isaiah 56:7 KJV, God writes "*Even them will I bring to my holy mountain, and make them joyful in my house of prayer: their burnt offerings and their sacrifices shall be accepted upon mine altar; for mine house shall be called* ***<u>an house of prayer for all people".</u>***

He says "a house of prayer for all people". Jesus quoted this same verse in Matthew 21:13 when he cleared the money-grubbing money-changers out of the temple...*a House of Prayer.* One can almost tell the difference between a praying church and every other one! You can distinguish them by their fruit and the lives changed. You can distinguish them by the personal and corporate revivals going on there.

In almost every one of these instances, praying families are involved. Families have always and will always be the backbone of America. The Praying Family is the spinal fluid. For most of America's colorful history, it has always been the family and the family that worships together, stays together.

Family worship was instituted from early Biblical times. Abraham built an altar to the Lord (Genesis 12:7; 13:4). He did not build it in a 2000 seat sanctuary with jumbo TV screens but in the wilderness as he kept on moving.

My favorite military hero – God's General himself – Joshua, son of Nun, said in Joshua 24:15 "as for me and my house, we will serve the Lord", i.e. family worship. There is a special anointing when the Spirit of God appears where two or four or five in a family sit around and talk about the Lord. He shows up in unity when we pray and praise Him for all His blessings...and not just at the Thanksgiving meal.

Arthur W. Pink was an intense Puritan-like Calvinist who lived in the early part of the 20th century. Born in England, he came to the United States to study at Moody Bible Institute in Chicago. He later became a world traveling preacher. His works rank amongst some of the most spiritually uplifting for the believer. He has the best Biblically based writing on Family Worship ever.

In part, this what the late great evangelist wrote:

> *"An old writer well said, "A family without prayer is like a house without a roof, open and exposed to all the storms of Heaven." All our domestic comforts and temporal mercies*

issue from the loving-kindness of the Lord, and the best we can do in return is to gratefully acknowledge together, His goodness to us as a family.

Excuses against the discharge of this sacred duty are idle and worthless. Of what avail will it be when we render an account to God for the stewardship of our families to say that we had no time available, working hard from morn till eve? The more pressing be our temporal duties, the greater our need of seeking spiritual succor. Nor may any Christian plead that he is not qualified for such a work: gifts and talents are developed by use and not by neglect.

Family worship should be conducted reverently, earnestly and simply. It is then that the little ones will receive their first impressions and form their initial conceptions of the Lord God.

Great care needs to be taken lest a false idea be given them of the Divine Character, and for this the balance must be preserved between dwelling upon His transcendence and immanency, His holiness and His mercy, His might and His tenderness. His justice and His grace.

Worship should begin with a few words of prayer invoking God's presence and blessing. A short passage from His Word should follow, with brief comments thereon. Two or three verses of a Psalm may be sung. Close with a prayer of committal into the hands of God. Though we may not be able to pray eloquently, we should earnestly. Prevailing prayers are usually brief ones. Beware of wearying the young ones. 10

The advantages and blessings of family worship are incalculable. First, family worship will prevent much sin. It awes the soul, conveys a sense of God's majesty and authority sets solemn truths before the mind. It brings down benefits from God on the home. Personal piety in the home is a most influential means, under God, of conveying piety to the little ones.

Children are largely creatures of imitation, loving to copy what they see in others. "*He established a testimony in Jacob and appointed a law in Israel. which He commanded our fathers that they should make them known to their children: That the generation to come might know them, even the children which should be born; who should arise and declare them to their children: That they might set their hope in God, and not forget the works of God, but keep His commandments*" (Ps. 78:5, 7).

How much of the dreadful moral and spiritual conditions of the masses today may be traced back to the neglect of fathers in this duty? How can those who neglect the worship of God in their families look for peace and comfort therein? Daily prayer in the home is a blessed means of grace for allaying those unhappy passions to which our common nature is subject.

Finally, family prayer gains for us the presence and blessing of the Lord. There is a promise of His presence which is peculiarly applicable to this duty: see Matthew 18:19, 20. Many have found in family worship that help and communion with God which they sought for with less effect in private prayer." 10 ***A W. Pink***

DOUG MAZZA

In September 2006, I was beginning the first chapters of this book and did not know where the Lord wanted to take it. I contacted several ministries which are led by both men and women as I intend this book for all people, just as the Bible is. One of the ministries I felt particularly led to was Joni and friends.

If there is someone who lives the Grace and Love of God through suffering, it is Joni Eraekson Tada. In my conversations with her representative Steve Appel, the Lord led me in another direction. We had a few conversations about a gentleman named Doug Mazza.

This name may not jump out at Americans like Lee Iacocca does, but Doug has had a tremendous impact on a certain demographic of the car-buying public. After leaving the military, he was on a fast track into the corporate business world and landed successfully on the team which introduced Mitsubishi cars to the United States.

At age 39, he was the senior executive officer of Suzuki, North America. Doug is the man who introduced the Suzuki Samurai to America. It is amazing to think this off-road vehicle was priced at only $6200 when he launched it in America! He later went on to become the Chief Operating Officer of Hyundai N.A...

This Captain of American industry was such a business genius, he was written about in Harvard Business Review Journals, the New York Times etc. All of this changed at the birth of his third son, Ryan. Ryan was born with Crouzon Syndrome.

Crouzon is genetic deformity or disorder of the skull which only affects 16 newborns in one million. It was this disorder which brought this man of power and blessing to his knees. Doug grew up in the church but never had a personal relationship with Christ. Ryan was not supposed to live past two or three days. He is now 28 years old. He is blind and only 100 pounds but as Doug says "I am never closer to God than when I am with Ryan".

But does a man go from in control of a multi-billion dollar International company to making a statement like this on his own? NO! He was broken before God when Ryan was given to him from God. CEO Mazza's world was turned upside down. Like most people, he cried out to God when things went wrong.

Again, like most people, Doug said he negotiated his way out of problems and knew he could depend on this concept of the Holy One. Like most North Americans, he believed Jesus Christ was the son of God but it was only "head knowledge".

This question would come out of his angry moments when dealing with Ryan's many surgeries and close calls would get to him. As a man who was used to being in control, this was something he could not recognize. He was accustomed to staff "who would come, when he said come and go, when he said go". This was one business deal he could not negotiate on his terms.

Most business executives always want to have the last word. He tried this tact with God, asking "what do you want from me?" God told him "I want you"!

The now former CEO said "God said 'you want to be in control? I will give you something to be in control of. You will be in control of ...you would be in control of whether or not you will give me your life and trust in me". How about this answer from God! He has spoken to us several times in a similar manner!

From viewing his testimony and other things from resources sent me by the Joni and Friends organization, it is obvious God taught Doug a huge Life Lesson. The more Doug cried out to God questioning the suffering and pain of his dear son Ryan, the more God told him "I love Ryan more than you do". The more Ryan seemed to slip away into comas etc, the more God showed up.

God took him through brokenness as the high flying Chief Executive Officer gradually became Christ's Evangelizing Official. He left the corporate world. Being a volunteer all the while, along with his wife Lorraine, Doug signed on with Joni and Friends.

Every Christian knows Joni and her amazing story. Here is a woman who will have a front row seat in Heaven, I guarantee it. A paraplegic who paints with her teeth and has written over 35 books, Joni has inspired millions worldwide. Her wheelchair and other ministries have brought hope and comfort to countless worldwide.

It was to this mission God led Doug Mazza. He took the reins of Joni's ministry and God used his business talents to direct him into the International Mission field. From the plush carpeted boardrooms of Southern California, Doug can now be found in the voodoo infested mud of Haiti. There he brings Christ through word and deed. You can multiply this worldwide to his current calling.

He is the arms and feet of Joni. First he had to know suffering and brokenness. He had to learn about the Almighty Loving Creator Jesus Christ and His Father, our Father. He learnt through reading the Bible to Ryan for decades. He learnt from sometimes fervent prayer. After learning personal suffering and brokenness, then he had to learn from Joni's story.

The world could never understand a God who would leave a woman stuck in a wheelchair for almost four decades; a woman who can not attend to herself without help...this woman who declares her suffering is nothing compared to what Christ suffered on the Cross. Only God's true elect can even begin to fathom it. This God and Christ are worthy of the all faith and confidence and power and praise and Glory!

Once Doug identified with her spiritual, physical and emotional suffering and matched it with the One on the Cross, he was ready for service. You see, God can not use someone who is not broken to everything. God chooses the road to brokenness. Some are more painful than others. The more painful, the larger the call for service is!

Doug has taken Joni and Friends into a successful and thriving ministry WITHOUT compromising and huckstering. My new friend and future author Donna Rousseve, the Communications director at Joni and Friends, Agoura Hills, California reported how much God has blessed them out there. Doug was transitioning his staff of 65 into a fine new building at this writing and the Lord blessed the Joni ministry. They are set to become even the more effective in their Disability ministry worldwide. When God wants a work done, He provides!

Friends, all our righteousness are filthy rags. None of us come to the table with our hands clean. Thank God in Heaven for the riches of Christ Jesus. I take the words of Psalm 51: 7-10 NKJV to heart all the time. In it David *says "Purge me with hyssop, and I shall be clean; wash me, and I shall be whiter than snow. Make me hear joy and gladness, the bones You have broken may rejoice. Hide Your face from my sins, and blot out all my iniquities. Create in me a clean heart, O God, and renew a steadfast spirit within me"*

The key is brokenness, the keyhole is suffering. The deadbolt cylinder is us. The plug is the Word of God. The cut on the door frame is the mission field. But the Door Handle is Jesus Christ. Nothing turns without Him.

Those verses above from Psalm 51 are so rich in teaching and practice. "Make me hear joy and gladness (that) the bones You have broken may rejoice". Doug and Joni; Joe White who battled Leukemia and stands victorious in Christ....my heroes of the Faith know the joy and gladness from being made to suffer like Christ. We are constantly being broken and Jesus leads us through various levels of suffering.

So consider it gain, my dear friends, when trials come. He is sending out a message He has something for us in mind. He has something which you could never imagine in your wildest dreams. He has something which will take you on the Greatest Adventure of your life. He gets the Glory; we get to bask in it, under His protection. I dare anyone in this world to show me anything better than this!

Doug Mazza II knows this now. Joni and Donna and their friends know it. Michelle McGowan and her wonderful "IN HIS HANDS" Adoption Ministry in Springfield, Illinois knows it too. Michelle has a heart as big as Oklahoma for orphans to the extent of taking herself on a daring mission's trip to the orphanages in cold heartless, communist China. This is the same China which aborts these baby girls and treats the surviving ones like disposables in orphanages. People like Michelle are unknown to the world in their work on behalf of the least of these, but God knows who they are. Great is there reward.

My friends thank you for allowing me to bend your ear through all these pages. This has been the work of my life. I never had so much fun. Yet I have never been so inspired. For the countless sleepless nights of sitting here while the Holy Spirit poured it out of me, I thank the Lord for Him choosing me to write His book, for such a time. To God be the Glory, great things He hath done.

(The following bonus chapter contains four random thoughts and comments about things which have been impressed upon me over the years. Hope you read them!)

Now unto Him that is able to keep you from falling, and to present you faultless before the presence of His glory with exceeding joy, to the only wise God our Savior, be glory and majesty, dominion and power, both now and ever. Amen. (Jude 24, 25 KJV)

CHAPTER 11

SMORGASBORD!

He has showed you, O man, what is good.
And what does the LORD require of you?
To act justly and to love mercy
and to walk humbly with your God.
(Micah 6:8, NIV)

ITEM 1:

THE REAL AMERICAN MAN

American manhood has always been defined in terms of rugged individualism. It is a mindset burnt into the fabric of American life from the can-do days of men like President Theodore Roosevelt who epitomizes American Ascendancy in the world. As the 20th Century became America's century, more and more, American manhood began to be redefined in a number of ways – some of which God has never ordained.

In a sign of the coming Culture of Celebrity, Hollywood described a real he-man as someone with the onscreen exploits of silent screen actor Rudolph Valentino or the kick- down- the- door rough and tumbling John Wayne.

The first half of the century gave us men's men and what some called Christian men like General Douglas MacArthur, General George Patton, and General Dwight D. Eisenhower.

Actually, of all the men named above, only General MacArthur made more than one huge public confession for the Lord. The good General was both a man's man and God's man!!

According to the Public Broadcasting Service (PBS) series on the American Experience called "MACARTHUR", the General's biggest disappointment was not being able to convert the entire island of Japan to Christianity! He said "true democracy can exist only on a spiritual foundation," and will "endure when it rests firmly on the Christian conception of the individual and society." 1

If a U.S. General talked like that today in this era of anti-Christian bigotry and universalism, they would call for his head on a platter! In the same PBS TV documentary, he also said this about the Philippines "A Christian nation, the Philippines stand as a mighty bulwark of Christianity in the Far East, and its capacity for high moral leadership in Asia is unlimited." 1

There are many examples of speeches made by MacArthur where he shared testimony to the Lordship of Jesus Christ.

America was defined by many events in the first half of the 20th Century. These ranged from the Glory Days of Teddy Roosevelt to World War 1; from the Roaring 20's and its lawlessness to the Great Depression and on to World War II.

Each time period gave us men who stood out and, even today, are cited as the epitome of American manhood.

None of us could ever forget Saturday afternoon westerns with the great Audie Murphy, the most decorated soldier of World War II. Audie joined the United States Army in 1942 at the age of 18. He was only 5 foot 5 inches tall and weighed 110 lbs! But he managed to kill 240 German soldiers and received this country's highest honors. 2

John Wayne was not an actual Military hero, but had the profile of patriotism and passion for the American way of life. His movies are not only favorites of aging fifty year olds like me, but our children as well. They spelled American, where our ideals are "Good will always triumphs over Evil."

Wayne believed in American exceptionalism and even wrote a book called "America, why I love her"! He reigned supreme as the example of American manhood until the 1970's when Mr. Cool took his place!

Clint Eastwood hit the consciousness of America like a lightning bolt as Dirty Harry Callahan, in the Dirty Harry series of movies. Almost overnight, Eastwood, the strong, silent hero signified what most of us wished we could be: self-assured, brave and fearless; a type of man who made up his own rules, lived by them and of course, won the battle for our side – the good guys!

Since the "Dirty Harry" days, we have had U.S. Presidents like Ronald Reagan ('the bombing begins in five minutes" through an open mike); George H.W. Bush (who delights in jumping out of airplanes in defiance of his 80 years!) and his son, the current President George W. Bush (who flew and landed a jet on a carrier off San Diego in 2003, which not too many politicians can do)!

All these leaders had one thing in common – the Frontier Spirit. They see life in black and white terms, with the Hand of Almighty God over everything. The religious beliefs of each of these three acknowledged men of the West (in the case of the Bushes, New England transplants) are well known.

Both Reagan and President G.W. Bush are acknowledged born-again Christians. The latter's father, President G.H.W. Bush professes similar beliefs.

However the men, whom the popular culture has held up as our icons over these many years, have views which almost coincide with those of our Deist Founding Fathers!! (Webster's dictionary defines "Deism" as a movement or system of thought advocating natural religion, emphasizing morality, and in the 18th century *denying the interference of the Creator with the laws of the universe or simply put – 'God created the earth and walked away")!* 8

John Wayne and Clint Eastwood did not outright deny the Creator Jesus Christ.

But when Wayne had an opportunity to state his beliefs, he said " "I've always had a deep faith that there is a supreme being....there has to be....The fact that He's let me stick around a little longer, or She's let me stick around a little longer, certainly goes great with me!!!" (Huh??) 3

Clint Eastwood also had his chance to explain his beliefs to David Frost once on national TV and said this when asked by Frost "if God was important to him", Clint said" 'I'm just not a member of an organized religion. But I've always felt very strongly about things, I guess. Especially when I'm out in nature. I guess that's why I've done so many wide open films in nature. But religion is, I think, a very personal thing…." 4

The Founding Fathers George Washington, Benjamin Franklin were both Deists as well.Thomas Jefferson is the best known Deist. Washington's beliefs were detailed in a book called "Washington and Religion" by Paul F. Boller. In this book, eyewitnesses to the great Washington said : "often said in my hearing, though very sorrowfully, of course, that while Washington was very deferential to religion and its ceremonies, like nearly all the founders of the Republic, he was not a Christian, but a Deist…!!" (Pastor Arthur Bradford). 5

Jefferson is no better. He once considered himself to be a Unitarian as well as a deist. Here is what he said about the Bible and God's Truth in discussing the book or the Revelation "… (they are) merely the ravings of a maniac, no more worthy nor capable of explanation than the incoherencies of our own nightly dreams." (From Charles B. Stanford's book *'The Religious Life of Thomas Jefferson.'*) 6

He called the book of Revelation "manic ravings" that contained their "incoherencies". (Webster's Dictionary defines a Unitarian as "one who believes in the oneness of God as opposed to traditional Christian belief in the Trinity or the Father, Son, and Holy Spirit"). 7

These facts surprise a lot of Christians and even preachers who keep contending that our Founding Fathers were the "biggest Christians and evangelists" in the world! But "facts is facts!" In fact it was Deism and Unitarianism which began this country's slide into 20th Century moral relativism

EASTWOOD'S WORDS TO LIVE BY!

George Washington's leadership of the Continental Army which freed this country from British Oppression was typical Clint Eastwood. In fact the first president could be the original Dirty Harry!

The Crossing of the Delaware River led by him on Christmas night, 1776 into Trenton, New Jersey, is something right out of a True American hero book!

Here are some of the men who crossed the Frozen Delaware with General Washington: James Madison, James Monroe, Aaron Burr and Alexander Hamilton (who later shot at each other in the most famous duel of all time) as well as future Supreme Court Justice John Marshall and Prince Whipple, the most famous black man of the American Revolution.

Whipple was born in Amabou, Africa, brought to America as a slave, and signed up for Freedom with the Continental Army. 9

Hollywood could not have scripted a better real life adventure, which only Americans can do, period! Today's superhero Clint Eastwood a few years ago released his own TEN RULES A MAN SHOULD LIVE BY. Some of them can apply to the courage of The Continental Army crossing the Delaware, and while they sound somewhat good, they are not Scriptural. Judge for yourself.

Here they are:

1. Call your own shots
2. Be fearless
3. Keep moving
4. Love your job
5. Speak softly
6. Don't be predictable
7. Find a good woman
8. Learn to play the piano
9. You are what you drive
10. Avoid extreme makeovers

(First published in Men's Journal, February 2004 edition) 10

Let us examine this to see how it squares with being a man or woman of God. God is not a self-described Libertarian like Eastwood (one who believes in absolute free will and unrestricted liberty of thought and action; *Webster's*).

A child of God does not live on his or her own free will, but IN the Will of the One who saved us, because *"He who overcomes, I will make him a pillar in the temple of My God, and he will not go out from it anymore; and I will write on him the name of My God, and the name of the city of My God, the new Jerusalem, which comes down out of heaven from My God, and My new name" (Jesus in Revelation 3:12).*

A child of God does not run wild with the thoughts of this world, no matter how well intentioned, but has a mind of *"bringing every thought captive into captivity to the obedience of Christ' (2 Cor. 10: 5b; NKJV).*

A child of God does not go off doing our own thing because on Judgment Day *"each man's work will become evident; for the day will show it because it is to be revealed with fire, and the fire itself will test the quality of each man's work." (1 Cor. 3:13).*

EASTWOOD'S RULES, MODIFIED BY THE WORD OF GOD:

1. Let God call the shots (Psalm 119:26)
2. Be Fearless because of Christ (2 Timothy 1:7)
3. Don't keep moving; *"Be still and know that I am God."(* Psalm 46:10)
4. Love the Lord Your God (Matthew 22:37) and NOT worldly things.
5. Season your speech: *"Let your speech always be with grace, as though seasoned with salt, so that you will know how you should respond to each person"* (Colossians 4:6).
6. Don't be predictable, be transparent *"But above all, my brethren, do not swear, either by heaven or by earth or with any other oath; but your yes is to be yes, and your no, no, so that you may not fall under judgment"* (James 5:12).
7. Men, pray the Lord to lead you to the wife He selected for you, before the Foundation of the World; women, vice versa, the same; *"He who finds a wife finds a good thing and obtains favor from the LORD"* (Proverbs 18:22).

8. Rejoice in the Music of the Lord: *"speaking to one another in psalms and hymns and spiritual songs, singing and making melody with your heart to the Lord"* (Ephesians 5:19).
9. If you are the driver, the wrong man's driving! Secondly, you are who you are in Christ. You are not who the world defines you (which is by what you do for a living) but you are *"those who have been sanctified in Christ Jesus, saints by calling, with all who in every place call on the name of our Lord Jesus Christ, their Lord and ours"* (Ephesians 1:1).
10. Don't avoid "extreme makeovers"! *"Jesus answered, "Most assuredly, I say to you, unless one is born of water and the Spirit, he cannot enter the kingdom of God. That which is born of the flesh is flesh, and that which is born of the Spirit is spirit. Do not marvel that I said to you, 'You must be born again.' The wind blows where it wishes, and you hear the sound of it, but cannot tell where it comes from and where it goes. So is everyone who is born of the Spirit."* (John 3:5-8, NKJV).

One book I recommend to anyone who is interested in the beliefs of several of our great celebrities of the past and present is "What Hollywood believes" by one of my favorite people – Ray Comfort (Genesis Publishing, 2004). What you see in the book about people, whom you once thought were Christians would surprise you!

In the final analysis, it is obvious. The Real American man is a sold out, submissive, surrendered, smiling, Spirit-filled son of the Son of God. The Real American man is Christ's man. The Real American woman is all of that and the daughter of Christ. Together as a body of Christ we are now part of the Last Adam. When we return to the Garden of Eden in the New Heavens and Earth with Christ our Savior, King and Priest, we shall be once again be called man (Genesis 5:2).

Scripture says we will have a new name and live forever with Him. The Angel in Revelation 22 says "*the Kingdom of God is now with man*"....that is us my friends – but only if we are truly sons and daughters of Jesus Christ. There is no other way. There is no other religion and He is the Beginning and the End. He is the Lord of my life. He is all I need. He is my Sustainer, Redeemer, Counselor, Priest, King and Commander in Chief. I am ready to die for Him. How do I know all this? BECAUSE HE, WHO BEGAN A GOOD WORK IN ME, LIVES IN ME! AMEN

THE FOLLOWING IS A LIST OF 177 NAMES OF JESUS CHRIST. Why does the world hate Him? Why do European and other Western secularists want to keep His name out of everything in every day life? Why are peaceful Gideons prosecuted in the Florida Keys for passing out Bibles on public sidewalks, in violation of the First Amendment? Why are Christians murdered and persecuted in India, Pakistan, China, Africa and other pagan cultures? Why? Because of the Name! Read this list prayerfully. Look up the verses and you will know why the world hates us....because they first hated Him. And, by the way, He will come to judge the world....and the prince of darkness grim, tremble not for him, because his judgment and those who are his followers is sure!

177 Names of Christ and Verses [11]

1. Abraham's Seed	Genesis 22:18; Galatians 3:16
2. Advocate	1 John 2:1
3. Almighty	Revelation 1:8
4. Alpha and Omega	Revelation 1:8; 22:13
5. Amen	Revelation 3:14
6. Angel	Genesis 48:16; Exodus 23:20-21
7. Angel of God's Presence	Isaiah 63:9
8. Angel of the Lord	Exodus 3:2; Judges 13:15-22
9. Apostle	Hebrews 3:1
10. Arm of the Lord	Isaiah 51:9; 53:1
11. Author and Finisher of our faith	Hebrews 12:2
12. Author of eternal salvation	Hebrews 5:9
13. Beginning of the creation of God	Revelation 3:14

14. Beloved	Ephesians 1:6
15. Beloved Son	Matthew 12:18
16. Blessed and only Potentate	1 Timothy 6:15
17. Branch	Jeremiah 23:5; Zechariah 3:8; 6:12
18. Bread of Life	John 6:35, 48
19. Bridegroom	Matthew 9:15
20. Bright and Morning Star	Revelation 22:16
21. Captain of Salvation	Hebrews 2:10
22. Captain of the Lord's Host	Joshua 5:14-15
23. Carpenter	Mark 6:3
24. Carpenter's Son	Matthew 13:55
25. Chief Cornerstone	Ephesians 2:20; 1 Peter 2:6
26. Chief Shepherd	1 Peter 5:4
27. Christ	Matthew 16:20; Mark 14:16; Luke 23:2
28. Christ Jesus	Acts 19:4; Romans 3:24; 8:1; 1 Corinthians 1:2, 30
29. Christ Jesus our Lord	Romans 8:39; 1 Timothy 1:12
30. Christ of God	Luke 9:20
31. Christ the Lord	Luke 2:11
32. Commander	Isaiah 55:4
33. Consolation of Israel	Luke 2:25
34. Cornerstone	Matthew 21:42; Ephesians 2:20
35. Counselor	Isaiah 9:6
36. Creator	John 1:3
37. David	Jeremiah 30:9; Ezekiel 34:23
38. Dayspring	Luke 1:78
39. Deliverer	Romans 11:26
40. Desire of all nations	Haggai 2:7
41. Door	John 10:7
42. Elect of God	Isaiah 42:1
43. Eternal life	1 John 1:2; 5:20
44. Everlasting Father	Isaiah 9:6
45. Faithful and True	Revelation 19:11

46. Faithful Witness	Revelation 1:5; 3:14
47. First and Last	Revelation 1:17; 2:8
48. Firstborn	Psalm 89:27; Hebrews 1:6; Revelation 1:5
49. Forerunner	Hebrews 6:20
50. Fountain	Zechariah 13:1
51. Glory of the Lord	Isaiah 40:5
52. God	Isaiah 40:9; John 20:28
53. God blessed forever	Romans 9:5
54. God's fellow	Zechariah 13:7
55. Good Shepherd	John 10:14
56. Governor	Matthew 2:6
57. Great High Priest	Hebrews 4:14
58. Head of the Church	Ephesians 5:23; Colossians 1:18
59. Heir of all things	Hebrews 1:2
60. High Priest	Hebrews 4:14
61. Holy Child	Acts 4:27
62. Holy One	Psalm 16:10; Acts 2:27; 3:14
63. Holy One of God	Mark 1:24
64. Holy One of Israel	Isaiah 41:14; 54:5
65. Horn of salvation	Luke 1:69
66. I AM	Exodus 3:14; John 8:58
67. Image of God	2 Corinthians 4:4
68. Immanuel	Isaiah 7:14; Matthew 1:23
69. Jesus	Matthew 1:21; 1 Thessalonians 1:10
70. Jesus Christ	Matthew 1:1
71. Jesus of Nazareth	Matthew 21:11; Mark 1:24; Luke 24:19
72. Judge	Acts 10:42; 2 Timothy 4:8
73. Judge of Israel	Micah 5:1
74. Just One	Acts 7:52; 22:14
75. King	Zechariah 9:9; Matthew 21:5
76. King of Glory	Psalms 24:7-10

77. King of Israel	John 1:49
78. King of Kings	1 Timothy 6:15; Revelation 17:14
79. King of peace	Hebrews 7:2
80. King of righteousness	Hebrews 7:2
81. King of saints	Revelation 15:3
82. King of Salem	Hebrews 7:1
83. King of the Jews	Matthew 2:2; 27:37; John 19:19
84. King of Zion	Matthew 21:25
85. Lamb	Revelation 5:6,12; 13:8; 21:22; 22:3
86. Lamb of God	John 1:29,36
87. Lawgiver	Isaiah 33:22
88. Leader	Isaiah 55:4
89. Life	John 14:6; Colossians 3:4; 1 John 1:2
90. Light of the world	John 1:8; 8:12
91. Lily of the valleys	Song of Solomon 2:1
92. Lion of the tribe of Judah	Revelation 5:5
93. Living bread	John 6:51
94. Living stone	1 Peter 2:4
95. Lord and Savior	2 Peter 1:11; 3:18
96. Lord Christ	Colossians 3:24
97. Lord God Almighty	Revelation 15:3
98. Lord God of the holy prophets	Revelation 22:6
99. Lord Jesus	Acts 7:59; Colossians 3:17
100. Lord Jesus Christ	Acts 11:17; 16:31; 20:21
101. Lord of all	Acts 10:36
102. Lord of glory	1 Corinthians 2:8; James 2:1
103. Lord of Hosts	Isaiah 44:6
104. Lord of Lords	1 Timothy 6:15; Revelation 17:14; 19:16
105. Lord our righteousness	Jeremiah 23:6; 33:16
106. Man of sorrows	Isaiah 53:3

107.	Mediator	1 Timothy 2:5
108.	Messenger of the covenant	Malachi 3:1
109.	Messiah	Daniel 9:25; John 1:41
110.	Mighty God	Isaiah 9:6
111.	Mighty One of Israel	Isaiah 30:29
112.	Mighty One of Jacob	Isaiah 49:26; 60:16
113.	Morningstar	Revelation 22:16; 2 Peter 1:19
114.	Most Holy	Daniel 9:24
115.	Nazarene	Matthew 9:23
116.	Offspring of David	Revelation 22:16
117.	Only begotten	John 1:14
118.	Only begotten Son	John 1:18
119.	Our Passover	1 Corinthians 5:7
120.	Potentate	1 Timothy 6:15
121.	Power of God	1 Corinthians 1:24
122.	Prince	Acts 5:31
123.	Prince of life	Acts 3:15
124.	Prince of peace	Isaiah 9:6
125.	Prince of the kings of the earth	Revelation 1:5
126.	Prophet	Matthew 21:11; Luke 24:19; John 7:40
127.	Rabbi	John 1:49
128.	Rabboni	John 20:16
129.	Ransom	1 Timothy 2:6
130.	Redeemer	Job 19:25; Isaiah 59:20; 60:16
131.	Resurrection and life	John 11:25
132.	Rock	1 Corinthians 10:4
133.	Rock of offence	1 Peter 2:8
134.	Root of David	Revelation 5:5; 22:16
135.	Root of Jesse	Isaiah 11:10
136.	Rose of Sharon	Song of Solomon 2:1
137.	Ruler of Israel	Micah 5:2
138.	Savior	Luke 2:11; 2 Peter 2:20; 3:18
139.	Savior of the body	Ephesians 5:23

140.	Scepter	Numbers 24:17
141.	Second Adam	1 Corinthians 15:45
142.	Second Man	1 Corinthians 15:47
143.	Seed of David	2 Timothy 2:8
144.	Seed of woman	Genesis 3:15
145.	Servant	Isaiah 42:1; 52:13; 53:11; Acts 4:30
146.	Servant of Rulers	Isaiah 49:7
147.	Shepherd	Mark 14:27
148.	Shepherd and overseer of souls	1 Peter 2:25
149.	Shepherd of Israel	Psalm 80:1
150.	Shiloh	Genesis 49:10
151.	Son of David	Matthew 9:27
152.	Son of God	Luke 1:35; John 1:49
153.	Son of Joseph	John 6:42
154.	Son of man	John 5:27
155.	Son of the Blessed	Mark 14:61
156.	Son of the Father	2 John 1:3
157.	Son of the Highest	Luke 1:32
158.	Star	Numbers 24:17
159.	Stone of stumbling	1 Peter 2:8
160.	Sun of righteousness	Malachi 4:2
161.	Sure foundation	Isaiah 28:16
162.	Surety	Hebrews 7:22
163.	Teacher	Matthew 23:8; John 3:2
164.	Tender plant	Isaiah 53:2
165.	True God	1 John 5:20
166.	True light	John 1:9
167.	True vine	John 15:1
168.	Truth	John 14:6
169.	Vine	John 15:1
170.	Way	John 14:6
171.	Wisdom	Proverbs 8:12
172.	Wisdom of God	1 Corinthians 1:24

173.	Witness	Isaiah 55:4; Revelation 1:5
174.	Wonderful	Isaiah 9:6
175.	Word	John 1:1; 1 John 5:7
176.	Word of God	Revelation 19:13
177.	Word of life	1 John 1:1

ITEM 2:

WDJW (what did Jesus write?)

John 8: 3-11 NIV reads: "*The teachers of the law and the Pharisees brought in a woman caught in adultery. They made her stand before the group and said to Jesus, "Teacher, this woman was caught in the act of adultery. In the Law Moses commanded us to stone such women. Now what do you say?" They were using this question as a trap, in order to have a basis for accusing him.*

But ***Jesus bent down and started to write on the ground with His finger****. When they kept on questioning Him, He straightened up and said to them, "If any one of you is without sin, let him be the first to throw a stone at her."* ***Again he stooped down and wrote on the ground.*** *At this, those who heard began to go away one at a time, the older ones first, until only Jesus was left, with the woman still standing there. Jesus straightened up and asked her, "Woman, where are they? Has no one condemned you?" "No one, Sir," she said. "Then neither do I condemn you," Jesus declared. "Go now and leave your life of sin.""* (Emphasis mine).

Look at the two bold underlined sentences again. Both times Jesus wrote on the ground with His Fingers. When the pastor of Springfield Bible Church, John Standard was preaching out of John 8 on this passage, and came up to this, the Spirit of the Lord gave me a revelation which still floors me. It is completely within the realm of possibility once I obeyed!

No one, no theologian or writer or preacher can prove what Jesus wrote on the ground. Neither can I. All I am saying is what the Lord directed me to on this Sunday morning during the message, and I believe it.

Look at Daniel 5:25-28 in this default version of this book – the Literal New American Standard Bible: *"Now this is the inscription that was written out: 'MENE, MENE, TEKEL, UPHARSIN.*

> *26 This is the interpretation of the message: 'MENE'—God has numbered your kingdom and put an end to it.*
> ***27 'TEKEL'—you have been weighed on the scales and found deficient.***
> *28 'PERES'—your kingdom has been divided and given over to the Medes and Persians"*. (Emphasis mine)

It is my contention, from listening to the Lord and His directing me immediately to this Scripture, that Jesus wrote **TEKEL** in the dirt that day!

In John 8:16, John specifically says *"Jesus bent down and* ***started to write on the ground with His Finger****"*. The last time we saw the handwriting with a Finger is Daniel 5:5 "*Suddenly* ***the fingers of a human hand appeared and wrote*** *on the plaster of the wall, near the lamp stand in the royal palace. The king watched the hand as it wrote"*.

Is this out of the realm of His possibility? During a fast a few years ago, He revealed, (and I stand on this), to me He wrote the 10 Commandments on Mt. Sinai on the tablet. He is called the Word of God and in the Beginning was the Word. He is the Creator of all things. I know He wrote the Tablets. He was in the Pillar of Fire. He was the Rock that Moses struck in anger. In fact Moses had to die before they got to the Promised Land because of this disobedient sin! 1 Corinthians 10:4 says the Rock He struck was Christ. So Christ was everywhere on earth in Spirit before His humble Birth in Bethlehem.

Sure John 8:16 may be the first time the God/Man Jesus was seen physically to write something on earth, but His was the hand in Belshazzar's palace on that day!

Why do I say He wrote "TEKEL"? This means "you have been weighed in the scales and found DEFICIENT"!! Now, before I got saved, I was TEKEL...and not tickled! In fact the world is too pickled in its own corruption to see what the Son of Man is saying to them. Conversely Daniel was told by the Angel of God, he is "*highly esteemed*" in Daniel 9:23 – the opposite of TEKEL!

Therefore when Jesus wrote TEKEL on the ground, He had the same message for the Pharisees....namely "men...teachers of the Law and Pharisees, you hypocrites....who are you to attempt to stone this woman....I have weighed <u>YOU</u> in the scales and you have no moral authority to do this! You are more in desperate need of a Savior as she is, now back off"!!

Am I nuts? I don't think so! I just love Jesus! In my humble opinion, this answers the question: "WHAT DID JESUS WRITE, or WDJW"?

<u>ITEM 3:</u>

<u>THE REAL REASON THE AMERICAN INDIAN IS EXTINCT</u>

This is not meant to diminish the wanton wiping out of an entire race of people. In fact the American Indian is still very much alive today. Unfortunately most live in dire poverty on reservations where alcoholism and hopelessness run rampant. Indian gaming casinos have not helped the matter much either.

There are a lot of Christian ministries now toiling in reservations in North Dakota, Oklahoma and Minnesota where my friend Lynn Wilson has her "Hope for the First Nations" ministry just bringing fruit by bushel after bushel, into the Kingdom. However both Lynn and my brother James Nesbit have encountered not just stumbling blocks and obstacles to ministry but a Spiritual warfare which is real and evil!

Lynn has had several episodic events where the Indian medicine men were involved. James went on a Great Lakes Tour in the Fall of 2006 where he and a team of prayer warriors circled every Great

Lake in North America and claimed it back from the devil. He did the same at Niagara Falls. He is currently on a tour of America's Great Rivers with a solid American Indian Ministry Leader Jim Chosa (www.daychief.org). Both men on a mission to pray over these rivers for protection and release of God's Hand upon America.

What is an Indian Medicine man, you ask? We have all seen them in the movies etc. What the world may not know is his powers are supernatural and NOT from the Holy God Almighty! His 'duties' are to heal diseases (hence the term 'medicine man'); locate lost things and get 'spiritual' favor for his tribe for general welfare or any battle or whatever they did.

They 'accomplished' this by worshipping at altars, similar to the pagan Baals of the Bible, by way of spirit dances, mind altering drugs like peyote etc....you have heard the phrase "heap good medicine". What do you think that is?! These medicine men use things like those harmless looking 'dream catchers' to catch the spirits as well as other thing we need to know nothing of. Suffice it to say, all of this violates the first Two Commandments given by Jesus on Mt. Sinai.

These (Exodus 20: 2-5 NKJV) are plain enough and anyone who sins against them are in danger of hell:

> *2 **I am the Lord your God**, Who has brought you out of the land of Egypt, out of the house of bondage.*
>
> *3 **You shall have no other gods before or besides Me.***
>
> *4 **You shall not make yourself any graven image [to worship it]** or any likeness of anything that is in the heavens above, or that is in the earth beneath, or that is in the water under the earth;*
>
> *5 **You shall not bow down yourself to them or serve them; for I the Lord your God am a jealous God**, visiting the iniquity of the fathers upon the children to the third and fourth generation of those who hate Me.* (Emphasis mine)

The beliefs of the American Indian were not of the Holy One of Israel. In fact much of today's New Age mysticism has similar roots in the worship of beings. These are not of Christ and come not just from Eastern religions but earth religions of the Indian. We all know about their belief in the Great Spirit in the Sky. These people's gods were the sun, moon, (13) the rain, the earth and all its created matter including animals.

Does any of this sound familiar?!! Nowadays we have the entire world bowing at the altar to the false gods of global warming, Earth Day and its pagan goddess ghia as well as its assorted animal gods. A certain religion worships a cow while its people starve! And so on and so on.

Again, this is not meant to be brutal as these people suffered a lot of Broken Treaties and injustice. HOWEVER, like the pagan-worshipping Canaanites, the Lord has a way of clearing out those who do not believe in Him. He did it in Central and South America. He is coming in Justice on the Day of Wrath to do it again!! Praise God!

There is nothing viler than the human sacrifice the Aztecs and Mayan cultures performed in the long, pre-Western civilization history of the Americas. Nothing. From the blood sacrifices of virgins and babies to wanton murder, these cultures were just like the lost Israelites who joined with those around them and participated in the practices of Molech.

God was so disgusted and fed up with the House of Israel, He sent His prophets, Jeremiah, Hosea and Ezekiel to prophesy of His coming Wrath against them. God allowed a godless, powerful army of Babylonians to destroy Israel and sent them into captivity for their wickedness. This is what happened to the American Indian to a certain extent.

Manifest destiny (14) was the philosophy which says Providence (or God) allowed the obvious (manifest) and certain (destiny) to occur as America expanded. I believe this. While the American Indian was not dealt with in most instances very fairly, this Earth belongs to God and He can do with it what He pleases.

No mysticism from the pit of hell; no man-made philosophy will prevail against the Church of the Lord Jesus Christ. There are now a number of Christian Missionaries making inroads into these reservations. The Missionaries of Christ are using the Word of God instead to break strongholds. Jesus said whatever we bind on earth will be bound in Heaven and so it is at this time. When He returns, He will set the rest of it right.

Our missionaries deserve all our prayers and intercession because they are up against something ingrained in a culture which has oppressed the tribes as much as, or more than any broken treaty!

ITEM 4:

GLOBAL WARMING, A SLAP AGAINST GOD!

Why is the Global Warming hysteria a slap against Almighty God? Here is what God said in Jeremiah 14:22 NKJV: *Are there any among the idols of the nations that can cause rain?*

Or can the heavens give showers?
Are You not He, O LORD our God?
Therefore we will wait for You,
***Since You have made all these*.**

However the arrogance of man is really stunning! But it has been so since Lucifer, the angel of light fell from heaven. In his pride, he thought himself greater than God. The created fallen angel considered himself greater than his creator. So it is with fallen man.

For generations, scientists, philosophers and now politicians considered themselves smarter than God. Why? They think anyone who believes in the inerrant Word of God is a rube, hick, hayseed or a plain old dummy. I love what He says in 1 Corinthians 1:27 " *but God has chosen the foolish things of the world to put to shame the wise, and God has chosen the weak things of the world to put to shame the things which are mighty".*

Look at this again "BUT God".....The three letter word "but" means more than it says! It contrasts the idiocy of the elite of the heathens in the United Nations, in media and Academics as well as assorted politicians who are now in a battle against skeptics of Global Warming. These people are in direct and permanent rebellion against God Himself and Jesus Christ, the Creator, in particular!!

The "but" in this verse, means this....no matter what these people do as far as government policy etc...they will answer directly to Him who sits on the Throne. My friends, they will not like what comes down for their rebellion!

The following brief argument comes out of Job 38 NKJV.

The Global Warming Hysteria proponents say man has altered the earth

God says: "*Where were you when I laid the foundations of the earth?*

Tell Me, if you have understanding." (verse 4)

The Global Warming Hysteria proponents say the seas are rising and New York City will be under water!!

God says: *"who shut in the sea with doors, when it burst forth and issued from the womb... When I said, 'This far you may come, but no farther, and here your proud waves must stop!'"* (verses 8 and 11).

Here are some more verses of this Chapter. While these "wise" in a worldly sense are only wise until their judgment at the Great White Throne of God and they may consider His Word as irrelevant; He is still God and there is none like Him! Which one of these Global Warming Worshippers can answer any of the following questions, in their folly? If your friends are captured by the sin of global warming belief, run these verses by them from Job 38:

22 "Have you entered the treasury of snow,
Or have you seen the treasury of hail,
23 Which I have reserved for the time of trouble,
For the day of battle and war?
24 By what way is light diffused,
Or the east wind scattered over the earth?
25 "Who has divided a channel for the overflowing water,
Or a path for the thunderbolt,
26 To cause it to rain on a land where there is no one,
A wilderness in which there is no man;
27 To satisfy the desolate waste,
And cause to spring forth the growth of tender grass?

28 Has the rain a father?
Or who has begotten the drops of dew?
29 From whose womb comes the ice?
And the frost of heaven, who gives it birth?
30 The waters harden like stone,
And the surface of the deep is frozen.
31 "Can you bind the cluster of the Pleiades,
Or loose the belt of Orion?
32 Can you bring out Mazzaroth in its season?
Or can you guide the Great Bear with its cubs?
33 Do you know the ordinances of the heavens?
Can you set their dominion over the earth?
34 "Can you lift up your voice to the clouds,
That an abundance of water may cover you?
35 Can you send out lightnings, that they may go,
And say to you, 'Here we are!'?

To read more of the account of Creation (to flesh out the account of Genesis 1 and 2), please read the entire chapters of Job 38-41.

The leadership of the National Association of Evangelicals has gone on record supporting this secular, humanist hoax of Global Warming. They do not speak for those of us who believe in Biblical Christianity. We see this theory as an abomination against our all-powerful God!

By doing so, they have sided with those who are in rebellion against the very Bible and Word of God these preachers claim to preach from! They have challenged the Sovereignty of God. Thus, I humbly submit, this Global Warming scam is a slap against a Holy God. As He says in Matthew 24:7 "...in various places, there will be famine and earthquakes..." None of these things have anything to do with so-called ice caps melting as mankind breathes in and out! Jesus was describing these very days, the last days!

FOOTNOTES FOR THE TWO MINUTE WARNING:

INTRODUCTION:

Footnote:

Oswald Chamber: My Utmost for His Highest *http://www.rbc.org/utmost/index.php?month=11&day=15&year=07*

CHAPTER 1:

1. http://en.thinkexist.com/
2. http://home.snu.edu/~hculbert/commit.htm
3. Ray Comfort: Sermon series "Faith Comes by Hearing" (no copyright).
4. John Calvin, Commentary on the Book of Romans (public domain): http://www.ccel.org/ccel/calvin/calcom38.html
5. Thomas M. Knox; sailor extraordinaire
6. Horatio Spafford "It is Well with My Soul" (public domain)
7. www.terrax.org/sailing/glossary
8. O Victory in Jesus (Hymn, public domain)
9. Sermon series, Southland Christian Church, Lexington, Kentucky. Pastor Mike Breaux (February 1997, no copyright)
10. "Just a Closer Walk with Thee" (Hymn, Public Domain)
11. http://www.puritansermons.com/charnock/charindx.htm

12. Youtube.com (public domain)
13. All "Famous Last Words" except Footnote 12 are from: The Evidence Bible: Ray Comfort; Bridge-Logos Publishers, Gainesville, Florida, USA. Copyright 2003; page 1504, page 1505, in part.
14. All word definitions are from www.websters-online-dictionary.org

CHAPTER 2:

1. http://en.wikipedia.org/wiki/Voltaire (Public Domain) and * The Evidence Bible: Ray Comfort; Bridge-Logos Publishers, Gainesville, Florida, USA. Copyright 2003; page 1504
2. Dr.Voddie Baucham: The Everloving Truth ; B&H Publishing Group (May 2004) pages 135-136
3. JOSEPHUS (Translated by William Whiston); Kregel Publications, Grand Rapids, Michigan , 1960, 1978 page 379, paragraph 3.
4. Further information on Origins of the Bible comes out of years of reading and studying about God's Word. No particular source quoted or material sourced.
5. www.iconocast.com/Gandhi_on_Management.htm (public domain) for Gandhi's 7 Deadly Sins.
6. PRAY MAGAZINE (ISSUE 55) JULY/AUGUST 2006,
7. http://shaw.thefreelibrary.com/
8. www.websters-online-dictionary.org for all definitions
9. ***NOTE: All information on the Origins of the Bible has been gleaned from a couple of decades of study and reading from many sources, sermons, documentaries etc. All other sources used have been footnoted above.***

CHAPTER 3:

1. Quote from General William Booth: http://www.revival-library.org/index.html?http://www.revival-library.org/quotes/prayer.htm

2. Touching Lives TV Ministry; Dr. James Merritt, Cross Pointe, the Church at Gwinnett Center, Duluth, Georgia.
3. Path to Personal Revival, page 23 by Randy Heinsch; Grace Conquest Ministries, Peoria, Illinois. Used by Permission.
   Webster's Online Dictionary: www.websters-online-dictionary.org where definitions are mentioned.

CHAPTER 4:

1. "Revival Fire" by Paul Baloche
   Copyright 1996, Integrity's Hosanna Music
   Fair Use (Section 107 U.S. Copyright Law, Title 17 U.S.Code)

2. Hcfish: http://www.founders.org/FJ05/article3.html

3 Dr. Walter D. Zorn and S. Edward Tesh "The College Press NIV Commentary on Psalms Vol. 1 College Press Publishing Co. 1999 Page 139
4. http://en.wikipedia.org/wiki/Category:Ancient_Roman_military_clothing re :(**all** references to the uniform of the Roman soldier etc.)
5. http://en.wikipedia.org/wiki/Revival_(religious)and www.wikipedia.com (all references to the Great Awakenings and historical data on these revivals)
6. www.websters-online-dictionary.org (for all word definitions).
7. All references to author Claude King and his materials on Revival are from the National Day of Prayer Coordinator Conference I attended; October 2006; Focus on the Family, Colorado Springs, Colorado.

CHAPTER 5:

1. http://quotations.about.com/cs/inspirationquotes/a/Leadership12.htm

2. Bobby Welch, YOU THE WARRIOR LEADER, Broadman & Holman Publishers, Nashville, Tennessee 2004. Page2
   Ibid pages 89, 90 and 91 in part
3. All references to Dr. Steve Farrar and his materials are used by Permission from Dr. Farrar.
4. http://www.livingwaters.com/articles_ray_archive/articles_ray_03-02-04_whatbattle.shtml*
5. http://pptkids.org/index-20050422.php
6. http://en.wikipedia.org/wiki/Moody_Bible_Institute
   Further credits:
   www.answers.com/topic/acknowledgement
   http://www.wisdomquotes.com/cat_courage.htm
   http://www.m-w.com/dictionary/visionary

CHAPTER 6:

1. http://www.wisdomquotes.com/cat_wisdom.html
2. www.promisekeepers.org
3. www.wikipedia.com
4. R. Albert Mohler Blog: Friday, June 09, 2006 "More on Marriage, Ministry, and Credibility"; www.albertmohler.com
5. Stu Weber, Four Pillars of a Man's Heart: Bringing Strength into Balance (Sisters, Oregon: Multnomah, 1993) page 13
6. Gary Chapman: The Five Love Languages. Northfield Publishing, Chicago, Illinois; 1992, 1995 and 2004 Page 15 and Page 18.
7. Dr. Walter D. Zorn and S. Edward Tesh "The College Press NIV Commentary on Psalms Vol. 1 College Press Publishing Co. 1999 page 338

CHAPTER 7:

1. Dr. Jerry Falwell's Fourth Quarter Ministry: Thomas Road Baptist Church **http://sermons.trbc.org/20010805.html**

and the Liberty Journal (Fall 2001), Liberty University, Lynchburg, Virginia / www.liberty.edu

2. Dr. James Dobson's Focus on the Family Radio Broadcast, Colorado Springs, Colorado.
3. Jean Coleman, the Society for the Study of Androgen Deficiency, London, England (http://www.andropause.org.uk/Articles/aboutus.asp)
4. Bob Corbett, "What is Existentialism" March 1985. Philosophy Dept. Webster U., St. Louis, Mo. http://www.websteruniv.edu/~corbetre/philosophy/ **(Used by permission)**
5. Ladies Home Journal, March 2005, "Learn to love yourself" by Rick Warren, Pastor, Saddleback Church
6. Chuck Swindoll's "Insight for Living" Radio Broadcast, Plano, Texas.

CHAPTER 8:

0 http://quotes.zaadz.com/pericles

1 The Reformed Reader: http://www.reformedreader.org/history/christian/ahob2/chapter04.htm **(Used by permission)**

2 *All information on the Wightman Family Heritage and Abraham Lincoln courtesy:
Ronald Wightman (cousin to the Lincolns!)
Salt Lake City, Utah
www.wightmanfamily.com/holmes.html
(Used by permission)

3 www.websters-online-dictionary.org for all word definitions.

CHAPTER 9:

1. Webster's Online Dictionary (www.websters-online-dictionary.org)
2. No Place for Truth by Dr. David Wells (Eerdmans, 1994) pg 300

3. Holiness by Dr. Joel Beeke (Banner of Truth Publishing Co.: 1994): http://www.monergism.com/ directory/link_category/Holiness-Personal/
4. http://theworldfrommywindow.blogspot.com/2007/03/joel-beeke-on-why-you-should-read.html

CHAPTER 10:

1. http://en.wikipedia.org/wiki/Rat_race
2. Dr. Steve Farrar "Overcoming Overload", Multnomah Books (2004) pages 153-154
   ibid pages 155-156. All books and materials by Dr. Steve Farrar are used by exclusive permission.
3. http://www.familiesandwork.org/summary/over-work2005.pdf pages 2, 3
4. http://www.mayoclinic.com/health/stresssymptoms/SR00008_D
5. http://www.businessmeninchrist.com/Bernie-column-20070212.php
6. *Don't* Quit from The Complete Speaker's Sourcebook by Eleanor Doan page 207 © 1996, Zondervan Treasures; Zondervan Publishing House
7. John Calvin; 'Instruction in Faith, John Calvin's "own 1537 digest of the Institutes; Section 8 "The Law of the Lord"'.
8. Hymn "Leaning on the Everlasting Arms" by Elisha Hoffman and Anthony Showalter, 1887
10. http://www.mindheart.com/deeper/proskuneo.php
11. All quotations by Arthur W. Pink are used by permission by PBM Desktop Publishers, Granbury, Texas. Copyright Providence Baptist Ministries.
12. All resources concerning Doug Mazza are used by permission of Joni and Friends.

CHAPTER 11:

1. Public Broadcasting Service, The American Experience "People and Events – MacArthur" WGBH-TV, Boston (1999)
2. www.wikipedia.org "Audie Murphy."
3. "What Hollywood Believes", Ray Comfort, Genesis Publishing Group (2004)page 66
4. "CLINT, the Life & Legend", Patrick McGilligan St. Martin's Press, NY (1999)page 29
5. "Washington and Religion", Paul Boller, Southern Methodist University Press (1963) (http://www.positive-atheism.org/hist/quotes/washington.htm)
6. "The Religious Life of Thomas Jefferson", Charles B. Stanford, University of Virginia Press, (1987) and, in part, http://www.iusb.edu/~journal/1999/Paper9.html
7. http://en.wikipedia.org/wiki/Thomas_Jefferson .
8. Webster's Encyclopedic Dictionary, 1941
9. www.americanrevolution.org/delxone.html
10. Men's Journal, New York, NY, February 2004 edition.... republished by the Hawaii Reporter and www.newsmax.com
11. http://www.promiselandchrysalis.com/templates/System/details.asp?id=30821&PID=242607
12. All Dictionary definitions are from www.websters-online-dictionary.org
13. http://www.religion-cults.com/Ancient/America/america.htm (public domain)
14. http://en.wikipedia.org/wiki/Manifest_Destiny

Printed in the United States
200007BV00005B/106-192/A

9 781602 665613